D0800530

looking back

Modern America
in Historical Perspective

Stephen Mark Halpern
City University of New York

Rand McNally College Publishing Company
Chicago

Rand McNally History Series
Fred Harvey Harrington, *Advisory Editor*

To My Wife Sheila
and
Benjamin and Kate

Contents

Acknowledgments

Grateful acknowledgment is made to the following for permission to quote from copyrighted material:

The Belknap Press of Harvard University Press: for *Century of Struggle: The Woman's Rights Movement in the United States* by Eleanor Flexner. Copyright 1959, 1968 by Eleanor Flexner.

The University of Pennsylvania Press: for *Backwoods Utopias: The Sectarian Origins and the Owenite Phase of Communitarian Socialism in America, 1663–1829* by Arthur Bestor. Copyright 1970, by the Trustees of the University of Pennsylvania.

Dover Publications: for *The People Called Shakers* by Edward Deming Andrews. Copyright 1953, 1963 by Edward Deming Andrews. Also, for *Heavens on Earth: Utopian Communities in America, 1689–1880* by Mark Holloway. Copyright 1966.

Preface

Each chapter in this book explores a theme in American social history. The topics included have produced a great deal of discussion and debate within recent years, and they affect a large segment of the American people. One need only scan a newspaper or magazine to confirm the nation's preoccupation with ecology, technology, women's liberation, the city, communes, leisure and higher education. These subjects are likely to concern us for many years to come.

I have tried to respond to the demand for lively and relevant history by presenting a contemporary view of each subject before discussing its historical development. To facilitate this, each chapter has been divided into two parts. In part one, I discuss how and why a subject has come to our attention, what its social importance is, and how it is likely to affect us in the future. In part two, I explore the subject as a theme in American social history, with emphasis on the main events and ideas that shaped its evolution. The first part of each chapter is intended to serve as an introduction and consciousness-raiser which will encourage people to ask historical questions. The second part is intended to provide historical information and a thematic understanding of the subject being explored.

None of the chapters in this book are complete histories of the topics under consideration. Rather, they are introductory essays which seek to develop a sense of historical perspective and understanding. Part of this perspective involves seeing that what we call modern has historical antecedents, and that what we think is novel and promising may have been tried and found wanting in the past. To know this is not to diminish the importance of our own time, but to recognize that in dealing with the present we must consider the powerful influence of the past.

looking back

The Sorcerer's Apprentice

1

The Machine in American Life and Thought

Modern technology is a major force, perhaps *the* major force, in our lives today. It shapes and influences the way we produce goods, carry on business, communicate, move about and enjoy our leisure time. It shapes and structures our system of politics, our values and ethics, and subtly affects our aesthetic sensibilities. Technology is omnipresent in our lives today, so much so that we hardly recognize its power, potential, and constraints. It is a force to be reckoned with, lest it become like the sorcerer's apprentice, a marvelous genie out of control.

TECHNOLOGY AND HISTORY

Across the span of human history mastery of technology and technical innovation have defined the character of civilizations and played a

part in their rise and fall. We differentiate paleolithic and neolithic societies by the tools they used. Egyptian pharaohs based their power on their skill in solving irrigation problems and interpreting meteorological and astronomical events. The Romans applied technology to warfare, road building and city architecture, and dominated most of the known world for a thousand years. Even in the Middle Ages when agriculture was the dominant mode of life, technology played a critical role. Kings and princes may not have known how to keep accurate time, cure toothaches or obtain hot running water, but they successfully mined and smelted ores, improved bows and arrows, fortified their castles and developed a systematic census. Medieval peasants worshipped in vast Gothic cathedrals made possible by new methods of quarrying, moving and hoisting stone.

Although the Renaissance witnessed important advances in technology—among them printing with movable type and the use of lenses to view the universe and see microorganisms—and the Enlightenment made educated people aware of Newton's laws and the method of science, it was not until the nineteenth century that average people began to feel the influence of technology in their everyday lives. For many, the abandonment of farming and entrance into a factory began their acquaintance with the new machines. For others, it was the arrival of a steam locomotive or the appearance of the telegraph which ushered them suddenly into the modern age. For many, mechanization and industrialization produced a feeling of alienation and personal insignificance as new mechanical forces transformed their lives. The Luddite rioting in England in the early 1800s in which workers set fire to factories and wrecked their machines, is a dramatic example of people striking out at technological forces they could not understand.

The nineteenth century witnessed some of the most important technical advances of any era, among them the factory and railroad, the telegraph, telephone and electric light and the phonograph, photograph and sewing machine. Technical innovation transformed the way people worked, altered social institutions such as the family and accelerated the trend toward political unification, yet it left traditional concepts of time, space and the structure of matter fundamentally unchanged. In the twentieth century, however, such achievements as harnessing atomic energy, deciphering the genetic code, journeying into outer space and developing systems based upon automation and cybernation, triggered an intellectual and cultural revolution of immense significance, a revolution which called into question traditional beliefs and which made technology a prime factor in social change.

> The geographical explosion of technology has created the first worldwide civilization; and it is a technological civilization. It has shifted the power center of the world away from Western Europe thousands of miles to both West and East. More important still, modern technology in this century has made men reconsider old concepts, such as the position of women in society, and it has remade basic institutions—work, education, and warfare for example. It has shifted a large number of people in the technologically advanced countries from working with their hands to working . . . with their minds. It has changed the

physical environment of man from one of nature to the man-made big city.[1]

We sometimes forget that as recently as 1914 there were no airplanes, computers, television sets, transistors, plastics, antibiotics, radio-tele-scopes and very few automobiles. The whole fabric and texture of life in pretechnological society, even in nineteenth century society, was fundamentally different from our own.

TECHNOLOGICAL CIVILIZATION

One simply has to glance around to realize how much technology permeates and influences our lives. We live in comfort using a vast array of appliances until a fuse blows or a blackout throws us into confusion. We travel quickly over great distances until precious gasoline is withheld by a boycott or a government decree. Our interest compounds, our paychecks arrive on time, our mail is sorted correctly until a computer fails, or an electric cable snaps. "Only sixty years ago, men depended on nature and were primarily threatened by natural catastrophes," writes Peter Drucker. "Men today depend on technology, and our major threats are technological breakdowns. The largest cities in the world would become uninhabitable in forty-eight hours were the water supply or the sewage systems to give out."[2]

It is not simply our physical dependence upon machines that characterizes technological civilization, but the force exerted by technology upon our values, life styles and institutions. In the realm of religion, for example, the advance of technology has allowed men "to experience themselves, their power, and their relationships to nature and history in terms of open possibility, hope, action and self-confidence. The symbolism of such traditional religious postures as subservience, fatefulness, destiny and suprarational faith begins . . . to seem irrelevant to our actual experience."[3] In the realm of personal decision making, the "scope of individual choice and action today are greater than in previous times, in the choice of consumer products, marital partner, occupation, place to live, objects of loyalty, and allegiance to religious, political, and other social groups.[4] In the

---

[1] Peter Drucker, *Technology, Management and Society,* Rev. ed. (New York, 1971), pp. 76–77.
    [2] *Ibid.,* p. 87.
    [3] Emmanuel G. Mesthene, *Technological Change; Its Impact on Man and Society* (New York, 1970), p. 58.
    [4] *Ibid.,* p. 85.

realm of politics technology alters the way power is used, the way people perceive their leaders, and the manner in which leaders are held accountable. All politicians know, for example, how computers and statistical poll-taking have altered their profession. Similarly, they are aware of television's power to influence public opinion and affect voting behavior.

The enormous power of technology to do the work required by modern society has led many people to conclude that technological civilization is an unalloyed blessing, conferring more power, more wealth, more food and longer life with each passing year. The proponents of technology point to the "green revolution," plans to harvest the oceans, advances in medicine and pharmacology and expanding knowledge of the universe as examples of the benefits gained by technological sophistication. There are many critics of technology, on the other hand, who see in the advance of technology more evil than good. For Eugene Schwartz, for example, "Science and technology have become established myths of . . . those . . . who sought to abolish myths in the name of reason. Science has become a secular religion, technology its temple, efficiency its dogma."[5] For Jacques Ellul technology "enslaves modern man," and "effaces all individual and even all collective modes of expression." It is an autonomous force, too powerful, too diffuse and too complex to control.[6] For writers such as George Orwell and Aldous Huxley the tendencies in technological civilization toward conformity, amorality and technocratic fascism, lead ultimately to dehumanization and perhaps the downfall of human society. In *1984* and *Brave New World* these writers present a nightmare vision of society that has put too much faith in technique, order, rationality and control.

A more balanced view of technological society, which avoids simple affirmation or condemnation, is offered by Alvin Toffler, in a recent best seller entitled *Future Shock.* "We cannot and must not turn off the switch of technological progress," he writes. "Only romantic fools babble about returning to a 'state of nature' ." Toffler recognizes the benefits of technology but is also one of its most severe critics for he believes that technology speeds up our lives to the point where our nervous and social systems cannot handle the greatly accelerated pace of change. Technological civilization, he asserts, has created a new disease, the disease of future shock. "Future shock is the dizzying disorientation brought on by the premature arrival of the future." It is

---

[5] Eugene S. Schwartz, *Overskill: The Decline of Technology in Modern Civilization* (Chicago, 1971), p. 4.

[6] Jacques Ellul, *The Technological Society* (New York, 1964).

"a time phenomenon, a product of the greatly accelerated rate of change in society." Toffler charts how technology forces us into an increasingly transient world in which people, places and things mean less and less with each passing day. He shows us people constantly on the move, buying and disposing of things, changing marital partners and life styles in a society in which there is no permanence, only change. According to Toffler there is no area of life that is not touched by technology "yet the horrifying truth is that, so far as much technology is concerned, no one is in charge." If we are to avoid "the malaise, mass neurosis, irrationality and free-floating violence already apparent in contemporary life" we must begin to tame technology. We must make "super-decisions" about our future, he writes, or else suffer the consequences of future shock.

TECHNOLOGICAL IMPACT: SOME SPECIFIC EXAMPLES

While the broad implications of technological civilization have been and will continue to be analyzed, the impact of specific technologies on people and the environment have also been described. Marshall McLuhan has shown, for example, that television is not only a source for information and entertainment, it is a revolutionary technology that alters the way we think. Once print shaped our modes of perception but today electrons stimulate our consciousness giving us a desire for "wholeness, empathy, and depth of awareness."[7] Similarly a NASA scientist has pointed out that although computers enable us to work with complex mathematical models and calculate at unprecedented speeds, these machines may soon catch up with humans in their ability to reason and think and threaten the primacy of man. By 1999 we "should produce a machine that has the memory size and complexity of the human brain. . . . These solid-state brains, functioning with quasi-human intelligence will inaugurate the age of man-machine symbiosis."[8] Medical scientists have also pointed out how new machines which prolong life, raise all sorts of questions about definitions of life and death and the ethics of terminating life. It is becoming more and more obvious that as technology solves one set of problems it poses several others.

The computer is a case in point. Its power to calculate and store

---

[7] Marshall McLuhàn, *Understanding Media: The Extensions of Man* (New York, 1964).

[8] Robert Jastrow, "Man in Space or Chip in Space," *The New York Times Magazine*, January 31, 1971.

information is formidable and consequently it is used in a great variety of situations. Data banks, for example, gather information on millions of people without any limitations or constraints. At a congressional hearing in 1971 investigating these information systems, Senator Sam Ervin held up a two-inch square of microfilm which contained 773,746 words, the same as the 1,245 page Bible on his desk. Ervin was driving home the point that computers have almost limitless ability to store information, information that a government could use against its citizens if their privacy were not properly safeguarded. Professor Arthur Miller told the hearing that "Americans are scrutinized, measured, watched, counted, and interrogated by more government agencies, law-enforcement officials, social scientists, and poll-takers than any time in our history." Allen Westin, the author of *Privacy and Freedom,* and Ralph Nader have also pointed out how a "dossier dictatorship" can evolve. Computer technology is not, of course, the proper object of these critic's attacks. It is the harmful use to which this new technology may be put that causes them concern.

Some of the most cogent critics writing about the impact of technology have been scientist-ecologists who have raised our awareness of the relationship of technology to the health of our environment. Barry Commoner, for example, has detailed the negative impact of new technologies on our environment in a number of important works. In *The Closing Circle* (1971) he concludes that new technologies which emphasize synthetic compounds, nonbiodegradable substances and high energy consumption are responsible for much of our environmental pollution.

> The overall evidence seems clear. The chief reason for the environmental crisis that has engulfed the United States in recent years is the sweeping transformation of productive technologies since World War II. . . . Productive technologies with intense impact on the environment have displaced less destructive ones. The environmental crisis is the inevitable result of this counterecological pattern of growth.[9]

Dr. René Dubos, a Nobel scientist, has also written about the environment and has summed up the feeling of many of his colleagues when he said, "Technological civilization has raised standards of living for large numbers of people, but paradoxically it has also lowered the quality of life in many places. . . . Electronic gadgets, plastic knicknacks and processed foodstuffs do not compensate for the degrada-

---

[9] Barry Commoner, *The Closing Circle* (New York, 1971), p. 177.

tion of nature into wastelands, of bright atmosphere into murky skies, of free behavior into regimented life."[10] Environmentalists such as Commoner and Dubos have cast their nets broadly attacking traditional attitudes and assumptions, patterns of behavior and specific technological innovations. They have challenged the safety of nuclear reactors which through accident or faulty design could lead to massive radioactive contamination. They have attacked the automobile as the prime polluting agent in the nation. Their most important contribution has been to criticize from within, using the hard facts of science itself to show us the fallacy of following technology blindly.

TECHNOLOGY ASSESSMENT

The tendency of many individuals both inside and outside the scientific community to view the pace and direction of technology with alarm is a direct result of technology's awesome influence and power. It is one thing to develop nuclear energy and quite another to produce a doomsday bomb. It is one thing to study the functions and structure of genes and quite another to engage in "genetic engineering." As we arrive at the threshold of creating life in laboratories, developing new chemical agents and planting tiny computers in the human brain, many people want to know about the physical, social, political and ethical ramifications of given technologies.

It was with this in mind that the House of Representatives Subcommittee on Science, Research and Development headed by Emilio Q. Daddario began to explore the concept of technology assessment in 1967. Technology assessment, according to the committee, would help identify "the undesirable by-products and side effects of technology in advance of their crystallization" and inform "the public of their potential in order that appropriate steps may be taken to eliminate or minimize them." The committee held hearings, took expert testimony and reported out a bill but no action was taken for several years. The debate over the pros and cons of a supersonic transport in 1970–71, however, over building an oil pipeline from Alaska's North Slope, and the uproar over mercury deposits in the nation's lakes and streams sensitized public opinion and gave technology assessment a new urgency. Five years after the Daddario bill was presented the Congress passed the Technology Assessment Act of 1972. It set up an Office of Technology Assessment to advise the Congress. It created a

---

[10] René Dubos, "The Roots of Counter Culture" *The New York Times,* September 24, 1972, p. 13.

Technology Assessment Advisory Council of distinguished citizens and scientists. The new Office published a preliminary report on its activities in May, 1973 acting on its mandate to help Congress secure information concerning "the physical, biological, economic, social and political effects of new technologies, and to utilize this information . . . in the legislative assessment of matters pending before the Congress."[11]

How will technology assessment work in actual practice? Has this kind of activity been attempted before? The Office of Technology Assessment will work with the Environment Protection Agency in undertaking environmental impact studies. It will work with the National Science Foundation to determine the probable consequences of new technologies. It will also undertake its own technological forecasting by subsidizing research and collecting and interpreting data from private industry, "think tanks," government agencies and university laboratories. Although some critics have questioned the viability of such activity, proponents of technology assessment point out that certain government agencies have already engaged in this activity and found it worthwhile. An officer of the National Science Foundation, for example, wrote in the *New York Times* that his organization "recently solicited proposals for technology assessment in the areas of solar and geothermal energy development; electronic banking and the cashless, checkless society, the replacement of chemical pesticides by biopesticides; alternative work schedules, and the strategies and methods for energy conservation."[12] In other words, the Technology Assessment Act of 1972, was merely institutionalizing an already existing, although uncoordinated, government function.

Although technology assessment deals in possibilities and probabilities, and has yet to work out a firm methodology, a recent study undertaken at M.I.T. and funded by the Club of Rome,[13] provides an example of how sophisticated forecasting social and economic trends has already become. The project sought to determine how recent trends in economic and population growth will affect the world in the near future. The method employed was to develop a world model of growth (a systems approach) and feed into a computer all the factors and their variables that would affect the model over time. The con-

---

[11] For background on the Technology Assessment Act of 1972 see *U.S. Code Congressional and Administrative News,* Vol. 2, 92nd Congress, Second Session, 1972, p. 3568.

[12] *The New York Times,* April 22, 1972, III, p. 12.

[13] The Club of Rome is an informal international association devoted to discussing and analyzing "the major problems facing mankind." See *The Limits of Growth* (1972), Foreword.

clusion of the researchers, published as *The Limits of Growth* (1972), was that mankind faces an uncontrollable and disastrous collapse of its society within 100 years unless it moves speedily to establish a "global equilibrium" in which growth of population and industrial output are halted. Obviously, this apocalyptic prognosis raised many questions about the methods and assumptions of the M.I.T. project. Nevertheless, the world model concept was an important contribution to the new field of future studies, and a methodology which holds promise for those interested in technology assessment.

TECHNOLOGY AND THE FUTURE

No one can properly forsee where the new forces of technology will lead us. We may hope that the prophets who describe a future in which human beings resemble machines and where beauty, spontaneity and individuality cease to exist are just as wrong in their assessment as those who believe we should abandon all technology as the only way to save our humanity. It is horrible to contemplate a future in which the elements of nature, love and poetry are extinguished but just as horrible to give up technologies which can feed those in need and cure people fatally afflicted.

Our best course, it seems, is to refine our capacity to assess technology and then attempt to tame it. We cannot accept the implications of future shock. We cannot afford to let technology evolve outside the context of traditional values and ethics. Nor can we allow a new technocratic elite to control the levers of power and render our democracy obsolete. We have in the words of Alvin Toffler to make "super-decisions" about our future. "In the past, culture emerged without premeditation. Today, for the first time, we can raise the process to awareness. By the application of conscious technological policy . . . we can contour the culture of tomorrow."[14]

THE ORIGINS OF AMERICAN TECHNOLOGY

In 1776 the United States was not an industrial, technological society. For two centuries Great Britain insisted that the colonies serve her interests and this meant providing natural resources for England's mills and factories. As a consequence of restrictive trade laws, the colonists had little choice but to avoid manufacturing and concentrate on har-

---

[14] Alvin Toffler, *Future Shock* (New York, 1970), p. 433.

vesting America's great natural wealth. The colonists exported furs, timber, tobacco, potash, livestock, whale and fish oil, rice and indigo. They produced pig iron but sent it to England where it was fashioned into useful implements. About the only endeavor that required technological know-how was shipbuilding which was extensive in the Northeast. Most Englishmen thought of Americans as agriculturalists, and indeed they were.

In the years between the American Revolution and the Civil War, however, Americans began to perfect their technical skills. During this period the cotton gin and mechanical reaper were invented, revolutionizing the production of cotton and wheat. Factories using the power of stationary steam engines were built, and steamboats, canals, railroads and the telegraph transformed the way Americans communicated, traveled, and transported goods. American technology, of course, developed gradually. Many minds and hands were at work, much experimenting took place and a good deal of borrowing of ideas as well. Americans were fortunate, however, in having the right mix of physical, economic, political and cultural factors that favored industrial and technological development.

America's break with England in 1776 was an important factor which influenced the course of technical development. Until the Revolution, Americans either had their hands tied by mercantilist restrictions on manufacture or were in awe of British invention and technology. The War for Independence, however, and the subsequent need for self-defense and economic self-sufficiency, forced American craftsmen and mechanics to devise their own methods of manufacture and solve technical problems on their own. The American shipbuilding industry, for example, began to build larger ships and adopt new production techniques during the naval war with France in 1798. The War of 1812 created a need for weapons, uniforms, wagons and equipment met by native manufacturers. The opening of the trans-Appalachian West, which began with independence, stimulated road and canal building on the frontier. Independence initiated the search for native answers to technical problems and gave Americans a pride in native products. It also permitted Americans to trade freely with other countries, and to study foreign methods of manufacture hitherto unknown.

The scarcity of labor in America also promoted technological development. Between 1800 and 1840, during the first phase of industrialization, many manufacturers realized that young men favored farming as a vocation and turned to women and children to fill their factories. They also turned to new machines which held out the promise of reducing reliance on human labor. Oliver Evans demonstrated the effectiveness of mechanization as early as the 1780s by building a wheat mill in which chains, hoists, screw devices and gears lifted, sifted, ground and loaded grain. Eli Whitney, in 1798, began producing rifles for the American government by using machines, and a minimum of human labor. The British Committee on Machinery which visited American armories and factories in the 1850s noted that "everything that could be done to reduce labour in the movement of materials from one point to another was adopted. This includes mechanical arrangements for lifting materials . . . from one floor to another, carriages for conveying material on the same floor, and such like."[15] In 1851 another British observer wrote: "The laboring classes are comparatively few in number, but this is counterbalanced by . . . the eagerness with which they call in the aid of machinery in almost every department of industry. Wherever it can be introduced as a substitution for manual labor it is universally and willingly resorted to. . . ."[16] Technology, in sum, was America's answer to a shortage of willing factory hands.

A third factor in the evolution of American technology was the enormous native market for manufactured goods. There were no internal tariffs or restrictions on the flow of raw materials or finished products. There was need for every imaginable item from cheap cotton cloth to furniture, farm implements, wagons, watches and items used in the home. Mechanical ingenuity was well rewarded when it resulted in cutting costs on some essential product; innovations in transportation in a nation the size of America were consistently sought. Europeans, on the other hand, found it hard to compete in the American market because high tariffs made their exports expensive. Also their finely-wrought products had limited appeal in a society that wanted cheap, simply-designed goods.

Still another factor contributing to interest in and diffusion of technology was the high degree of physical and social mobility in America that motivated Americans to try new methods, make things better, bigger and faster. Mechanics moved around a great deal, passing secrets, learning new techniques, sharing ideas. Patent laws were initially lax and the courts were slow to act to prevent infringements. The French traveler Alexis de Tocqueville noted that "Restlessness of character seems to me to be one of the distinctive traits of this people. The American is devoured by the longing to make his fortune; it is the unique passion of his life. . . ." De Tocqueville attributed the spirit of innovation, of inventiveness and daring to the fact that Americans have "no inveterate habits, no spirit of routine; [the American]

---

[15] J. E. Sawyer, "The Social Basis of the American System of Manufacturing," *Journal of Economic History* 14 (1954): 372.

[16] H. J. Habakkuk, *American and British Technology in the Nineteenth Century* (London, 1962), pp. 6–7.

is less afraid than any other inhabitiant of the globe to risk what he has gained in the hope of a better future. . . ."[17] From de Tocqueville we discern the spirit of a people on the make, a spirit necessary for inventiveness, innovation and technical progress. The fact that we were a frontier society, no doubt, also shaped popular attitudes towards tools and machines. How else could one populate and conquer a wilderness without mechanical allies in the struggle for survival?

Finally, Americans would not have embraced technology with such enthusiasm if technology had not been compatible with religious beliefs, political ideals and other commonly held values. In fact, American optimism, materialism, and the work ethic were conducive to interest and faith in technology. William McGuffey told the children who read his school books that hard work was good for them.

> Work, work, my boy, be not afraid
> Look labor boldly in the face;
> Take up the hammer or the spade
> And blush not for your humble place.[18]

Protestant ministers, while uneasy about the theory of evolution, nevertheless preached that science and technology were religion's allies in man's search for material and spiritual progress. Even the democratic ethos reinforced an interest in machines and technical innovation. In America, many believed that machines would one day provide material necessities to all the people and even luxuries once enjoyed by an aristocratic elite.

REAPING PROFITS: THE FARMER AND THE MACHINE

Throughout the eighteenth century American farmers clung to old implements and old ways of doing things. As immigrants they had brought to the New World tools that sufficed at home: plow shares, two- and three-prong hay and grain forks, scythes, reaping hooks, steeled axes, winnowing fans and spades. Over the years these tools underwent minor changes to meet new agricultural conditions, but the idea of mechanized farming was not seriously considered.

> The land was broken with a crude wooden plow drawn by oxen or horses. The harrow used to break and level the upturned

---

[17] Quoted in Habakkuk, p. 112.
[18] Quoted in Stuart Bruchey, *The Roots of American Economic Growth, 1607–1861* (New York, 1965), p. 197.

clods was roughly made of wood in the shape of a V, containing wooden teeth. Grain was sown by hand, cultivated laboriously with crude tools, reaped with a sickle, and threshed with a flail or trod by horses.[19]

Despite primitive methods, surpluses were produced, accounting for the lack of interest in mechanization. Too few farmers had the time or money to invest in new inventions, anyway. The old methods seemed good enough.

In the early decades of the nineteenth century, however, as the demand for American foodstuffs increased, it became obvious that agriculture could benefit from advances in technology. Farmers began reading Jared Eliot's treatises on "Field-Husbandry" which described Jethro Tull's seed drill and his ideas on the use of fertilizers. They began to use cast iron plows although some still feared these new devises would poison their soil. The most important technological innovation in farming, however, came in 1837 when John Deere displayed a steel plow which could cut easily through tough prairie sod and scour (clean) as it moved. Deere's invention was an instant success and thereafter hostility to iron and steel farm implements disappeared. Deere began mass producing his "singing plow" (it vibrated in the soil) and by 1858 his factory at Moline, Illinois was producing 13,000 plows a year. Shortly thereafter Deere began to design and manufacture other mechanical devices and work at expanding his company which was already known for revolutionizing farming techniques.

Another wedding of technology and agriculture occurred in 1831 when Cyrus McCormick successfully harvested a small field of wheat with a mechanical reaper of his own design. It was a wood frame device pulled by a horse. As it moved, a wheel turned against the ground providing the power to drive other wheels through a series of connecting belts. The heart of the reaper was a vibrating horizontal knife which cut the wheat as it was pushed against the knife by a windmill-like device called the reel. A series of wooden fingers protruded in front of the knife so that the wheat would be separated and set up properly for cutting. As the reaper moved across a field a swath was cut and the wheat fell onto a platform in the rear.

Despite the fact that McCormick had worked out the essentials of reaping, his new invention had no market in his home state of Virginia. Little wheat was grown there and the reaper could not work

---

[19] A. C. Bining and T. C. Cochran, *The Rise of American Economic Life,* Fourth ed. (New York, 1964), p. 54.

effectively wherever the topography was uneven. In 1847, therefore, he and a partner set up a factory in Chicago, near the farms of the Great Plains. Here in a region that was flat and where farms were large, mechanical harvesting attracted attention. The reaper could increase harvesting capacity by well over 1000 percent. Two, three or four reapers used in tandem could harvest quantities of wheat unimaginable before. McCormick's invention was a tremendous success and, notwithstanding the competition from another reaper inventor, Obed Hussey, McCormick sold over 5,000 reapers within three years after his move to Illinois. In 1856 alone his factory produced and sold 4,000 mechanical harvesters. At the start of the Civil War 80,000 to 90,000 reapers were in use on Middle Western farms, many of them manufactured at McCormick's Chicago factory.[20]

With the introduction of McCormick's reaper, American agriculture entered the era of mechanization. The reaper was followed by other labor- and time-saving devices: mowers and binders, steam threshers, mechanized plows and all-purpose combines. In the 1880s these machines made possible "bonanza farms" where tens of thousands of acres were harvested within a matter of days. By contrast, the 233 man hours needed to produce a hundred bushels of wheat in 1840 took 152 man hours in 1880 and only 108 man hours in 1900. The value of farm machinery rose from 152 million dollars in 1850 to 271 million dollars in 1870, to 750 million dollars in 1900.[21]

The reaper facilitated large-scale farming and by the Civil War turned the West into the "breadbasket" of the nation. National production of wheat rose phenomenally: 84 million bushels in 1839, 173 million bushels in 1859, 289 million bushels in 1869, up to 502 million bushels in 1880. Western states produced 50 percent of these totals by 1860 and continued to increase their capacity thereafter. Not only wheat, but corn, oats, barley, and soybean production soared.

The new technology transformed the West from a remote frontier area into a vital section, politically and economically. The railroad, of course, was essential in this transformation. But mechanization of agriculture was the cornerstone of Western importance for it gave farmers the wherewithal to harvest the vast acreage of the Great Plains. Agricultural technology created an economy of abundance, something unheard of in other parts of the world. Abundance, in turn, allowed Americans to eat better and it gave the United States surplus commodities for export. Mechanization of agriculture had political impli-

---

[20] *Ibid.,* p. 286.
[21] U.S. Bureau of the Census, *Historical Statistics of the United States, Colonial Times to 1957* (Washington, D.C., 1960), pp. 281, 285.

cations as well. Western wheat fed northern troops during the Civil War and made the British, who depended upon American grain, hesitate to recognize the South. In sum, the mechanization of agriculture shaped western development, and made the West an important sectional force in national affairs.

SOUTHERN AGRICULTURE AND THE COTTON GIN

In the autumn of 1792 a young Yale college graduate, Eli Whitney, traveled south to Georgia to take up a job as a tutor. Finding that his employer intended to pay him only half his negotiated salary, Whitney refused the teaching position and accepted instead an invitation to visit the plantation of Mrs. Nathanael Greene, widow of General Nathanael Greene of Revolutionary War fame. While learning about southern society and manners, Whitney was also instructed in the problems facing southern agriculture. Tobacco exports had fallen off since the Revolution and the soil would not yield adequate surpluses of long fibered cotton. Green seed or upland cotton, however, grew well, but it took a slave an entire day to clean the seeds from a pound of cotton. Mrs. Greene suggested to Whitney that he apply his mechanical talents to solving this problem and he accepted the challenge.

Encouraged by Mrs. Greene and her plantation manager Phineas Miller, Whitney set to work in one of the farm's shops. Within six months he built the prototype of his cotton gin (engine). The gin consisted of a cyclinder containing tiny protruding wires mounted in a box. As the cylinder rotated, the wires passed through a series of slats, tearing at the cotton but leaving behind the seeds, which were too large to pass through the slats. The clean cotton was swept from the wires by a brush mounted over the wires rotating in the opposite direction. The first gins were operated by hand; subsequent models were adapted to horse and steam power.

Whitney's gin could process fifty pounds of cotton in a day. Later, improved models could process even more. As gins came into use, pirated and copied by unscrupulous farmers, cotton production in the South spiraled: 10,000 bales in 1793, 100,000 in 1801, 533,000 in 1825, 1.06 million in 1835, 2.1 million in 1850, and almost four million in 1860. The dollar value of cotton production was enormous and cotton became the largest export staple of the nation. The South produced seven-eighths of the world's cotton on the eve of the Civil War. No wonder, it was hailed in the South as "king."

Whitney's invention provided southerners with a new technology which made wide-scale cotton production possible. One consequence was that large sums began to be invested in cotton and cotton agriculture spread throughout the entire South engulfing the southern frontier states as well. Another consequence was that slavery, which some observers predicted would die out in the early 1800s, gained a new economic rationale. The price of slaves rose, importations increased and the slave population boomed. Even farmers operating with a few slaves made profits because of high cotton prices.

Overemphasis on the cultivation of cotton, however, retarded the South's agricultural and industrial development. With easy money coming from cotton, there was no obvious reason for planter's to diversify; some continued to grow tobacco, rice and sugar but few believed that farming crops other than cotton was worthwhile. Ownership of land remained the measure of a man's worth; capital, poured into land and slaves, was not available for industrial enterprise. A few southerners operated textile mills. Lumber and flour mills, iron and coal mines also dotted the South. On the eve of the Civil War, however, less than ten percent of the nation's manufactured goods came from below the Mason-Dixon line.

To say that the cotton gin was solely responsible for retarding Southern agricultural and industrial development is, of course, an exaggeration. Southerners could have taken some of their profits from the export of cotton and used it to promote home industries. They could have lessened their dependence on the industrialized North, had they not clung so strongly to agrarian ideals. The cotton gin did not create a slave South, nor did it force southerners to evolve a one-crop economy. It did not change the South as much as it intensified forces already strong in southern society.

THE BIRTH OF AMERICAN MANUFACTURING

Before the American Revolution there were virtually no factories in America. Work was done in small shops by independent craftsmen and mass production was unknown. In 1790, however, the first factory for spinning cotton thread was built at Pawtucket, Rhode Island. It was the creation of an ambitious English mechanic named Samuel Slater.

Slater had left England with hopes of getting rich in America. Familiar with the machines in the factory of Jedediah Smith, a cotton manufacturer and partner of the inventor Arkwright, Slater smuggled out plans for spinning cotton by relying on his exceptional memory. Having arrived in Philadelphia in 1789, he accepted an offer from a group of Quaker businessmen to get some old spinning machinery working, but when Slater saw their condition he proposed to his sponsors that he build new machines, on Arkwright's principles, from scratch. Working closely with a skilled blacksmith and several carpenters who were sworn to secrecy, Slater began his ambitious project. By December 1790, his factory was complete; the first to manufacture cotton thread by water-driven machinery.

The success of Slater's cotton-thread machines encouraged imitation. By 1815 there were 213 factories in the Northeast operating 130,000 spindles. The textile industry did not really become firmly established, however, until a group of merchants, the Boston Associates, set up a factory which spun thread and wove cotton cloth on a massive scale. The Associates, led by Francis Cabot Lowell, established their first textile factory at Waltham, Massachusetts. The Lowell mills returned such a handsome profit that Lowell was encouraged to undertake other projects. In 1823 the Boston Associates began building a new manufacturing complex at a high falls on the Merrimack River which they named after the recently deceased Lowell. By 1850 Lowell was a city of 32,000 workers tending 300,000 spindles and 9,000 power looms.[22]

The adoption of the factory system was an important technical advance over old methods of production which relied upon workers living in different locations, performing highly specialized tasks. Brought under one roof, they were easily available, and with machines taking over complex tasks, cheap unskilled labor (women and children) could be recruited. Despite the fact that factories seemed ideal for textile manufacture, however, it was by no means certain that they could mass produce products that required precision work. It was not until a group of New England gunsmiths applied the concepts of standardization and interchangeability to manufacture, that it became possible for thousands of items to be mass produced by machine.

Historians have traditionally attributed the development of manufacture utilizing interchangeable parts to Eli Whitney, who convinced the American government in 1798 that he could produce 10,000 muskets for the United States army within two years. The idea of interchangeable parts was not new—it originated in France with a man named Blanc—but Whitney hoped to perfect it and give it practical application in America. Setting up a small factory in what later became Whitneyville, Connecticut, he began to design and build machines that would turn out parts *so identical* that each one would be *interchangeable* among the rifles he produced. Whitney's progress was slow—he produced only 500 rifles between 1798 and 1800—and

---

[22] Mitchell Wilson, *American Science and Invention, A Pictorial History* (New York, 1954), p. 89.

it took him ten years, rather than two, to manufacture the promised number of rifles. Nevertheless, when he completed his project he had the satisfaction of knowing that he had made a major contribution to the art of manufacture in America. By the time of his death in 1825, precision manufacture by machine and interchangeability were accepted as essential principles of American industrial technology.

Recent research has shown that Whitney alone was not the father of the concept of interchangeable parts nor even its finest practitioner. The United States arsenals at Springfield and Harper's Ferry employed machines to make identical parts and other gun manufacturers such as Asa Waters, Lemuel Pomeroy, Simeon North and John Hall contributed to the development of standardized manufacture.[23] Along with Whitney these men paved the way for what became known as the American System of Manufacturing. It was based on factory mass production with machines turning out standardized (and therefore interchangeable) parts. The system required considerable capital for tooling up but once the machines were designed and created they could produce parts and products cheaply and efficiently.

The American system was applied to a broad field of products after rifle manufacture proved its effectiveness. Machines were invented to manufacture nails and screws, lamps, bedposts, furniture parts, even biscuits. Interchangeability was particularly important in the manufacture of watches and clocks, padlocks, keys, sewing machines and railroad apparatus. The system was ideally suited to a people who demanded cheap, durable products free of frills and fancy detail still characteristic of European manufacture. Europeans, in fact, were so impressed by the American system that committees were sent to the United States to study American methods of manufacture. One committee reported to the British House of Commons in 1854 that American products were sometimes crude but that production methods were excellent. "In the adaptation of special apparatus to a single operation in almost all branches of industry, the Americans display an amount of ingenuity, combined with undaunted energy, which as a nation we would do well to imitate."[24]

As a consequence of adopting factory production, and developing and refining standardized manufacture, Americans were ready to make important industrial strides in the middle decades of the nineteenth century. They had learned the lessons taught by Whitney and Lowell. They had seen how a market could be developed and ex-

---

[23] Robert S. Woodbury, "The Legend of Eli Whitney," *Technology and Culture*, 1, No. 3 (1960), pp. 235–251.
[24] Sawyer, "Social Basis," p. 374.

ploited by producing items cheaply and efficiently. When the Civil War finally resolved the issues of sectionalism and slavery, American industry and technology moved forward rapidly. By the time the nation prepared to celebrate its centennial in 1876, it was already considered one of the most technologically advanced nations in the world.

TECHNOLOGY AND INDUSTRY: 1850–1920

During the second half of the nineteenth century and the first two decades of the twentieth American industry came of age. The Lowell mills, the shops of Whitneyville, and many of the nation's other manufacturing establishments were replaced by giant new factories which produced everything from locomotives to safety pins. Hardly a year passed without thousands of applications pouring in upon the United States Patent Office, applications seeking protection for new machines, gadgets, chemical and electrical devices which would make some phrase of factory production more efficient or life more comfortable and easier to live. Eight hundred and eighty-three patents were issued in 1850 to American inventors. Two decades later the number reached 12,137. By the turn of the century, patents were being issued at the rate of 25,000 a year. Literally, this was an age of invention, an age in which the machine became an integral part of American society and culture.

There were thousands of inventions and technological developments which revolutionized American industry between 1850 and 1920; given adequate space we might discuss many of these. Because the list is long, however, it is necessary to isolate those technical developments which had broad impact and which encouraged additional invention and mechanization. The development of a method for making high-grade steel was one of these; so was the creation of basic industries such as coal, oil, and electricity. The sewing machine merits attention because it paved the way for the ready-made clothing and shoe industry. Henry Ford's assembly line, introduced in 1914, also deserves mention because of its impact on all subsequent methods of manufacture.

MAKING HIGH-GRADE STEEL

During colonial times the primary material used in manufacture and building was wood. A few iron foundries existed which turned out pig iron but it was not until after the War of 1812 that iron production gained significantly. Then experiments with new fuels—soft and hard coal and coke—and with mechanical methods of blowing hot air into iron increased iron output. By 1860, over a half-million tons of pig iron were produced in 377 furnaces, ten times the amount produced in 1810.[25] Another half-million tons of bar iron were also produced in 1860.

The production of steel, however, remained small because iron masters had not perfected a method of reducing the carbon content in iron below two percent, the point at which iron becomes tough, elastic steel. Actually a Kentuckian named William Kelly had developed a steel-making process in the 1850s, but a patent war with Henry Bessemer, an Englishman using some of Kelly's techniques, thwarted dissemination of Kelly's process. Bessemer received his own patents for making steel in 1856 and some years later convinced Andrew Carnegie that his process for producing steel was efficient and economical. In the early 1870s Carnegie was ready to act on Bessemer's advice. Converters of the Englishman's design were installed at Carnegie's new steel works near Pittsburgh, Pennsylvania. They proved so effective that other steel manufacturers quickly followed Carnegie's example.

The Bessemer process involved passing a stream of cold air through molten iron in a large pear-shaped container called a converter. Oxygen from the air combined with carbon in the iron and the end product was burned off as carbon dioxide. A European refinement of the process, soon adopted, involved the addition of a mixture of manganese, silicon, iron, lime and zinc to further control the carbon content in the steel. When the steel's quality was judged acceptable, it was removed from the converter and poured into molds.

The Bessemer process, although widely used, was only one among several steel-making processes adopted in the United States. Another was the open hearth method in which molten iron was poured into huge shallow bowls and samples were taken to test for carbon content. Still another was the crucible process in which steel, made in pots, was lifted from the furnace before the metal was poured into molds. During the 1880s and 1890s new methods of separating ores by electromagnetism, of pounding steel with steam hammers and of rolling steel were also introduced. As a result of these improvements steel production during the last quarter of the nineteenth century soared. By 1880 American production of steel surpassed British output. By 1914 twenty-five and a half million tons of steel were being

---

[25] Bining and Cochran, *Economic Life,* p. 240.

produced, a far cry from the 12,000 tons of steel produced back in 1860.

In the 1870s and 1880s huge iron ore deposits were discovered in Michigan, Wisconsin and Minnesota. These discoveries assured steel producers that the raw material for making their product would continue to exist in abundant supply. Soon steel was being used in the manufacture of a wide range of machines; in boilers for steam engines, in bridges, buildings, and ultimately in automobiles. Steel threshers, binders, tractors and barbed wire became familiar items on every farm. Steel replaced iron in weapons manufacture, in shipbuilding and in thousands of household tools and gadgets. Not until the rise of the plastics industry in the 1930s was there such a multitude of applications for a single primary product. With steel the metallurgical industry was born and an entirely new and complex technology came into being.

COAL AND OIL

American industries thrived during the eighteenth and nineteenth centuries because they had abundant supplies of iron ore and never lacked natural sources of energy. Water power ran the mills of colonial America and wood and charcoal provided cheap, available fuel. After 1800 an interest developed in the potential of coal when Jesse Fall of Wilkes-Barre, Pennsylvania demonstrated that coal could be used as a fuel in the manufacture of nails. When steam engines came into use in the 1830s and 1840s, coal became America's chief source of energy. It ran stationary steam engines and locomotives. As coke, it was the principal fuel in iron manufacture. By the mid-nineteenth century, coal was being used domestically, to heat ovens, and to keep houses warm.

Coal production boomed in the middle decades of the nineteenth century and continued at an upward trend for the rest of the century. By 1914 the United States was producing twenty-five percent of the world's coal supply, reckoned conservatively at half a billion tons. Advances in coal technology in the twentieth century gave coal production fresh importance. Perfumes, dyes, TNT and nylon were developed from elements in coal tar and coal gas. Aspirin and other drugs were also by-products of coal technology. Although by the 1930s oil threatened coal's supremacy, coal remained a major source of domestic energy. Of the forty thousand trillion BTUs consumed in the United States in 1956, for example, coal still accounted for over thirty percent of the total.

Another important energy source developed in nineteenth-century America was oil, which, before its properties as a fuel and an illuminant were known, was sold as a remedy for colds and aches by self-styled "doctors."

The first man to experiment with oil as a substitute for whale oil in lamps was Samuel Kier, a Pittsburgh druggist who discovered oil seeping from his salt well on the Allegheny River in 1849. Kier sent a sample of this oil to a University of Pennsylvania professor and received word that the oil might be refined and used as a lighting agent in lamps. Not long after, two businessmen, George Bissel and Jonathan Evelyth, approached Benjamin Silliman Jr. of Yale and asked him to evaluate the commercial potential of oil. After Silliman reported that oil had such potential, Bissel and Evelyth joined in a partnership with Colonel E. L. Drake and began drilling for oil at Titusville, Pa. In May, 1859 oil was "struck" at a level of sixty-nine feet. By early summer the small well was producing twenty-two barrels of oil a day.

During the 1860s and 1870s, oil fever spread throughout the eastern United States as fast as gold fever had spread in the West two decades before. Speculators bought up every available acre of land in the vicinity of Oil Creek, Pennsylvania and erected primitive drills and rigs. Unlike gold diggers, however, most of these speculators were modestly successful. Oil production averaged two to three million barrels during the 1860s and then shot up to 20 million barrels by the early 1880s. Known as kerosene, oil became the principal lighting agent in American homes. It was also used as a lubricant and after 1870 refineries began turning out by-products such as wax and gasoline which found their way to market.

Drilling for oil and especially refining oil, became a major industry during the last quarter of the nineteenth century and emerged in the twentieth as one of the giants along with steel, railroading and mining. By 1880 giant refineries, most controlled by John D. Rockefeller, produced millions of barrels of oil for use in industry and in an ever-widening number of manufactured products. Oil was an excellent fuel and a successful competitor with coal. It was transportable through pipes which greatly facilitated distribution. Refined into gasoine, it became the principal fuel of transport in the twentieth century. In the 1920s the lessons learned in petroleum manufacture were applied to the emerging petrochemical and plastics industries which quickly elaborated complex technologies of their own. In the short span of fifty years, oil became the principal source of energy in the United States and a form of "liquid gold" for many oil producing nations.

ELECTRICITY

For the first three quarters of the nineteenth century few men thought that electricity had energy potential. Scientists in Europe and America experimented with it, tamed it for use in the telegraph, built dynamos to generate high voltages, but found few practical applications for it until the late 1860s. Then, experimenters in England built the first successful arc lights to replace gas burning in coastal lighthouses. This was followed by the development of electric street lighting in the 1870s. These giant arc lights, however, were crude mechanisms, requiring large amounts of electric current and burning with an unpleasant glare. Electricity hardly seemed destined to replace gas lighting until 1877, when Thomas Alva Edison began thinking about using electricity to light people's homes.

By this date, Edison was a well-known inventor. He had developed a device to send multiple signals over telegraph wires. Excited by the possibilities of subdividing electric current to reach many users, he began to experiment with passing electricity through substances in evacuated glass bulbs, something others had tried before. He stated his objective in these words:

> Object: E to effect exact imitation of all done by gas, to replace lighting by gas by lighting by electricity. To improve the illumination to such an extent as to meet all requirements of natural, artificial and commercial conditions. Previous inventions failed —necessities for commercial success and accomplishment by Edison. Edison's great effort—not to make a large light or a blinding light, but a small light having the mildness of gas.[26]

Having set his goals, Edison experimented with vigor and tenacity. He instructed his workmen to create the best possible vacuum in his bulbs. He tried hundreds of elements as lighting agents until he hit upon an appropriate filament. This was a piece of cotton thread, fastened to a platinum wire covered with carbon. Further refinements lengthened the illuminating life of these filaments. In October, 1879 Edison and his assistants succeeded in burning one of his lamps for thirteen-and-one-half hours. In November, a patent for a carbon filament lamp was applied for and the press trumpeted the news. Edison had succeeded in making "A Light Without Gas or Flame, Cheaper

---

[26] Matthew Josephson, *Edison* (New York, 1959), p. 181.

Than Oil." "Success," the newspapers proclaimed, "in a Cotton Thread."[27]

To prove that electric lighting could compete with gas, however, Edison had to build a successful distributing system, and produce electricity cheaply enough for general use. To accomplish this, he opened a headquarters in lower Manhattan, purchased a plot of land on Pearl Street to house his new generating equipment, and began the arduous task of laying cables, training men and refining his devices to meet new situations. It took him a year and a half before the kinks in his system were ironed out but finally, at 3 p.m. on Monday September 4, 1882, steam was channeled to one of his huge dynamos and the switch to produce electric current was thrown. Far from being a momentous event, this first commercial use of electric lighting went largely unnoticed. Edison's Electric Illuminating Company on that day delivered current to only 85 customers using a total of 400 lamps!

This small beginning, however, presaged the dawn of the electric age. Within ten years millions of Edison lamps were in common use and central and isolated power stations (for factories, and the homes of the wealthy) were springing up throughout the nation. By the late 1880s competition in the electric lighting field was stiff, for alternating current, which could be transmitted over long distances unlike Edison's direct current, promised new commercial applications. In 1892 all the major Edison competitors, except the successful George Westinghouse, agreed to consolidate with the Edison system and the giant General Electric Company was born. Edison, deep in debt from financing his lamp and dynamo companies, sold out for cash and left the electric light industry for good. Fed up with patent wars and the machinations of financiers, he turned his fruitful mind to perfecting a phonograph and giving the world the first motion pictures.

SINGER AND FORD

Edison was an inventive genius first and a businessman second. Isaac Singer, the manufacturer of sewing machines and Henry Ford the automobile tycoon, were businessmen first and second. They find their way into the history of American technology not because of their inventive genius (although Singer did invent an improved sewing machine) but because they helped revolutionize the art of manufac-

---

[27] *Ibid.*, p. 223.

ture and marketing. Singer introduced the sewing machine into industry and into the home, one of the first appliances to be sold to the consumer on a massive scale. Ford, of course, is known for bringing the automobile into the reach of the average citizen. He did this by adopting the assembly line system in producing the Model T and Model A.

Isaac Singer did not invent the sewing machine. This was the creation of a Frenchman, Thimonnier, who developed a stitching machine in the 1820s and made uniforms for the French Army in the early 1830s.[28] Thimonnier's invention was not well known in America and the need for such a machine inspired native invention. Walter Hunt, a prolific inventor (he invented a bullet with a self-contained explosive and the safety pin) developed the idea for a sewing machine but his prototype was crude and could not sew a straight seam. Elias Howe, however, was more successful. Over a period of years he invented a machine which could stitch mechanically, and proved its usefulness in competition with five seamstresses. He patented his invention in 1846 but had to wait three years before the full value of his machine was recognized.

Isaac Singer, a successful manufacturer of machinery, was also inspired to invent a sewing machine in the late 1840s. His model, patented in 1851, contained several improvements over Howe's invention. Singer's machine employed a foot treadle in place of Howe's hand crank. Also, his needle stitched vertically, an improvement over Howe's horizontal stitcher. Nevertheless, Howe proved the priority of his patents in court, forcing Singer to devise a strategic compromise. This shrewd businessman proposed a merger of all existing sewing machine patents with appropriate royalties paid to Howe. Singer effected the merger and thereafter had control of the nascent sewing machine industry in America.

Singer's genius lay in the manner in which he promoted his machines. He opened elaborate showrooms, advertised with incredible sums of money and soon became known to every housewife in America. His sewing machines became a household fixture, allowing women to make clothing that was both economical and attractive. Sewing machines were also adopted for commercial use and by the 1860's ready-to-wear clothing factories were springing up throughout the Northeast, ushering in the age of standardized clothing manufacture (and ushering out the skilled tailor). The Singer method of manufacturing and selling became the model of successful business

---

[28] Wilson, *Science and Invention,* p. 130.

in the nineteenth century. He produced in quantity, sold within the range of the average citizen, and advertised like mad. Americans are familiar with these marketing techniques in the 1970s.

Singer's techniques were not lost on the young Henry Ford when he decided to produce automobiles in 1906. Hardly the first in this field, Ford's innovations were mainly in exterior design (a short car with high clearance), increased engine power, and selling at the right price. Initial success with the Model T—sold for around $900 in 1910 —led Ford to rethink how he could produce more cars, faster. With the help of two engineers, C. W. Avery and William Klarin, Ford reequipped his factory with electrified conveyor belts which moved his car chassis past workers and parts arranged in proper sequence. Workers thereafter remained in place on the assembly line, performing specialized functions again and again. In 1914 the Ford plant at Highland Park, Michigan turned out an assembled car in ninety-three minutes. The same job had taken fourteen hours the year before.

Ford was hailed as a prophet by Americans and Europeans in the 1920s and his message was clear: "Machinery, is the new Messiah," he declared, asserting that machinery could create unprecedented abundance and usher in the millenium. Ford's proof for these assertions was his personal success, his ability to pay his workers high salaries (actually, to keep down labor turnover), and the improved living standard of his customers. Few disputed Ford's conclusions and his assembly-line system became the model for American industry in the early twentieth century. With Ford, American industrial technology reached new perfection, and the businessman-engineer reached new esteem. The Model T was another machine, in a long list of machines, that became associated with prosperity and progress in American thought.

TRANSPORTATION

In our day of jet travel and quick movement by automobile, it is difficult to conceive of an America in which life was lived close to home and in which travel and transport posed difficult problems. Throughout most of the eighteenth century, for example, travel on land was long and arduous. The Boston-New York trip, made in the fastest stage coach of the day, took three days and another five if the destination was Washington, D.C. Transportation of bulky goods was confined to floating them down rivers, with delivery time dependent upon the swiftness of currents and the adeptness of crews. Good roads were few and far between, and where they existed were plagued by flooding and erosion. In the West hand-hewn trails provided the only routes for regular travel.

In the years following the American Revolution, however, a number of advances were made in the technology of travel. Turnpike companies, for example, took advantage of new methods of paving, grading and draining roads, as well as new bridge building techniques to improve roads which were financed out of tolls. The federal government helped build a free road, the Cumberland, which stretched 600 miles from Pennsylvania to Illinois, thereby opening a route for westward migration. Improvements in travel by stage, and the establishment of regularly scheduled trips, also facilitated easier travel. On the Boston—New York—Philadelphia—Washington axis numerous stage companies competed with one another to offer comfortable rides and cut travel time.

A major improvement in commercial transportation in the post-1812 era was made possible by canals. Canals offered advantages over roads because they facilitated the transport of very heavy cargoes at cheap rates. Connected to rivers, canals extended the distances over which goods could be transported. Canals also stimulated regional economic development wherever they were built. The difficulty with canals, however, was their costly construction, especially in areas that were rocky or of uneven terrain. Despite this drawback, the 1820s and 1830s witnessed enormous activity in canal building, primarily in the North and West, but also in the South.

The greatest canal of all, the one which demonstrated the importance and profitability of canals, was the Erie (1817-1825) which stretched 363 miles from Albany to Buffalo, connecting Lake Erie with the upper Hudson River. The Erie Canal represented the greatest feat of American engineering of its day, accomplished with back breaking work, patience and inventive imagination. To build the "big ditch" new plows with special blades were devised and new hoists were erected to move boulders and vast quantities of earth. Special machines were developed to pull down trees and rip up stumps. These mechanical aides enabled construction crews to overcome major physical obstacles and work at optimum speed. In 1825, eight years after the canal was begun, the project's patron, Governor De Witt Clinton, made a triumphant tour along the canal and down the Hudson to New York City. The opening of the canal was marked by fireworks, speech making, and the ceremonious pouring of kegs of water from famous rivers into New York Bay.

The Erie Canal cut traveling time from Buffalo to New York from twenty to six days and cut costs from 100 dollars a ton to 10 dollars a ton.[29] It opened up a major artery to the West and made New York the single most important port in the nation. Large quantities of freight could now be moved up the Hudson, across the canal, and through the Great Lakes as far as Indiana and Illinois. Other states quickly caught canal fever. By 1830 1,277 miles of canals were built; by 1840, 3,326 miles.

Another achievement of American transportation during the early nineteenth century was the invention and successful operation of steamboats. Several Americans had tried their hand at developing these craft in the late eighteenth and early nineteenth centuries. The most notable of these was John Fitch who built a steamboat employing mechanically operated oars in 1786. Fitch's boat, however, was slow and cumbersome, and proved to be financial failure. It remained for Robert Fulton to prove that practical and profitable steamboats could be built.

Fulton is justly famous for demonstrating the efficacy of steam travel, even though his *Clermont* used an English-made engine and incorporated ideas tried by others before. The *Clermont* was a 160-ton side-wheeler, 142 feet long and capable of traveling steadily upstream. On its maiden voyage in 1807, it made the 150-mile trip from New York to Albany in thirty-two hours, an average of five miles an hour. The success of the *Clermont* encouraged Fulton to produce improved models which he put into service on the Hudson run. Not long after, however, other inventors introduced rival ships of their own. John Stevens, long at work on his own creation, successfully put his *Phoenix* into service on the Delaware River in 1808. Other inventors brought forward improved ships which were faster and more efficient. In 1811 the *New Orleans* made its descent on the Ohio and Mississippi rivers from Pittsburgh to New Orleans. This was the first steamboat to travel in the West, a region which soon embraced steam travel enthusiastically.

Steamboats swiftly conquered America's rivers. There was abundant timber to build them and keep their engines burning. There were farmers anxious to send their produce to faraway markets, and merchants with goods to ship along the river routes. Sturdy, unadorned steamboats were built to carry cotton, hogs and grain. Small, sleek vessels were designed to travel in narrow straits. The most impressive steamboats were built for travelers and tourists who demanded comfort, elegance and luxury. In the lithographs of Currier and Ives we can still see their opulent staterooms, chandeliered ball-

---

[29] Bining and Cochran, *Economic Life,* p. 191.

rooms and open promenades.[30] Each ship was unique, with a style and spirit all its own.

Economically, steamboats were enormously successful. Their appearance brought sharp drops in freight rates, easy transport of bulky staples, relatively cheap, safe travel. Steamboats created the economic flowering of the Mississippi Valley and opened up access to areas along the rivers of the Pacific Northwest. But steamboats also had drawbacks. Their course of travel was dictated by nature. Their ability to move goods was considerable, but their speed beckoned for improvement. In winter rivers sometimes froze, and some rivers remained difficult, if not impossible to navigate. A method of transport which could carry goods over the shortest route, which would be cheap and dependable, and which could be built into a transportation *network* could easily challenge the supremacy of the river queens. The railroad proved to be just this method of transport.

THE RAILROAD

It is impossible to credit one individual with the invention of the railroad. Like so many other inventions, it was the work of many men, involving the adaptation and synthesis of old and new ideas. Carriages set on rails had been used for centuries in England and Europe to carry rock and metal ores from quarries and mines. Numerous experiments involving carriages on rails were made throughout the eighteenth and early nineteenth centuries. The search for a steam engine railroad began in the 1780s but it was not until the 1820s that locomotives demonstrated that they could pull better than horses. In 1829 George Stephenson's *Rocket* performed successfully in England. At about the same time the tiny, American built *Tom Thumb* pulled a group of passengers over thirteen miles of track built by the Baltimore and Ohio railroad. In 1830 *The Best Friend of Charleston* went into service on the Charleston and Hamburg Railroad. On its inaugural run, 141 excited passengers rode behind a locomotive built at the West Point Foundry in New York. A band, seated in the front carriage, played lively tunes, drowning out the hiss of steam. The railroad age, thus began, with style and pageant.

From the outset, Americans welcomed the new method of travel, even though the inconveniences were many. The first locomotives were cumbersome and slow; they belched sparks and lurched; they stopped frequently for repairs or to take on additional fuel. Early

---

[30] Marshall B. Davidson, *Life in America* (Boston, 1951), vol. II, pp. 224–243.

passenger cars were no more comfortable than the cramped stage coaches after which they were modeled; soot and smoke spilled through their windows, along with the noise of the locomotive and clanging wheels. Within two decades after their initial appearance, however, the railroads exhibited marked improvements. Iron and steel rails replaced wooden and iron covered rails. Powerful locomotives, with swivel trucks for negotiating steep curves, were introduced, along with cow catchers to clear the tracks, lights for night travel and whistles and bells for warning and signaling. Long and sleek passenger cars appeared with comfortable seats, improved ventilation, heating and rest rooms; broad windows for sightseeing also made travel more enjoyable. In the 1860s, when George Pullman introduced his sleeping cars, railroad travel reached a new pinnacle of comfort and luxury. Passengers could eat in elegant dining cars, read and chat in lounging cars, and retire for the night while speeding to their destinations at fifty or sixty miles an hour.

All these improvements did not come at once, however, and the railroads had their imperfections and critics. Somtimes they could be dangerous because weak bridges, excessively steep curves and hastily constructed rails caused accidents. Some people resented the intrusion of railroads into quiet, rural surroundings and decried the destruction of the forests to provide fuel and rail ties. Some travelers, especially Europeans, thought the railroads exhibited all the weaknesses of democracy, because everyone ate, slept, spit, and snored in the same class and in full view of everyone else. To most people, however, the railroads meant adventure and excitement. "The fierce-throated beauty of the locomotives," their speed and power, were high achievements of the age. People turned out to celebrate when the first trains arrived in their towns and continued to welcome the news, mail, the people and goods they brought with them.

By the 1840s there were already more miles of railroad in the United States than there were miles of canals. By the 1850s railroads began to stretch towards the Mississippi Valley, challenging the supremacy of the steamboats and then surpassing them in carrying freight and people. By the 1860s the transcontinental railroad was under construction and in 1869 the last spike was struck, linking the Atlantic and the Pacific coasts. During the next three decades the railroad spread its tentacles in an increasingly complex pattern across the United States. The stage coaches, the Pony Express, the freight wagon trains, and Indian tribes all disappeared before the rush of steam. The culture of the East, law and order, machines and settlers, inevitably followed wherever the rails were laid.

One may say without exaggeration that the railroad transformed America during these years. The need for vast quantities of coal, iron and steel, combined with the demand for rails, locomotives and passenger cars stimulated American industry. The need for investment capital and efficient organization and management encouraged the creation of new business and banking institutions. The opportunity to work on the railroads and settle the West encouraged immigration from Europe and Asia; settlement along railroad routes generated new demand for goods and services.

Railroad transportation also dramatically transformed the American market. Without the railroad the West would have remained sparsely populated and unproductive; with it, westward migration soared and western wheat poured into eastern markets and ports. The railroad enabled western ranchers to transport their beef to city markets; refrigerator cars invented in the late 1860s and early 1870s insured that the meat remained fresh. The railroads also encouraged merchants and manufacturers to think of their market in regional, and ultimately in national terms. The network of iron rails helped create one nation and one market out of a group of diverse and far-flung sections.

In addition to its economic influence, the railroad acted as a major social catalyst, altering how and where people lived, loosening regional ties, reinforcing the American habit of moving freely from place to place, quickening the pace of business and broadening personal contacts. All of these social adjustments had their positive and negative aspects, the inevitable result of fast and pervasive technological change. While most Americans welcomed the railroad, for example, a few sensitive critics recognized that it would soon bring the ills of town and factory to the countryside, and that it was only a matter of time before the American wilderness was destroyed. "That devilish Iron Horse, whose ear-rendering neigh is heard throughout the town," wrote Henry David Thoreau, "has muddied the Boiling Spring with his foot." For Thoreau, the railroad was more than a convenience and an instrument of progress. It was a machine which threatened to destroy the harmony of man's physical and spiritual landscape.

Thoreau's love of the individual, spontaneous and contemplative life made him fear the "devilish Iron Horse" and his fears were well founded; the railroads heralded the age of standardization, punctuality and uniformity. They could not be used freely like turnpikes; their cars, fares and routes were controlled by giant corporations which dictated rates and schedules to farmers and merchants. They made coordination, standardization, planning and sound organization into commerical paradigms which businessmen eagerly sought to introduce. They also ran on fixed schedules, forcing people to plan ahead, measure time and follow their watches and clocks more carefully. The railroads, moreover, spread a sameness and uniformity across the continent because the architecture, products and ideas of the East rapidly penetrated frontier areas. Towns did not develop out of their unique environments, over long periods of time, but sprang up quickly on the pattern of those down the track. The railroad helped create the uniformity of Main street in many American cities and towns.

The railroads thus had far-ranging effects, many of which could not have been foretold. They provided speed and efficiency but also monopoly and uniformity. They provided unprecedented mobility but demanded new discipline. They opened up new regions and areas of enterprise but also created new problems and tensions. In many subtle and unknown ways railroads changed the quality and fabric of life in nineteenth-century America.

COMMUNICATING ACROSS A CONTINENT

The striking advances in transportation effected by the steamboat and the railroad, were accompanied by profound changes in the realm of communications; together these amounted to a technological revolution which erased every obstacle set by time and distance. This revolution began with the invention of the telegraph in the 1840s and included the laying of a trans-Atlantic cable in the late 1850s, the invention of the telephone in the 1870s, the birth of the radio broadcast industry in the 1920s and finally the introduction of commercial television in the 1940s.

When Samuel F. B. Morse began work on his telegraph in 1832, he knew precisely what he wished to accomplish. "If . . . the presence of electricity can be made visible in any desired part of the circuit, I see no reason why intelligence might not be instantaneously transmitted by electricity to any distance." Morse found during five years of experiment, however, that having a goal and developing a mechanism to achieve it, could be quite different things. He was trained as a painter, knew almost nothing about physics and electricity, and was too poor to hire skilled assistants. Nevertheless, by 1837 he perfected a crude device for sending and receiving "intelligence." It consisted of a sender which made and broke a circuit in a coded sequence. The receiver consisted of an electrically activated pencil which made marks on a moving strip of paper.

After improving his invention by incorporating the suggestions of Joseph Henry, then the leading authority on electricity, Morse took his invention to the United States Congress; he wanted a subsidy of $30,000 to build an operational telegraph. The money was slow in coming, but after persistent petitioning (and selling part of his rights to a congressman who had influence) Morse received the subsidy he sought. Work on the first telegraph line began in 1843 and was completed in the spring of 1844. On May 24, 1844 Morse sent his first message over forty miles of wire strung between the Baltimore railroad station and the Supreme Court Chamber. It read, "What hath God Wrought."

Initially, telegraphy was viewed as a curiosity and the Baltimore-Washington line was idle. Soon, however, businessmen began to grasp its potential. Ezra Cornell made a fortune establishing telegraph lines extending into the Middle West and used part of it to found Cornell University. Henry O'Reilly, an Irish-born promoter, also became a telegraph tycoon. After 1844 about fifty private companies competed in the telegraph business until Hiram Sibley's Western Union Company (founded in 1856) began to buy them out. Western Union brought order, consolidation and monopoly to the telegraph business. By the early 1870s, telegraphy was nearly synonymous with Western Union.

The coastal cities of the East were the first to benefit from telegraph communication. By the 1850s most of the important midwestern cities were connected by telegraph lines. In July, 1861 work began on a Nebraska-California line which was completed the following October. Now messages which formerly took days, or even weeks, could be sent instantly over the newly-strung lines. The Pony Express which had revolutionized mail transport in the far West only a few years before, was immediately eclipsed. "When the telegraph reduced the time from the Missouri to the Pacific from ten days to a fraction of a second, its [the Pony Express] doom was sealed. America's most romantic experiment in transportation had met its master."[31]

Western Union operated 112,000 miles of telegraph wire in 1870; 234,000 in 1880; over one million in 1902. In 1870 it handled nine million messages; twenty-nine million in 1880; almost seventy million in 1902. These figures exhibit the dramatic upsurge in telegraph usage during the last three decades of the nineteenth century. Americans became accustomed to communicating over long distances and accustomed to receiving distant news with the morning paper.

Morse's invention bound the nation together even more tightly than the railroad's iron rails; the reality of instant communication altered government operations, business performance, and personal behavior and expectations. The telegraph became an instrument of war, serving northern and southern troops during the Civil War. It

---

[31] Ray A. Billington, *The Far Western Frontier* (New York, 1962), p. 290.

became an instrument of government; officials in Washington used the telegraph to maintain communications with officers and functionaries in the field. The telegraph revolutionized the recording and sending of news; "Dispatch by Telegraph" caught the eye and meant that copy was hot and relevant, even when the event or activity described occurred halfway around the world. It also greatly facilitated the communication of business information. The railroads used the telegraph to direct and reroute trains, flash instructions and dispatch repair crews. Financial institutions such as banks, insurance companies and stock exchanges operated on the strength of information sent over the "lightning wires." Big business in America grew up with the telegraph. It was a vital tool in establishing contacts between buyers and sellers, gathering market information and learning the latest financial and political news.

The telephone, invented by Alexander Graham Bell in 1876, had an importance and impact as far-reaching as that of the telegraph. In many ways it was superior to that instrument. It was not necessary to go to an office to place a call because telephones were located in homes and offices. It was not necessary to abbreviate or communicate in clipped phrases because one talked on the telephone naturally, just as one spoke to another person. The medium of communication was speech, not code, which offered all the richness and emotion of the human voice. By telephone one could urge, cajole, convince, explain, command, demand, announce and denounce with all the wit and eloquence at one's disposal. It was a truly personal instrument, equally adapted to proposing marriage or closing a business deal.

The growth of the telephone industry was slow at first, but by the 1890s it gained momentum. In 1891 there were 239,000 telephones in the United States; in 1899, 1,356,000. By 1910 the number stood at seven and a half million, by 1920, thirteen and a third million. Five persons per thousand had telephones in 1895; eighteen per thousand in 1900 and eighty-two per thousand in 1910. While these numbers are small compared to present-day figures (563 per thousand or one telephone for every two persons), they indicate a spectacular rate of growth. More people used telephones than owned them, of course, because friends and relatives offered their use freely.

The telephone was primarily an instrument for urban communication during its first years of use. It offered unlimited opportunities for business; bosses could speak to subordinates in distant offices, sales and strategy could be coordinated, contracts made on a personal basis. Telephones helped break the loneliness of those confined to home or bed and facilitated friendly human intercourse in crowded, sprawling cities. When rural installations began in the 1920s and 1930s, they helped relieve the isolation and loneliness of farm life.

The "Sunday Call" to friends and relatives became common throughout America during these years. It helped people to maintain friendships which were being threatened by the mobility offered by trains and automobiles.

Like the telephone, radio played a prominent part in speeding communication, disseminating information and promoting national feeling.

The radio was not an American invention; rather it evolved from the research and experiment of inventors in many lands. A German, Heinrich Hertz, was the first to detect the presence of radio waves (Hertzian waves) in the air; a Russian, Alexander Popov, experimented successfully with the first antenna for radio transmission; an Italian, Guglielmo Marconi, is credited with perfecting the means of transmitting and receiving radio waves—as code—over great distances; and a Canadian-American physicist, Reginald Fessenden, created radio as we know it by modulating radio waves to reproduce speech and music.

An important contribution to radio technology, however, was made by an American. Lee De Forest (1873–1961) developed the first practical method of amplifying weak radio signals by using a vacuum tube containing three electrodes. This triode, the Audion, was the precursor of all modern radio tubes which formed the basis of electronics until the advent of the transistor. De Forest also pioneered in the field of broadcasting; in 1910 he broadcast Enrico Caruso singing from the Metropolitan Opera House. A few years later he began daily broadcasting of news and music from his laboratory-studio.

The era of commercial radio began on November 2, 1920 when an East Pittsburgh station, KDKA, went on the air to inform listeners about the pending Harding-Cox presidential election. KDKA continued to broadcast regular programs and other stations quickly followed suit. The listening public was small at first, but the appeal of hearing music and entertainment rapidly swelled its numbers. Stations sprouted everywhere, better receivers appeared, and programming gained new sophistication. In 1926 the National Broadcasting Company was formed; CBS came into existence the following year. In 1927 Congress created the Federal Radio Commission (reorganized as the Federal Communications Commission in 1934) to oversee licensing and regulate broadcast traffic. By 1930 almost fourteen million American families owned radio receivers, and 618 stations were on the air.

Within a few years after its introduction, radio became an integral part of American life. It became the only source of news and information for those who could not read and for those who lived far from urban centers. It brought news, sports events, music, entertainment, church services, advertisements and agricultural instruction into the home. A mayor, senator or governor could address his constituency, argue a cause or promote his candidacy. The president of the United States could, for the first time in history, address the entire American people. Franklin D. Roosevelt made extensive use of radio to foster calm and dedication during the depression years and World War II. Every succeeding president used the radio (and more recently, television) as an instrument of politics, persuasion and government.

Radio had the effect of promoting national feeling and homogeneity. Products, heroes, entertainers and preachers became known nationally; people in different regions learned about important events simultaneously; big city values and attitudes filtered across the air waves into town and country. The radio connected Americans in hundreds of ways although regional differences, loyalties and dialects continued to survive.

Radio's phenomenal success was quickly duplicated by television once that medium was perfected and developed for mass consumption. Like radio, television was the product of several inventive minds working on the same problem. In December 1923 a Russian-American, Vladimir Zworykin, demonstrated a crude but practical device for transmitting images at Westinghouse laboratories. In 1929 Zworykin moved to RCA where he continued to perfect television transmission and helped develop the first television broadcasts. In 1927, Philo T. Farnsworth, working independently in California, invented a mechanism for transmitting static images and bits of film and received several important patents which advanced television's future. Herbert Ives of American Telephone and Telegraph demonstrated the feasibility of wire transmission of television in 1927, while in England B.B.C. technicians succeeded with their own television experiments. By the mid-1930s Allen B. Dumont had developed improved kinescope tubes as well as prototypes of television receivers which could be sold commercially.

In 1935 RCA decided to commit one million dollars to develop commercial television and thereafter one technical problem after another was rapidly solved. Choosing the 1939 World's Fair as the appropriate showcase for this new invention, RCA set up demonstration cameras and five- and nine-inch receivers at the Fair grounds and began broadcasting from its Radio City studio. On February 26, 1939, the first experimental program to the Fair featured a telecast of *Amos 'n' Andy*. On April 30 President Roosevelt formally opened the Fair and his speech was viewed on television by an excited audience. Thereafter a stream of studio programs including "plays, bits of opera, comedians, singers, jugglers, puppets and kitchen demonstrations" delighted World's Fair audiences. Not to be outdone, CBS and the

Dumont organization moved quickly from experiment to practice. They began telecasting in New York in 1939–1940 and Dumont began marketing receivers. By May 1940 there were twenty-three television stations operating in the United States.

Television had to wait for the end of World War II, a war which focused attention on radar, atomic energy and defense production, to make a second debut. When it did, however, the major networks were ready to exploit television's potential. Television sets began appearing in retail stores in 1946–1947. F.C.C. licenses were acquired and new broadcasting studios were rapidly established. New programs, now paid for by advertising, began to be broadcast daily.

> As sets appeared, taverns rushed to acquire them. Sports events proved an especially powerful attraction. In every television city, groups clustered around tavern sets. The program repertoire expanded. In January 1947 the opening of Congress was televised for the first time. . . . In May the *Kraft Theater* television drama series made its NBC debut. That summer the Zoomar lens got into action in a CBS telecast of a baseball game between the Brooklyn Dodgers and the Cincinnati Reds. Its ability to leap from a full-field long shot to a close-up of the pitcher working his wad of chewing tobacco caused a stir.[32]

By the late 1940s Americans had television fever. Within a few years millions lost interest in radio and millions more stopped attending the local cinema.

Television's rapid acceptance is reflected in some remarkable statistics. Within a decade of its introduction almost fifty million American homes had television receivers. It had taken radio twenty-five years to accomplish the same level of acceptance and the automobile nearly half a century. By 1974 ninety-six percent of all households owned at least one television set while nearly thirty percent had two or more. What alarmed some critics was the mesmerizing grip of television on the popular mind, a grip exerted equally on young and old. "The average American male at age sixty-five has spent three thousand days, or nearly nine years, watching television; a five-year-old American child has spent more hours before the set than a student spends in class during four years of college."[33] The new media, moreover, had far-reaching cultural effects. It was, as Marshall McLuhan said, a

---

[32] Erik Barnouw, *The Golden Web, A History of Broadcasting in the United States 1933–1953* (New York, 1968), p. 244.

[33] Russel Nye, *The Unembarrassed Muse, The Popular Arts in America* (New York, 1970), p. 408.

cool medium which would alter perceptions and our attitudes towards print. It was an instantaneous medium which reconnected and retribalized people into a "global village." Beyond this the quality of television programming was hotly debated as programs with scant educational or cultural content dominated television screens. The debate over television's influence and impact continues in the 1970s as broadcasters experiment with innovative formats and as Public Service Television begins to attract a new, more sophisticated audience.

CONCLUSION

From the first improvements in the plow, to the advent of television and travel in space, technology has shaped American society and culture. Because America was a frontier region with few restraints on individual initiative and experiment, because European immigrants were anxious to create material wealth out of a rich but untamed environment, because labor was scarce and all that was new and innovative came to be highly regarded—Americans turned to machines to create wealth and abundance. Machines became symbols of progress and power in the nation's literature, advertisements and magazines. Machines were perceived as tools which would strengthen and unify American society. Technology became linked in the popular mind with all the positive virtues: democracy, a high standard of living, the conquest of nature.[34]

While the majority of Americans throughout our history praised machines as instruments of progress, a few isolated individuals spoke out against the march of technology and all that it implied. "If the inventive genius of America . . . brings into being machine after machine . . . is not the laborer, here as in England, thereby liable at last, to be crowded out of the permission to work for his daily bread."[35] This was the English reformer Robert Owen speaking, articulating the fears of many American laborers who feared that machines would render their labor obsolete. "Things are in the saddle and ride mankind," wrote the poet Ralph Waldo Emerson, describing a society in which objects were coming to mean more than men and technical mastery more than spiritual growth. Owen and Emerson, Henry David Thoreau, and a few representatives of labor spoke out against the po-

---

[34] See, for example, Hugo A. Meier, "Technology and Democracy, 1800–1860," *Mississippi Valley Historical Review* 43 (1957)): 618–640; and Leo Marx, *The Machine in the Garden: Technology and the Pastoral Ideal in America* (New York, 1964).

[35] Quoted in Meier, p. 629.

tential destruction and dehumanization which accompanied technological advance, but their voices were hardly heard. The great majority of Americans believed that machines would create a nation of plenty and they welcomed inventions accordingly.

In retrospect, we can see that the dissenters voiced important criticisms. They were the first to recognize the negative effects of technology. They were the first to point to the destruction of nature, the devaluation of human labor, the reverence for power and mechanism in place of human and aesthetic concerns. Today, we are becoming aware that technology must be understood and tamed, in order to create a world in which machines serve people and people come before machines. To neglect this would be to fulfill Emerson's dire prediction.

> Things are in the saddle,
> And ride mankind.

> There are two laws discrete,
> Not reconciled,
> Law for man, and law for thing;
> The last builds town and fleet,
> But it runs wild,
> And doth the man unking.

SUGGESTIONS FOR FURTHER READING

A good introduction to the problems raised by modern technology is Emmanuel Mesthene's *Technological Change: Its Impact on Man and Society* (1970) and, edited by the same author, *Technology and Social Change* (1967). Also valuable are Barry Commoner, *The Closing Circle: Nature, Man and Technology* (1971); Victor Ferkiss, *Technological Man: The Myth and the Reality* (1969); Alvin Toffler, *Future Shock* (1970); Eugene Schwartz, *Overskill: The Decline of Technology in Modern Civilization* (1971); Irene Taviss, *Our Tool-Making Society* (1972); Robert H. Hamill, *Plenty and Trouble: The Impact of Technology on People* (1971); Jacques Ellul, *The Technological Society* (1964); Marshall McLuhan, *Understanding Media: The Extensions of Man* (1964); Michael Harrington, *The Accidental Century* (1965); Herman Kahn and Anthony Wiener, *The Year 2000: A Framework for Speculation on the Next Thirty-Three Years* (1967); and Theodore Roszak, *The Making of a Counter Culture* (1969).

There are very few comprehensive histories of American technology. Among the more useful are: John W. Oliver, *A History of Ameri-*

can *Technology* (1956); Roger Burlingame, *March of the Iron Men* (1938); Mitchell Wilson, *American Science and Invention: A Pictorial History* (1954); Waldemar Kaempffert, ed., *A Popular History of American Invention* (1924); and Carroll W. Pursell Jr., *Readings in Technology and American Life* (1969). Material on American technological development is also included in Marshall Davidson, *Life in America* (1951); A. C. Bining and T. C. Cochran, *The Rise of American Economic Life* (1964); A. Hunter Dupree, *Science and the Emergence of Modern America, 1865–1916* (1963); and the National Geographic Society, *Those Inventive Americans* (1971), a popular treatment. Hindle Brooke's *Technology in Early America* (1966) is a definitive bibliography with commentary.

Interpretive studies of American technology include: H. J. Habakkuk, *American and British Technology in the Nineteenth Century* (1962); Stuart Bruchey, *The Roots of American Economic Growth, 1607–1861* (1965); Eugene S. Ferguson, "On the Origin and Development of American Mechanical 'Know-How'," *Midcontinent American Studies Journal*, 3 (1962), 3–16; J. E. Sawyer, "The Social Basis of the American System of Manufacturing," *Journal of Economic History*, 14 (1954), 361–379; George H. Daniels, "The Big Questions in the History of American Technology," *Technology and Culture*, 2, No. 1 (January, 1970), 1–21; Robert S. Woodbury, "The Legend of Eli Whitney," *Technology and Culture*, 1, No. 3 (1960), 235–251; Hugo Meier, "Technology and Democracy, 1800–1860," *Mississippi Valley Historical Review*, 43 (1957), 618–640; Leo Marx, *The Machine in the Garden: Technology and the Pastoral Ideal in America* (1964).

There are biographies of most of the important American inventors and technologists. For a quick sketch consult Isaac Asimov, *Asimov's Biographical Encyclopedia of Science and Technology* (1964). Nontechnical and highly interesting are: Carleton Mabee, *The American Leonardo, The Life of Samuel F. B. Morse* (1943); Constance M. Green, *Eli Whitney and the Birth of American Technology* (1956); William T. Hutchinson, *Cyrus Hall McCormick* (2 vols., 1930 and 1935); Matthew Josephson, *Edison* (1959); Allan Nevins and F. E. Hill, *Ford* (1954–1957); Joseph Wall, *Andrew Carnegie* (1970); and Robert V. Bruce, *Alexander Graham Bell and the Conquest of Solitude* (1973). Greville and Dorothy Bathe's *Oliver Evans: A Chronicle of Early American Engineering* (1935) is a major work but very technical and detailed.

The history of American broadcasting is covered in a three volume work by Erik Barnouw. See Barnouw's *A Tower in Babel: A History of Broadcasting in the United States to 1933* (1966), *The Golden Web: A History of Broadcasting in the United States, 1933–1953* (1968), and *The Image Empire: A History of Broadcasting in the United States From 1953* (1970).

The Pursuit of Happiness

2

Communes of Today and Yesterday

Daily and hourly, television and the printed media introduce us to movements, events and ideas. This deluge of instant information often creates the impression that America is a land where history is synonymous with yesterday's news and where all that is going on is indeed new and pioneering. Those familiar with American history, however, are afforded a different perspective. Much that seems new is really a resurgence or revitalization of past influences and ideas. This is especially true of the subject of this chapter: the commune phenomenon in American thought and culture.

It is estimated that there are somewhere between 2,000 and 3,000 communes of various types in America today and that their total population numbers upwards of 150,000 people. They exist in every re-

gion of the United States, in cities as well as remote rural areas, and have inspired admiration, hostility and interest far greater than their size and numbers would suggest. We know a good deal about communes and their activities because both the establishment and the underground media have provided us with full and lively coverage. Sociologists, too, have rushed to write about communes and their implications for society, but if one is wary of academic analysis, one may turn for information to the newsletters, broadsides and graphic creations of the commune members themselves.

The communes of contemporary America by no means share the same structure, style of living and goals. Richard Fairfield who has written about the commune movement extensively differentiates between Marxist, anarchist, and ideological communes, those founded on scientific theory, modern religious communes, hip communes, group marriage communes, service communes and youth communes.[1] Sonya Rudikoff writes that some groups are "revolutionary, some anarchist, some organized on specific Yoga, Buddhist, Sufi or other principles, some based on sexual reform, some on dietary reform, some on Skinnerian ideas, some on drugs, or encounter theory, or extrasensory perception. There are women's communes, there are urban workers' collectives in various professions, there are recreations of Indian tribes, there are the Jesus Freaks, the Children of God, the Havurat Shalom."[2] The first impression that one gains from studying modern communes is that they offer a highly diverse and everchanging variety of alternatives to living life in mainstream society.

Consider the following examples:

> At Twin Oaks, a commune in Virginia established on the principles outlined in B. F. Skinner's *Walden Two,* a group of people devote themselves to communal living and support themselves by making hammocks out of cotton rope. They appoint managers to oversee all communal activities—including a "Generalized Bastard" whose job is to hear and redress grievances. Members live a productive, well-ordered existence. Children are raised by a Child Raising Manager and the biological parents are not permitted to discipline their own children. Work is mandatory although extra incentives are offered to those doing the most difficult or boring work.

> At the Hog Farm Commune in Taos, New Mexico there is no apparent order or structure. Fairfield reports "The Hog Farm is about 75 people living on 14 acres of land in New Mexico, all taking care of each other and this hog and her friend." The Hog Farm received national attention when its members doled out food and tender-loving-care to many hungry and doped-up kids at the Woodstock Festival in August, 1969. Since then hordes of curious strangers have visited the Hog Farm Commune demanding free food and lodging. At this writing the commune's future is uncertain.

> The Lama Foundation in the hills of northern New Mexico is a

---

[1] Richard Fairfield, *Communes USA* (Baltimore, 1972).

[2] Sonya Rudikoff, "O Pioneers! Reflections on the Whole Earth People," *Commentary* (July, 1972): 66.

religious, educational community devoted to teaching and learning what's basic. Each resident family must have the wherewithal to build its own separate housing. There is a residency requirement of one working season before membership in the commune is granted. The Foundation runs a school which teaches plumbing, carpentry, and crafts. It also publishes books on architecture *(The Dome Cookbook)* and books on spiritual subjects.

Pulsa is the name of an artists' commune located at Harmony Ranch in Oxford, Connecticut. The group consists of men and women interested in "producing an art experience by organizing various sound and light activities in environments." Several members of the Pulsa group teach at Yale University.

Harrad West is the name of a group living experiment begun in Berkeley, California in 1968. Its goal is to develop an alternative to the nuclear family and the monogamous marriage by developing multilateral relationships among adults. "Our shared ideals include a belief in openness and honesty between people, responsibility for one's own feelings and concern for others." Regular group therapy is an integral part of this cooperative living experiment.

A group of young men and women living on Ridge Street on New York's Lower East Side formed a commune in August, 1970 that may or may not still be in existence. Its composition and character, however, was similar to countless other urban communes. Members contributed $50 to $75 each month to a common fund. Individuals shared household goods, chores and cooking. The commune had little formal structure, few rules and no spiritual or ideological unity. The commune, nevertheless, was viewed as an answer to the loneliness and alienation many of its members experienced in the big city.

The Himalayan Academy, situated near California's Nevada City, is a cooperative community led by an American convert to Yoga. Members take vows of poverty and celibacy and train for the priesthood. They give up their worldly possessions to follow the teachings of their guru and to pursue study and meditation in the context of living and sharing with others.

COMMUNES AND THE COUNTER CULTURE

Despite the apparent diversity of contemporary communes, their members share a common outlook and set of values that social critics have identified as the world view of the counter culture.[3] This world view is expressed in the language, dress and ritual favored by commune members. It is also expressed in the art, crafts and architecture of the commune movement. A composite portrait of these values and ideals adds up to a statement of cultural dissent, a rejection of mainstream society and all that it stands for.

Perhaps the most important component of the communal world view is the rejection of scientific, technological society and the attraction to preindustrial, even primitive styles of living. The preference for naturally grown fruits and vegetables, for living without heat and electricity, for making clothes and furniture by hand expresses disenchantment with modern tools and machines. Commune architecture, with its adobe dwellings, woodframe buildings, geodesic domes, teepees and shacks, emphasizes an aesthetic based on simplicity, primitiveness and the human scale. This rejection of technological society extends into almost every facet of communal life and thought. The notion that man should master his physical environment is replaced by the idea that individuals should live cooperatively and in harmony with their surroundings. The notion that time should be ordered and used effectively to produce material wealth is replaced by the idea that one should follow emotional imperatives and the clock of nature. Where modern society seeks more and more complexity and technological sophistication, the communal answer is to simplify and get back to basics. Both consciously and unconsciously the members of communes have said no to the demands and imperatives of the modern scientific state.

Accompanying this rejection is a rejection of rationalism and all that it is perceived to stand for. To a great many of the young commune members reason is synonomous with atomic bombs, Minuteman missiles, computers, impersonal bureaucracies, a systems- rather than a value-oriented approach to decision making, and a politics guided by whiz kids and technicians. This distorted and highly selective reading of the meaning of rationalism has led members of many communes to turn to alternative cognitive modes. The widespread interest in Buddhism, Yoga, Zen, Taoism and American Indian Religion is one expression of this antirationalism. Antirationalism often merges

---

[3] Theodore Roszak, *The Making of a Counter Culture* (New York, 1969); and Keith Melville, *Communes in the Counter Culture* (New York, 1972).

with irrationalism as suggested by communal interest in astrology, folk magic and herbal medicine, the belief in the occult and the ready acceptance of mystical revelation, extrasensory perception and other psychic phenomena. The children of computer specialists, economists, doctors and engineers are clearly rejecting something they dislike or do not understand and finding refuge in the subjective and the irrational.

The rejection of time as it is used and conceived in modern society and the emphasis on the immediate experience is another component of the communal world view. Although a number of communes assign tasks and structure the day's activities, the vast majority prefer to remain open-ended and to allow people to do their own thing. The ordering of time is viewed as an imposition from without, as duplicating the activity of factory and office; consequently high value is placed on random activity, serendipity and play. The play element, in fact, is one of the distinguishing characteristics of communal life. To some of the younger members play comes naturally, as an extension of childhood. To others it is pursued purposefully as a statement of what life should be all about. Overall, the emphasis on play and random activity may be viewed as another statement of dissent, of rejection of demands imposed by work schedules, production deadlines, and the discomforts of hearing the 6 A.M. commuter alarm-clock.

Commune members place a high value on the search for personal identity and self-realization, placing the individual rather than the group at the center of the communal quest. Individualism is apparent in the unusual names that commune members take for themselves (Lord Byron, Peter Rabbit), in their distinctive dress, and preoccupation with mechanisms and panaceas that lead to greater sensitivity and insight. Getting oneself "together," and taking one's "trip," are regarded as important and sacrosanct. As one might expect, the emphasis on individualism leads to conflicts with collectivism. Many communes fail to succeed because individuals are unwilling to subordinate themselves to the group. This is one of the major problems and inner tensions in the commune movement today.

There is nevertheless, considerable importance attached to interpersonal communication brunting some of the less desirable effects of an exaggerated individualism. Keith Melville has noted that "there is a thirst among the young for genuine encounter in any form."[4] He cites the instant sense of community seemingly present at rock festivals and the demands for "campus community" as examples of this desire.

---

[4] Melville, *Communes,* p. 21.

Within the communes themselves the attempt to come to grips with alienation and loneliness is dealt with in group therapy sessions, mutual criticism sessions, communal dining and work, the sharing of ritual, music making, and experiments with group sex and the sharing of sexual partners. There is also much emphasis on touching, communi-: cating and loving. To some extent these attempts to overcome alienation and loneliness are not unique; they have parallels in the larger society which has also taken eagerly to encounter groups, sensitivity training, and similar mechanisms which promise less loneliness and more personal fulfillment.

ORIGINS

It is no accident that communes grew and proliferated during the late 1960s and early 1970s. The decade that began with President Kennedy's call for a politics of participation, with the promise of desegregation, a war on poverty and the Peace Corps, rapidly degenerated into a decade scarred by political assassination, ghetto riots, rising crime and the war in Indochina. Young people who had taken seriously the call to make America better found that they were incapable of "changing the system," and turned from participation to active confrontation. The mid-1960s saw the rise of the Students for a Democratic Society, of Black Power, of the Weathermen, the Yippies (Youth International Party) and the televised violence of the 1968 Democratic National Convention. It witnessed the first organized assault on the universities, and the spectacle of draft resistance, draft card burnings and antiwar demonstrations. Almost overnight it seemed as if the educated and articulate young had rejected the values and political assumptions of American society.

Television's daily reporting of the war in Vietnam had a great deal to do with the development of both radical activism and hippie disengagement during the 1960s. The litany of death and destruction described day in and day out created a mood of moral indignation, frustration and anger. The young received this news within colleges and universities where they could collectively feel its impact and organize to protest. As the war in Vietnam dragged on and on it seemed to expose the unresponsiveness of government and the weaknesses in American society. The Congress failed to regain its voice in warmaking decisions; the raucous protest of the peace movement seemed to go unheard. Young people drifted into two distinct camps: those who advocated a "New Left" political program and violent action to stop the war (the militants and radicals), and those who favored total disengagement and the adoption of alternative life styles (the Hippies).

During the late 1960s radicalism and activism lost some of their appeal as the politics of confrontation became identified with extreme leftists and die-hard revolutionaries. The Weathermen's attempts to bomb banks and corporate headquarters only created the specter of more police power; their advocacy of violence discredited the entire radical and reform student movement. Consequently, activism began to be replaced by withdrawal and rejection; political rhetoric by an apolitical outlook; the call to change society was replaced by the call to change oneself first. More and more young people began to experiment with drugs, to flock to communities like Haight-Asbury in San Francisco or the East Village in New York, to gather at Rock Festivals, Be-Ins, Love-Ins or Festivals of Life. It was during the years after 1967 that the values and symbols of the counter culture took on their distinctive form and meaning.

The commune movement thus emerged as one expression of cultural and political dissent, as a movement among the disaffected, the disillusioned and the alienated. Many of the people attracted to communal living were involved in the drug scene while others had tried and rejected drugs. Others had become disenchanted with New Left politics; still others were dropouts from colleges and universities which they felt resembled impersonal bureaucracies rather than communities of students and scholars. The unifying bond within the counter culture and the commune movement was rejection of the values of American society; the goal, "to discover new types of community, new family patterns, new sexual mores, new kinds of livelihood, new esthetic forms, new personal identities on the far side of power politics, the bourgeois home, and the consumer society."[5] As one communal member put it, "Our purpose is to abolish the system (call it the Greed Machine, Capitalism the Great Hamburger Grinder, Babylon, do-your-jobism) and learn to live cooperatively, intelligently, gracefully (call it the New Awareness, anarchism, the Aquarian Age, communism, whatever you wish).[6]

COMMUNES: PROS AND CONS

The commune movement in contemporary America has not inspired objective discussion and analysis. The movement is hailed by advocates in the counter culture, and by sympathetic social critics who are turned off by what they consider the dehumanizing tendencies in

---

[5] Roszak, *Counter Culture,* p. 66.
[6] Melville, *Communes,* p. 18.

American society. The movement, on the other hand, is vilified by people who see the communes as the refuge of pampered youngsters, freaked-out gurus, and lost souls. Because the communes represent a new way of life founded upon a rejection of mainstream society, they inevitably inspire partisan debate.

An objective assessment of the communes must take account of both their positive and negative aspects. One positive aspect of the commune movement is its recognition that there are fundamental weaknesses in a society which is swamping people physically and emotionally by its reckless pursuit of material wealth. Commune members have rejected the hallowed axioms of competition and capitalism because they believe people have become subordinate to the productive processes and that "things are in the saddle and ride mankind." They reject the notion that every technological gain is a progressive step because they see around them the pollution and ecological stress created by scientific and industrial innovation. The search for community, for individual self-expression and for immediacy, is an expression of discontent with a society that is increasingly mobile and impersonal and which advertises personal happiness and fulfillment without really promoting it. In their dissent and disenchantment with the inadequacies of American society the communes are saying something important and fundamental.

Another positive dimension of the commune movement is its affirmation of spontaneity, sensuality and experience. The middle class and affluent youngsters who seek out the communal life are individuals who feel deprived; deprived of living in natural surroundings; deprived of human friendship; deprived of the opportunity to test themselves against the challenge of survival. How else can we explain the interest in farming, building one's own home, making furniture by hand, in baking bread and sewing clothes and the rejection of modern labor saving devices? How else can we explain the delight in play and nudity, the interest in the mysterious and the occult except by saying that these are experiences lacking in the urban and suburban environments from which many commune members come. Seen in the light of experiential deprivation, some of the bizarre and eccentric activities within the communes take on new meaning.

By their very existence the communes serve a positive purpose. They not only provide an opportunity for people to experiment with alternative life styles, but they serve notice on the society at large that all is not as it should be. By literally turning social conventions on their head, by rejecting the nuclear family, the concept of progress, the reverence for material wealth, and all the other ratified values of American society they offer a critique of our conventional wisdom.

Not all their criticisms are valid, of course, but they do goad people into examining attitudes and values that are too often accepted reflexively.

The negative aspects of communal life are also clearly apparent. Rejection of society is not a program nor a bond among people that offers strength and meaning. Communes have short life spans because individuals too often pursue their personal quests with little regard for communal survival. There is too much anarchism and too much individualism in most of the communes, too much spontaneous planting of gardens and too little careful cultivation and weeding. In the desire to flee the responsibilities of the straight world, there is too much rejection of all responsibility. This is one of the inherent weaknesses in the communes today.

Another weakness is the failure to replace the values and norms of American society with anything that approaches a workable, coherent way of life. Everything is tentative and experimental, whether it be setting patterns of work, working out living arrangements or developing agreed-upon alternatives to marriage and the family. A few of the religious and ideological communes have succeeded in putting a philosophy of life into practice but the vast majority of communes have failed in this respect. No doubt many of the people attracted to communes do not want a rigid philosophy or code to live by, but lack of any code creates confusion and builds in communal obsolescence and instability.

A third weakness within the commune movement is the failure to make the communes self-supporting and self-sustaining. Many settlements are begun by people with few skills appropriate to the environments they settle in. Subsistence farming is insufficient to pay off mortgages, or pay for the bare necessities of life. Too many commune members must work away from the communes, take odd jobs or accept food stamps and welfare. The very activities that would make communal life successful are rejected as coming from the mainstream society: planning, developing a budget, mechanizing production, specializing in some craft or product. A few of the communes do produce some item that earns them money. The vast majority, however, resemble rural crashpads rather than ongoing, productive communities.

The commune movement has not yet proved that it is a serious, self-sustaining attempt to promote alternative life styles. This is so because it is built on a number of contradictions. In rejecting the values of structure, order and planning for the future the communes have diminished their potential for stability, continuity and growth. In placing the individual at the center of their social experiments they have sapped their collective energies. Until rejection is tempered by more positive social and economic programs the communes will continue to experience inner tensions and a high degree of failure.

THE COMMUNES OF EARLY AMERICA

Those interested in modern-day communes cannot but be fascinated by their historic antecedents: 130 communes founded in America between the mid-seventeenth century and the Civil War based on a great variety of religious, economic and social beliefs. Many of these communes were tiny ephemeral social experiments, hardly known in their own day and barely recorded in our history. But others such as the Shaker communes, Brook Farm, New Harmony and the Oneida Community received considerable attention by social critics and popular writers and enjoyed remarkable longevity. In this section we will explore why communes were so popular in pre-Civil War America and why America provided such a fertile ground for their development. We will also examine the internal history of several early communes and determine in what ways these communes were similar to, and in what ways they differed from, present-day communes.

Between 1663 and 1860, 130 communes or communitarian settlements were begun in the United States.[7] Twenty-four of these were foreign-language religious communities; eight were secular foreign-language communities; twenty-two were Shaker Villages; ten were communities inspired by the philosophy of the Englishman Robert Owen; twenty-eight were communities inspired by the philosophy of the Frenchman Charles Fourier; and thirty-eight were English language communities guided by a variety of social ideas. Nineteen of these communes were founded in New England, twenty-three along the Middle Atlantic Seaboard, thirty-five in the Ohio and Upper Mississippi Valley, thirty-four in the Great Lakes Region, eighteen in the Trans-Mississippi West, and one in Tennessee.[8] Clearly, the commune movement in pre-Civil War America was popular and geographically widespread.

The idea of founding communities in which small numbers of people could gather and live according to some religious or social philosophy was not indigenous to America. Rather, it grew out of the religious controversies and persecutions that marred the history of

---

[7] Arthur Bestor, *Backwoods Utopias* (Philadelphia, Pa., 1971), Appendix, Statistical Summary.
[8] *Ibid.*

Europe since the inception of the Protestant Reformation in the six-teenth century. Religious sects inspired by their own special interpre-tation of the Bible, found themselves haunted and persecuted by the very authorities to whom they looked for support and for permission to worship freely. Unable to form their own churches, unable to im-plement the social and economic ideas that emerged from their inter-pretation of the scriptures, religious sects began to search first in Eur-ope, and then in the New World, for religious havens. Throughout the seventeenth and eighteenth centuries, the communes founded in America were exclusively religious communities, seeking the unre-stricted right to read and interpret the Bible as they and their leaders saw fit. The Labadist Community (1683), the Society of the Woman in the Wilderness (1694), the Ephrata Cloister (1732), the Moravian Brethren (1744), the Society of Separatists of Zoar (1817), and the Shakers (1787) are but a few examples of these early religious com-munes. In some instances these communes were founded entirely by European immigrants; in others, a handful of immigrants began com-munities which were enlarged by converts made in America.

European conditions in the early nineteenth century also provided the context and the motive for founding secular communitarian set-tlements in America. This was the era in which the disruptive influ-ences of the Industrial Revolution made themselves felt. Traditional patterns of agricultural labor were destroyed; polluting factories and crowded dwellings mushroomed in the new industrial cities; laborers found themselves at the mercy of unscrupulous entrepreneurs; all the old bonds of family and society were loosened. A few sensitive ob-servers, collectively called socialists, began to criticize the growing gap between rich and poor, the squalor and dehumanization created by rapid industrialization, the inhumanity of child labor and the il-literacy and irreligion found in all industrial communities. Robert Owen in England and Charles Fourier in France were but two of the early socialists who became convinced that the only way to reform society was to create entirely new model communities in which "every citizen [was] a genuine participant in the common effort—a co-operator in all the activities of the community and a beneficiary of all the social services it could provide."[9] These two socialists found enthusiastic support among individuals who were convinced the new industrial order was evil and destructive of human values.

Communitarianism thus stemmed from two European sources: the discontent of radical and dissenting religious sects which migrated to America to found communes; and the theories of European socialists

---

[9] *Ibid.,* p. 256.

who looked to America as a place to experiment with their communal projects. As a movement communitarianism proposed the reform of society through the creation of small separate communities. These communities would perfect social and economic arrangements so that they could be emulated and imitated by the rest of society. The communitarians rejected as foolish the notion that revolution could permanently reform society, just as they rejected the notion that reform through legislation would ameliorate society's ills. The essence of change, they believed, lay in the experimental community, in perfecting the microcosm. As the American socialist Albert Brisbane put it:

> The whole question of effecting a Social Reform may be reduced to the establishment of one Association, which will serve as a model for, and induce the rapid establishment of others. . . . Now if we can, with a knowledge of true architectural principles, build one house rightly, conveniently and elegantly, we can, by taking it for a model and building others like it, make a perfect and beautiful city: in the same manner, if we can, with a knowledge of true social principles, organize one township rightly, we can, by organizing others like it, and by spreading and rendering them universal, establish a true Social and Political Order.[10]

Although the origins of the early commune movement are to be found in Europe, it was in America that communitarianism took hold and prospered. One reason for this was that America had itself begun as a kind of experiment; an experiment in religious freedom, in representative government, in the welcoming of different nationalities. It was devoid of the burdens of history as Europeans understood it and it was hailed by some as the home of the "New Man." Well before the first commune was founded in America, the Plymouth colonists had experimented with communism, the Puritans with the creation of a religious commonwealth, and the Rhode Islanders with complete religious freedom. It was the newness and the experimental nature of American society itself that made it fertile ground for communitarian settlements.

The physical conditions in America also contributed to the growth and development of communes. Compared to Europe, America was an empty continent, waiting to be populated and developed. Land was cheap, opportunity abundant, religious freedom virtually assured.

---

[10] *Ibid.,* p. 231.

William Penn invited several of the early religious communes to settle in Pennsylvania so that his colony would prosper. The attractive farm country of New York State, of the Ohio Valley and the Great Lakes Region attracted commune leaders who came to America to shop for land. The emptiness and abundance of the New World not only attracted Europeans, but encouraged native Americans to pool their resources to purchase substantial tracts of land to begin their experimental communes.

Too much, however, can be made of the fact that cheapness and availability of land (the frontier) promoted the commune movement. Arthur Bestor has shown that the frontier "as an area of relatively cheap land or relatively few restrictions" could facilitate the creation of communes, but it could also encourage communitarians to disperse, to seek their wealth on individual farms or feel less need for community when the threat of persecution ceased to exist. He believes that the frontier promoted communitarianism in a more indirect and symbolic way. The frontier, he asserts, provided Americans with the knowledge that a great, undeveloped continent lay before them and that it was imperative that social, religious and economic institutions be perfected before all that territory was settled and frozen into rigid patterns.[11] It was not necessary to plant model communities directly on the frontier, but it was imperative that the work of reform be undertaken quickly so that settlers on the frontier would have examples and alternatives to follow. "The first half of the nineteenth century was the period when it was most natural for Americans to assert and to act upon the belief that the new society of the West could and should be shaped in embryo by the deliberate, self-conscious efforts of individuals and groups."[12] In this manner, Bestor believes, the frontier called forth the communal response.

FOREIGN-LANGUAGE SECTARIAN COMMUNITIES

Foreign-language religious sects were the first groups to establish communes in America. Their successes and failures marked out a path for other communes to follow. They were attracted to the American environment, as we have seen, by the plentiful supply of land, and by the assurance that they could practice their religion without interference from the established authorities. They adhered to a wide

---

[11] Bestor, "Patent-Office Models of the Good Society: Some Relationships Between Social Reform and Westward Expansion," *Backwoods Utopias*, pp. 230–252.
[12] *Ibid.*, p. 242.

spectrum of religious beliefs, all offshoots of the schisms and counter-schisms of the Protestant Reformation. Anabaptists, Baptists, Men-nonites, Quakers, Pietists and Quietists, in addition to a wide range of esoteric dissenting sects, ultimately planted communes in America. A few, such as the Shakers, were the personal creation of some individual who believed that he or she was divinely guided or inspired.

The earliest foreign-language sect to establish a commune in America was the Dutch Mennonites which planted a short-lived community at the mouth of the Hoorn Kill on the Delaware River in 1663. They were followed in 1683 by a group, inspired by the teachings of a Huguenot professor, Jean de Labadie, who purchased 3,750 acres of land on the Bohemia River in Maryland so that they could live according to the principles of primitive Christianity and communal ownership of property. In their communism and their asceticism the Labadists were typical of many of the early religious communes.

> Newcomers were obliged to put all their possessions and funds into the common stock, and when they left were required to surrender them. Their meals began with chanting and ended with silent and spontaneous prayer. Men and women ate apart from one another. Any dish that excited or delighted the palate was forbidden. . . . Household economy was so strict and the check on all individuals so detailed that a record was kept of how many slices of bread and butter were consumed by each person at each meal.[13]

Another of the early religious sects to found a commune in seventeenth-century America was The Contented of the God-Loving Soul, better known as The Woman in the Wilderness. This Pietist sect believed that the true Church was symbolized by a woman with two great wings who would fly into the wilderness at the moment of salvation. Led by a man named Johannes Kelpius, who blended Christian theology with a variety of millenial and superstitious beliefs, the brotherhood of The Woman in the Wilderness purchased land near Germantown, Pennsylvania in 1694 and began pursuing a life full of religious ritual centered around watching the heavens for a sign of the second coming.

> The religion of these men was a rich blend of Primitive Christianity, Theosophy, Rosicrucianism, and half pagan superstition.

---

[13] Mark Holloway, *Heavens on Earth: Utopian Communities in America, 1680–1880* (New York, 1966), p. 35.

> They believed in physical resurrection for everyone who led a virtuous life and adhered to the principles of Theosophy. From the Dark Ages they carried forward the mysteries of the Kabbalah, wore astrological amulets and talismans, . . . and used much of the mumbojumbo of medieval medicine. . . . The usual and necessary drudgery of any poor but self-sufficent community occupied a large part of their days, while their evenings were given over to esoteric studies, and their nights—turn and turn about—were often spent at the telescope.[14]

The Woman in the Wilderness was neither a successful nor long-lived commune. It proved, however, that even the most obscurantist sect could build a society of believers in America.

An equally religious but less mystical sect than The Woman in the Wilderness was the Ephrata Commune, a society of forty men and women led by Johann Konrad Beissel. This commune settled on land in Lancaster County, Pennsylvania in 1732 and constructed a series of communal dwellings without the use of any metal tool or metal building material. The Ephratans adhered to celibacy, a simple communism, maintained a regimen of hard work and prayer and eschewed any kind of worldly pleasure. They slept in sparsely-furnished rooms on plank beds, dressed in coarse woolen clothes and avoided any display of wealth. Unlike the more otherworldly communal sects, the Ephratans were interested in spreading their faith and published many books which were noted for their superior quality and fine appearance. Among these were hymnals, treatises on religion and theology, and the first German Bible in America. They also numbered among them several distinguished men of letters; one of whom, a Peter Müller, was asked by Congress to translate the Declaration of Independence into seven languages. The Ephratans not only built a successful commune, but prospered enough to found several branch communes. In 1920 there were still almost 200 practicing Ephratans in the United States.[15]

The Harmonists or Rappites were another of the German dissenting sects which sought refuge in the American wilderness. Their leader, George Rapp, was a practical man of great organizational ability. He brought his 600 followers to Pennsylvania in 1804, settled them on farms throughout Maryland and Pennsylvania and withdrew the most skilled among them to build a settlement on land twenty-five miles north of Pittsburgh which he had purchased the year before. By

---

[14] *Ibid.,* p. 41.
[15] *Ibid.,* p. 52.

February, 1805 the vanguard of mechanics and laborers had completed their tasks and Rapp gathered his followers to organize themselves into the "Harmony Society." They agreed to "adopt a uniform and simple dress and style of house; to keep thenceforth all things in common; and to labor for the common good of the whole body."[16] During the first year they erected loghouses, a church, a schoolhouse, a gristmill, a barn and some workshops. The following year they built a sawmill, tannery, storehouse and distillery. Being skilled agriculturalists they also planted corn, wheat, rye, hemp, and flax and began to cutivate merino sheep. Two years after its founding, Harmony was flourishing and secure.

The Harmonists were practical folk, not given to fanaticism, asceticism or abstruse theological speculation. They did, however, decide to adopt celibacy after a religious revival gripped the community in 1807. Believing that abstinence from sexual intercourse increased one's purity and spiritual awareness, they announced their intention to abstain from sex; married people continued to live together but in a celibate state and future marriages were forbidden. Surprisingly, this decision created little tension or dissatisfaction. A few Harmonists disapproved and left the sect. The rest seemed to be able to make the transition from conjugal marriage to celibacy with few problems or misgivings.

The Rappites remained in Pennsylvania until 1814 when they moved the commune to Posey County in Indiana. There, for ten years, they labored to build a fine community which grew to 700 persons by 1817. The Indiana site, however, had several disadvantages. Malaria haunted the community; neighbors were hostile and the commune had neither water communication with the outside world nor land suitable for vine culture. Therefore, in 1824, the commune made its third and final move back to a site only a hundred miles from their original settlement. By this time they had considerable experience in planning and building, and the Harmony commune, renamed Economy, rose rapidly and along well-conceived lines. The Duke of Saxe-Weimar visited Economy only two years after the commune's third move and was favorably impressed.

> The warehouse was shown to us, where the articles made here for sale or use are preserved, and I admired the excellence of all. The articles for the use of the society are kept by themselves; as the members have no private possessions, and every thing is

---

[16] Charles Nordhoff, *The Communistic Societies of the United States* (1875, reprinted, New York, 1965), p. 71.

in common, so must they, in relation to all their wants, be supplied from the common stock. The clothing and food they make use of is of the best quality. Of the latter, flour, salt meat, and all long-keeping articles, are served out monthly; fresh meat, on the contrary, is distributed as soon as it is killed, according to the size of the family, etc. As every house has a garden, each family raises its own vegetables and some poultry, and each family has its own bake-oven. For such things as are not raised in Economy, there is a store provided, from which the members, with the knowledge of the directors, may purchase what is necessary, and the people of the vicinity may do the same. . . .

Their factories and workshops are warmed during the winter by means of pipes connected with the steam-engine. All the workmen, and especially the females, had very healthy complexions, and moved me deeply by the warm-hearted friendliness with which they saluted the elder Rapp. I was also much gratified to see vessels containing fresh sweet-scented flowers standing on all the machines. The neatness which universally reigns is in every respect worthy of praise.[17]

The Rappites persevered in their simple faith and adherence to communism for many years. They weathered a schism caused by a "Count Maximillian de Leon" who seduced away a third of their members in 1832, and continued to prosper until old age and lack of new blood began to sap their energies. When Charles Nordhoff visited Economy in 1874 to gain first hand information for his study *The Communistic Societies of the United States,* he found it a clean and attractive community, but old and faltering. The gristmills and factories were quiet. The great hotel, once filled with travelers from nearby Pittsburgh, stood empty.

Once it was a busy place, for it had cotton, silk, and woolen factories, a brewery, and other industries; but the most important of these have now ceased; and as you walk along the quiet, shady streets, you meet only occasionally some stout little old man, in a short light-blue jacket and a tall and very broad-brimmed hat, looking amazingly like Hendrik Hudson's men in the play Rip Van Winkle; or some comfortable-looking dame, in Norman cap and stuff gown; whose polite "good-day" to you, in German or English as it may happen, is not unmixed with surprise at sight of a strange face; for, as you will presently dis-

---

[17] *Ibid.,* pp. 78–79.

cover at the hotel, visitors are not nowadays frequent in Economy.[18]

There were numerous other foreign-language sectarian communes founded in the United States during the years prior to the Civil War. Among these were the "General Economy" of the Moravian Brethren (Pennsylvania and North Carolina, 1744), The Society of the Separatists of Zoar (Ohio, 1817), Grand Ecore (Louisiana, 1834), Ebenezer Community (New York, 1843), Peace-Union (Pennsylvania, 1843), Bethel (Illinois, 1844), Amana (Iowa, 1855), and the Aurora Community (Oregon, 1856). All were distinguished by a desire to separate from the world to pursue an authentic, primitive Christianity. Most believed that communism reflected the economic arrangements of the early church. ("And all they that believed, were together, and all had things common." Acts 2:44) Many of the sectarian communes prospered through several generations, held together by a strong faith which fostered a common outlook and which stifled individualism and dissent. The foreign-language communes thus served as models for other groups, which, during the nineteenth century, separated themselves from the mainstream of American society in the hope of creating a perfect, or near-perfect society.

SHAKER COMMUNES

One of the most successful groups to establish communes in America was the Shakers, a sect whose religious beliefs led them naturally in the direction of communitarianism. The sect had its origins in the religious revivalism that swept England in the mid-1770s. A group of Quakers, led by James and Jane Wardley, broke with that sect when they found its theology and ritual unable to satisfy their emotional needs. The breakaway sect earned the title of Shaking Quakers because their worship included shaking and trembling, dancing and singing, and speaking in strange tongues. Among the Wardley's followers was Ann Lee, the daughter of a blacksmith who himself had joined the dissident sect. She was intensely devout, inclined to receiving visions and revelations, and her strong personality gradually impressed itself on the emotional, spiritually hungry group. One of these revelations enjoined the sect to abstain from sexual intercourse because Christ had appeared to show Ann the depravity of man's original sin. Another, directed her to go to America where the Church of

---

[18] *Ibid.*, pp. 64–65.

Christ's Second Appearing would be founded. Accordingly, she and a small band of followers left England in 1774. By then, Ann Lee's visions and prophecies had established her as the undisputed leader of the small Shaker sect.

The Shakers comprised only a handful of followers in America until the 1780s. Then as revivalism spread throughout the Northeastern states, the sect began to proselytize and attract converts. In 1776 the Shakers began their first commune at Niskeyuna (later called Watervliet) in New York State. After Mother Ann's death in 1784 Joseph Meacham, one of the Shaker elders, helped found eleven additional Shaker villages. Thereafter the sect grew substantially. "The United Society reached its zenith in the decade before the Civil War, when there were some six thousand members in eighteen branches and fifty-eight families."[19] Watervliet had a total of 2,668 members before it was dissolved in 1938. Union Village in Ohio had a total of 3,873 members before it was sold in 1912; New Lebanon had a total of 3,202 members before its dissolution in 1947.[20] Like many other sectarian and secular communities, the Shakers declined in numbers during the post-Civil War era. Yet it still had 1,000 practicing members in 1900. Five or six members remain today.

The Shaker faith was based on Mother Ann's statements and prophecies, her interpretation of scripture and some elements of traditional Christianity. The Shakers believed that Christ was God's first manifestation on earth; his second was in the person of Ann Lee. They believed that neither of these individuals should be worshipped in themselves, but that true believers could talk to them and commune with the spirits of all persons who had once lived. They also believed in spiritual healing, in speaking in strange tongues and in the appearance and exorcising of the Devil. They assert, writes Nordhoff, "that the second appearance of Christ upon earth has been; and that they are the only true Church, 'in which revelation, spiritualism, celibacy, oral confession, community, nonresistance, peace, the gift of healing, miracles, physical health, and separation from the world are the foundations of the new heavens.' "[21] These ideas circulated among several dissenting sects. The Shakers were unique, however, in their belief that God was both male and female and that male and female forces existed throughout the natural and spiritual world.

A cardinal principle of Shaker theology was celibacy. Mother Ann

[19] Edward Deming Andrews, *The People Called Shakers* (New York, 1963), p. 224.
[20] *Ibid.,* p. 290.
[21] Nordhoff, *Communistic Societies,* p. 118.

claimed she was instructed in this by revelation, but no doubt her own psychological problems with sex—an unwanted marriage and the death of all four of her children in infancy—contributed to her teaching that sexual intercourse was the root of many evils. The Shakers adhered to celibacy scrupulously and reinforced the rule by discouraging any contact between men and women. The Gospel Statutes and Ordinances circulated among the elders of the Shaker Villages, for example, read:

> The gospel of Christ's Second Appearing, strictly forbids all private union between the two sexes, in any case, place, or under any circumstances, indoors or out.
>
> 2. One brother and one sister, must not be together, alone, at any time, longer than to do a short and necessary duty or errand; and must not have private talk together at all, which they desire to have unknown to the Elders. Neither should brethren and sisters touch each other unnecessarily.
>
> 4. Brethren and sisters may not make presents to each other in a private manner.
>
> 7. Brethren and sisters may not pass each other on the stairs.
>
> 15. Sisters must not mend, nor set buttons on brethren's clothes, while they have them on.[22]

In this manner the Shakers guarded against sexual contacts and unions. They dealt with the problem of internal growth exclusively through accepting new members.

Shaker religious meetings were full of feeling and emotion providing outlets for pent up frustrations and sexual energy. In the early days they were characterized by " 'trembling, shaking, twitching, jerking, whirling, leaping, jumping, stamping, rolling on the floor or ground, running with one or both hands stretched out. . . . Also, hissing, brushing, and driving the devil or evil spirits out of their houses; . . . loud laughter, shouting and clapping their hands.' "[23] To these meetings came the spirits of the dead bringing good news, or announcing, through the medium of an enthusiast, that one among them had sinned. It was not uncommon for the Devil to visit these assemblies only to be exorcised by the shouts of "Shake! Shake! Shake!! There's a great spirit on you—shake him off! off! off!!." These rather

---

[22] Andrews, *Shakers*, pp. 266–267.
[23] Holloway, *Heavens on Earth*, p. 75.

frenzied activities were gradually replaced by more regulated, moderate behavior. Dancing in unison and chanting was common; so was the singing of hymns. As one magazine observed in 1796, "The contortions, grimaces, and promiscuous dancings, which marked and disgraced their conduct, when they first arose among us, have given way to a mode of worship, which tends to inspire sentiments of solemnity, rather than derision."[24]

An important component of the Shakers' success was their adherence to a strict code of personal behavior. This sect appealed to those individuals who were deeply spiritual and emotional yet required the steadying hand of authority to keep their passions in check. Life in Shaker communes was guided by a hierarchy of elders; individuals were grouped together in "families" where they could supervise one another; the rules of behavior were voluminous and incredibly detailed. The Gospel Statutes and Ordinances, for example, included rules for worship, for eating, for keeping the Sabbath, for behavior at Christmas and Thanksgiving, for the care of animals and buildings, for rising in the morning and retiring at night. The rules for the latter, for example, read:

> All are required to rise in the morning at the signal given for that purpose; and when any rise before the usual time they must not be noisy.
>
> 2. Brethren should leave their rooms, within fifteen minutes after the signal time of rising in the morning, unless prevented by sickness or infirmity.
>
> 4. There must be no unnecessary conversation after evening meeting, and none at all in bed, unless absolutely necessary.
>
> 8. All should retire to rest in the fear of God, without any playing, or boisterous laughing, and lie straight.[25]

No doubt some of these rules were broken. There is no evidence, however, that the Shakers found them burdensome or onerous.

The Shakers adopted communism in 1787 when they decided to live in separated communities and when the New Lebanon commune was being organized. Joseph Meacham, who presided over the sect at this time, worked out the details of the new economic arrangements first stated orally and codified in 1795. The New Lebanon community agreed "to stand as one joint community." The covenant stated:

[24] Andrews, *Shakers*, p. 66.
[25] *Ibid.*, pp. 269–270.

All the members that should be received into the Church, Should possess one Joint Interest, as a Religious right, that is, that all should have Just and Equal rights and Privileges, according to their needs, in the use of all things in the Church, without Any difference being made on account of what any of us brought in, so long as we remained in Obedience to the Order and Government of the Church....[26]

Shaker communism worked smoothly and satisfactorily. Members wore similar dress, ate communally and lived in roughly comparable quarters. They owned few possessions and willed what little they accumulated to the Church. The only problem that required solution were claims made against the community by those who returned to the outside world and wanted recompense for their possessions or labor. Meacham correctly perceived that these claims could involve extended litigation and decided to pay the disaffected a fixed sum provided they signed a waiver disclaiming any further demands. In 1799, to further protect the community, a new covenant was framed which resolved this problem.

And we do, by these presents, solemnly covenant with each other, for ourselves, and assigns, never hereafter, to bring debt or demand against the said Deacons, nor their successors, nor against any member of the Church, or community, jointly or severally on account of any of our services, or property, thus devoted and consecrated to the aforesaid sacred and charitable uses.[27]

The Shakers owed their economic success to their blending of agriculture and industry. Each family had its own farm and surpluses were sold for cash outside the community. Each commune also contained a number of workshops, each specializing in some craft or manufacture. In 1789, the New Lebanon commune already had "a tannery, fulling mill, clothing shop, chair factory, blacksmith shop, and cobbler's shop ... manufacturing such articles as saddles and saddlebags, harnesses, leather mittens, whips and whiplashes, dressed cloth, felt hats, chairs, coppers' ware, wrought nails, hoes, shoe and stock buckles, boots, and shoes."[28] Nordhoff writes that "some of the families make brooms, others dry sweet corn, raise and put up garden seeds, make medicinal extracts; make mops, baskets, chairs; one society makes large casks,

---

[26] *Ibid.*, p. 62.
[27] *Ibid.*, p. 69.
[28] *Ibid.*, p. 58.

and so on."[29] The Shakers are best remembered, however, for their simply designed buildings and furniture made entirely for their own use. The principles of utility and simplicity that guided their work became an important part of the American artistic tradition.

The Shakers were remarkable in many respects. They created eighteen self-sufficient communities, characterized by order, harmony and longevity. They were the first American society to stress the equality of men and women and to place women in important managerial positions. They were tolerant, accepting members from any race or faith who strove to follow the Shaker catechism. They evolved a distinctive style of arts and crafts which set new standards for simplicity and efficient design. Equally significant, they proved, perhaps more than any other group, that communism could succeed if people devoted themselves to some transcendant cause or ideal. They inspired many imitators, but few as zealous, well organized and practical as the communes founded by Joseph Meacham and the followers of Mother Ann Lee.

NEW HARMONY

The sectarian communes of early America were products of the fight for religious freedom in sixteenth- and seventeenth-century Europe. The Industrial Revolution, emerging a century and a half later, also called forth a communitarian response. This time, however, communes were founded not for religious reasons but to see if people could organize themselves to live productively and harmoniously without the baneful influences of industrial capitalism. One of these secular, experimental communities was New Harmony, Indiana, the brainchild of an English reformer named Robert Owen. It was begun in 1825 in the expectation that it would become a working model of a utopian society.

Robert Owen was born at Newtown, Montgomeryshire, Wales on May 14, 1771. After attending school for nine years he took a job in a Manchester cotton mill where he rose to the positoin of manager at the early age of nineteen. His managerial skills and business acumen ultimately brought him into partnership with a group of wealthy manufacturers who purchased the cotton mills of New Lanark, Scotland. By this time Owen had ideas of his own about how a successful factory should be run. Uppermost in his mind was the improvement of working conditions, especially those for young children working in the mills.

---

[29] Nordhoff, *Communistic Societies*, p. 149.

New schools and improved housing for workers were also part of his social program. Guided by a humanitarian outlook, Owen began developing New Lanark into a model industrial community.

New Lanark was not the worst of Britain's industrial towns but life there was bad enough. Poor housing and sanitation, widespread disease, illiteracy and the blight of child labor bore heavily upon the community's 2,000 inhabitants. Vice and heavy drinking were common among people who, six days a week, spent twelve to sixteen hours a day in the mills. Owen attacked these problems on several fronts. He reduced the hours of labor and improved factory conditions. He renovated existing housing and built new residences for workers and their families. He opened a company store where people from New Lanark could purchase items near their cost price. Owen also began a system of free public schools for children, one of the first such systems in· nineteenth-century England. Within a few years conditions at New Lanark substantially improved and Owen earned a reputation as a man with important, albeit radical, ideas.

In 1813 and 1814 Owen recorded his social and economic ideas in a book entitled, *A New View of Society: or, Essays on the Principle of the Formation of the Human Character, and the Application of the Principle to Practice*. This was only the first of a series of books, addresses and proposals in which he expounded his ideas. In *A New View of Society* Owen discussed his experiments at New Lanark and advocated a program of educating the poor. He also discussed the desirability of creating a public works program to help solve the problem of unemployment. Owen's view of society was that the physical and social environment shaped the individual; if one could rear people within a sound social and economic system, the human condition would naturally improve. Owen broke with the prevailing philosophy which held that individuals were responsible for all their personal successes and failures. He did not believe, for example, that poverty and illiteracy were due to the laziness or inferiority of the "lower orders." They were, rather, products of a system which denied workers a living wage, a healthy place to live, and a decent education.

As Owen's fame spread throughout England and Europe he launched a campaign to bring his reform program before Parliament. "In January 1815 he publicly proposed that Parliament enact a drastic measure prohibiting the labor of children under ten in factories, restricting the hours of work to ten and a half for children under eighteen years, requiring four years of compulsory education for all children employed, and appointing paid inspectors . . . to enforce the act."[30]

---

[30] Bestor, *Backwoods Utopias,* p. 68.

Owen was immediately attacked by those who thought his proposals threatened factory owners and the laissez-faire system. He ably defended his ideas before a committee of the House of Commons, but his proposals were modified and repeatedly held up from coming to a vote. Parliament finally adopted a plan for improving the conditions of workers, but by then Owen found the proposals unacceptable. He lost faith in the legislative path to reform and turned more and more to the communal ideal.

Owen's plans to found communities along reform principles crystalized during 1816 and 1817. In a series of pamphlets and broadsides written during these years his reform program was presented. The only way to change society, he asserted, was through the creation of a series of autonomous, but interlocking communes. These communes, ranging in size from 500 to 1500 individuals, would develop an economy based on cooperative effort. Trade would be carried on among communes eliminating the need for costly middlemen. Waste would be eliminated by efficient production; machines would serve rather than dominate men. Owen put a premium on accepting and utilizing science and the new technology in his communal societies. " 'MECHANISM AND SCIENCE *will be extensively introduced to execute all the work that is over-laborious, disagreeable, or in any way injurious to human nature...' "[31]

According to Owen the ideal commune should be housed in a giant enclosed rectangle with living quarters on all four sides. Churches, schools, shops and other institutional structures would be built across the center. Workshops would be located at a distance from the main complex so that noise and dirt would be minimized. In the architectural drawings made for Owen, his ideal community resembled a magnificent walled city which was self-contained and self-sustaining.

Within all these arrangements, however, no place was made for equality of living conditions. Owen maintained that equality was an ideal that could only be achieved slowly. Consequently, areas were set aside for rich and poor, discouraging intermingling of the classes. Only a few promenades outside the community structures were open for all to enjoy. Owen did not abandon this class-differentiated conception of community until the mid-1820s when more radical theorists convinced him that equality and communism should be introduced into community life right away.

For several years after the publication of his communitarian proposals Owen spent a great deal of time and money trying to convince

---

[31] *Ibid.*, p. 75.

people of their validity. He circulated his pamphlets among wealthy and influential persons, met and discussed his ideas with the sovereigns of Europe, and laid plans for establishing an Owenite community at Motherwell in Scotland. America had no place in his thinking until 1824 when word reached him that Harmony, the Rappite community in Indiana, was for sale. Owen was enthused over the prospect of purchasing an entire community with factories, residences, and cleared land. The proposal also came at a time when he was coming under attack for antireligious statements and when the Motherwell project seemed stalled. Accordingly, he decided to leave for America to inspect Harmony and negotiate with the Rappites in person. He departed from England on October 2, 1824 taking with him his second son William and Captain Donald Macdonald of the Royal Engineers.

Owen's social theories had been filtering across the Atlantic for several years; by 1824 they were known to a small coterie of academics and intellectuals who had learned about them from articles in English periodicals. When he arrived in New York on November 4, 1824 he was warmly greeted by supporters among American communitarians. He was also received by New York's cultural and political elite. After an exciting three weeks in which he inspected a Shaker village, visited Philadelphia and Washington and talked with President Monroe and other high government officials, he set out for Indiana to inspect Harmony and negotiate with Father Rapp. By January 3, 1825 Owen was satisfied the Harmony site was sound and a contract was signed giving him possession of 20,000 acres and a variety of shops, factories and buildings that could house approximately 700 people. For this Owen paid $95,000.

Despite the obvious advantages of inheriting a completely equipped and functioning community, New Harmony encountered problems from its inception. Its biggest problem was Owen himself, a man of speculative ideas interested more in speaking to audiences and converting people than getting down to the details of making his new community work. Owen left New Harmony the very day he took title to the community to make a whirlwind tour of the eastern states which included speeches before President Adams and members of Congress and the Supreme Court. During New Harmony's critical first year the proprietor absented himself for all but two months to travel and drum up support for his communitarian proposals. While he gained fame speaking before audiences in America and England, his son and Captain Macdonald had to wrestle with essential problems. Who should be allowed to join New Harmony? What system of property rights should prevail? How should lodgings and work be allocated? None of these problems received Owen's attention until he returned to New Harmony in April 1825.

During New Harmony's first year between 800 and 900 people flocked to the new commune asking to become members. In the absence of any method of selection all persons were permitted to remain. Economic arrangements were still vague and each individual interpreted for himself what he expected communitarian life to offer. During his visit of April 1825, Owen attempted to resolve some of these ambiguities by drafting a Constitution for a Preliminary Society. The document made some provision for selection of members. It also dealt with some of the details of labor credits and personal property rights. As to governance,

> [Owen] would direct the experiment himself during the first year, the members would share in its control during the second, and then, 'at the termination of the second year, or between that period and the end of the third year, an Association of Members may be formed to constitute a Community of Equality and Independence.' [32]

The Preliminary Society, however, never functioned according to plan. Probationary features which would have permitted Owen to select those best suited to successful communal living were never put into effect. On the crucial issue of distribution of wealth and property the Constitution of the Preliminary Society was silent. This was not an auspicious beginning for an experiment in living that was supposed to revolutionize the world.

Owen's failure to lay down clear guidelines for New Harmony did more to hinder the community's growth than any other single factor. The commune awaited his return in January 1826 with keen anticipation, hoping his presence and wise counsel would help them chart the society's future course. Upon his return, however, Owen did little more than officiate at the funeral of the Preliminary Society. In late January 1826 a new constitution was written which provided for more democracy and a "community of property," but which was actually vaguer on economic matters than the Constitution of the Preliminary Society which preceded it. The new constitution proved so unworkable that a month later the community agreed to return all direction to Owen for another year. In the meantime people had become so disillusioned with the progress of New Harmony that groups and cliques made arrangements to leave to found their own communes. In due order a Community No. II was founded, followed by a Community No. III and a Community No. IV. Owen, the heady idealist, believed these separa-

---

[32] *Ibid.*, p. 120.

tions were healthy and granted the first two communities land within his domain. When his sons William and Robert Dale proposed Community No. IV., however, his faith was tested. He refused to grant them land for the new experiment and the movement to create Community No. IV collapsed.

New Harmony was to go through a fourth and fifth reorganization before Owen left it in June 1827. It was also to experience serious financial problems which led to its demise. Failure to select the right individuals from the beginning meant that there were not enough skilled workmen to make the workshops and factories function productively. The absence of skilled farmers and foremen proved so disastrous that the community had to purchase most of its food from outside sources. Owen's early subsidies dulled people's desire to work, and the fact that each received the same recompense for labor provided no material incentive to do more than one's share. When Owen finally informed the commune of his intention to share the community's ownership and profit, provided they share in its debt and losses, most of the members fled from the responsibility. Only a few individuals were willing to put themselves in financial jeopardy to make the New Harmony experiment work.

For all its problems, however, there was a bright side to New Harmony life.

> It was a . . . varied, enlightened, liberal, and, to all appearances, pleasant life which New Harmony afforded its members. The isolation that embittered the lives of so many on the western frontiers was absent. The weekly dance on Tuesday nights, the concert on Thursday or Friday, the public discussion on Wednesday, the frequent lectures on everything from the circulation of the blood to the circulation of wealth, the unhampered discussions of religious ideas, the meetings of the Female Social Society and the Philanthropic Lodge of Masons, the parades and the drills, provided a round of activities hardly to be matched in any other hamlet of a thousand west of the Alleghenies.[33]

The community sponsored a lively newspaper, the New Harmony Gazette, which reported on community news and provided an open forum for unconventional ideas. The church and meeting houses were open to any preacher or philosopher who could attract a gathering. Undoubtedly, Owen's frequent lectures were also a source of excitement and amusement.

The community could also boast of having one of the most effec-

---

[33] Ibid., p. 168.

tive and innovative school systems in the American West. When Owen returned to Indiana by way of the Ohio River in 1826 he brought with him a "Boatload of Knowledge." William Maclure, past president of the Academy of Natural Science of Philadelphia, was on board. So was Thomas Say, an expert on insects and shells; Gerard Troost, a geologist; Charles Alexandre Lesueur, a well-known naturalist and Madame Marie Fretageot, a Philadelphia educator who adopted the methods of the Swiss pedagogue Pestalozzi. These individuals helped create a system of schools that combined classroom study with field work and research. They established a kindergarten, an infants school, "the first distinctive trade schools, the first system offering the same educational advantages to both sexes, and the first self-governing or 'free' school."[34] After Maclure argued with Owen over money and educational matters, Maclure succeeded in making the Educational Society self-governing, an act which strengthened it and increased its chances for survival. Under its auspices Maclure, Say, Lesueur and others pursued their research and published some of their finest work. It is ironic that Owen, who was so interested in educational reform, should have become an adversary of Maclure, whose Education Society was one of New Harmony's conspicuous successes.

New Harmony had ceased to function as a single community long before Owen left it in June 1827. At its third reorganization in May 1826 three independent communities were created—a School or Education Society, an Agricultural and Pastoral Society and a Mechanic and Manufacturing Society. Almost immediately cooperation among the three broke down and more separations took place. By May 1827 Owen was talking about "Ten Social Colonies of Equality and Common Property," a rhetorical gesture that barely masked New Harmony's failure. Undaunted by his inability to build a community under the best circumstances, Owen found solace in new visionary schemes. By 1828 he was planning a series of communes in Texas and New Mexico, a fantastic proposal that died an early death. Owen spent his later years in England and America trying to prove with words what he had been unable to prove with deeds. The Owenite phase of American communitarianism thus lost momentum and meaning after 1828. A few Owenite communes, founded during the days of New Harmony, struggled to survive. None of these, however, could reestablish Owenism as a viable social alternative. From 1830 through the early 1840s Americans turned away from new communal adventures. By the time communitarianism again captured people's imagination, it had new prophets and new followers.

---

[34] Holloway, *Heavens on Earth*, p. 114.

THE AMERICAN PHALANXES

The American belief that small communities held out promise for social and economic reform weathered the failure of New Harmony. Owen's defeat, it is true, stifled enthusiasm for founding new communities during the 1830s, but beginning in 1843 the communal fever was again widespread. From 1840 to 1860, for example, seventy-seven new communes were founded, compared to forty-seven communes founded during the preceding six decades. Many of these communes rejected radical economic doctrines in favor of cooperative arrangements and profit-sharing schemes. Twenty-eight of the post-1840 communes attempted to adapt the teachings of the French social philosopher Charles Fourier to American conditions. His theories of Association created even a greater stir than Owen's views on community fifteen years before.

Before his death in 1837, Charles Fourier drafted the most comprehensive and detailed program for community life of any of the early nineteenth-century reformers. Embittered by financial losses suffered by his family during the French Revolution, Fourier set out to invent a system of society that would inhibit revolution, distribute wealth more evenly, and provide people with a sense of purpose and fulfillment in their work. Unlike Owen, Fourier tied his social reform ideas to a complex cosmology. The universe, he believed, was a harmonious system built upon the symmetry of attraction and repulsion. In order for men to achieve happiness and social justice it was necessary for them to duplicate the tension and equilibrium in God's design. The place to begin was with associations of seven persons called Groups which would call forth, yet balance, competing interests among the seven members. By association, Groups would create larger bodies called Series which, in turn, would form Phalanxes containing between 1600 and 1800 persons. When some three million Phalanxes were created throughout the world peace and social justice would reign. Mankind would be united in language and life style, and benificent rulers would govern for the general good.

Fourier described his Phalanxes in great detail.

> The Phalanx should cover an area of about three square miles, of which the greater part will be given over to fields, orchards, and gardens. Somewhere on this estate will be the Phalanstery—the vast, three-story communal building that will house all the inhabitants of the Phalanx and provide them with every amenity they could possibly desire. The Phalanstery, like the groups and Series, will consist of a centre and two wings in which will be found apartments, a hotel, ballrooms, council-chambers, a

library, workshops, dining-hall, kitchens, nurseries, schools, recreation rooms, sanatoria, and so on. Granaries and stables will be housed in a building that will close the fourth side of the square—and in the quadrangle thus formed parades and festivities will be held, while from here also the Groups will set out each morning in orderly formation, with banners flying.[35]

Each phalanx was to be run as a cooperative society with individual members participating in the commune's total productivity. There was a formula for sharing profits, for classifying and allocating work, and for crediting members for the labor they expended. Although Fourier dreamed up a multitude of job categories, he insisted that individuals change their tasks several times a day. He believed that specialization of labor, as found in factories, dulled the senses and undermined morale.

It was not the complex and bizarre cosmology of Fourier that reached the American public in the 1840s, but his more practical and down to earth schemes. These were imported and popularized by Albert Brisbane, an American who converted to Fourierism in the 1830s, and studied with the master before his death. In the *Social Destiny of Man* written in 1840, Brisbane described the Phalanx system and lauded its potential for social reform. Brisbane's writings, in turn, converted Horace Greeley, editor of the *New York Tribune,* and with him a whole galaxy of reform-minded intellectuals. By 1842 the first of a series of Fourierist-inspired communities was being planned. Within the next few years dozens more were begun.

None of the American phalanxes, successful and unsuccessful, were able to implement even a modicum of Fourier's communal ideas. Most were undercapitalized, something Brisbane frequently warned against. Others began with good intentions but without the slightest idea of what skills were necessary to make a community productive. Still others purchased land that was difficult to farm and far from any settled community with which to trade. One after another the tiny undernourished Phalanxes failed. Apologists claimed that Fourier's ideas were not being faithfully followed. Detractors believed communal failures proved the folly of Fourier's ideas.

There were, however, notable exceptions to the list of failures. One of these was the North American Phalanx, established in 1843 at Red Bank, New Jersey. This community began with a membership of eighty and $8,000. Careful selection of members, a cooperative spirit and diligent work made the community successful. A three-story

---

[35] *Ibid.,* p. 136.

Phalanstery was erected. Seventy acres of orchards were brought under cultivation. A system of labor was introduced which rewarded individuals somewhat more for taking on the least desirable tasks. The North American Phalanx proved that a well-managed community could work. It lasted for twelve years and only went under after disagreements broke the ranks and a serious fire destroyed its shops and factories.

A dissident group that broke away from the North American Phalanx formed its own short-lived community, the Raritan Bay Union. Hardly an economic success, and too evanescent to merit extended discussion, the Union nevertheless created a school deserving of mention. In its day it was a pioneer in educational innovation. Its headmaster, Theodore Weld, was an antislavery activist; the prevailing philosophy of the school was to integrate school and life, "by making work and participation in the wider community part of the natural school experience of each child."[36]

> The school was run on the manual labor principle. Woodwork, agriculture, household skills and bookkeeping were added to the usual academic curriculum. Drawing, art, singing and instrumental music were a regular part of the students' activities. This was, for the period, an unusually rich curriculum, considered by many [to be] daring and experimental. Even more unusual was the coeducational and interracial aspect of the school. A contemporary observer noted: "It was a pioneer institution in many ways—the first in which young women were found educating their limbs in the gymnasium, rowing in boats, and making 'records' in swimming and high diving.[37]

Fourierism was not much in evidence at Raritan Bay Union. But the creative energies and opportunity to experiment released by community life were clearly apparent.

Probably the best known American community, Brook Farm, converted to Fourierism only after a period of relative success as a non-ideological commune. Brook Farm was founded by George Ripley, a former Unitarian minister, transcendentalist, and editor of a literary monthly, who believed that intellectual activity and manual labor within community would complement and enhance one another. With his wife and a small group which included Charles A. Dana

---

[36] Gerda Lerner, *The Grimké Sisters from South Carolina* (New York, 1971), p. 329.
[37] *Ibid.*

and Nathaniel Hawthorne, Ripley purchased 160 acres not far from Boston in 1841 to put his ideas to a practical test. Although working in the fields soon disabused Hawthorne and others of the idea that physical labor increased intellectual output, Brook Farm managed to attract and hold a number of teachers and artisans who developed a true communal spirit. A few workshops turned out tools and utensils. Farming provided enough food for the seventy to eighty inhabitants. The farm also published *The Harbinger,* a weekly magazine devoted to social and political topics. Some of the best known among the New England literati wrote for and subscribed to the community's periodical.

With more teachers than farmers it was inevitable that Brook Farm would develop excellent schools. It supported a kindergarten, a primary school and a college preparatory school. Emphasis was placed on personal motivation, close relations between teachers and pupils and blending manual labor with intellectual discipline. Students chose their own hours for study and were not subject to the harsh discipline then in vogue in other schools. A bonus of living in such an intellectual community was the opportunity provided students to converse with distinguished men and women who visited the farm during its early years. Brook Farm, like many other communes, manifested the concern for educational reform which was considered a prerequisite to any larger social transformation.

As Fourierism caught the reformer's imagination during the early 1840s, Brook Farm became susceptible to its rhetoric. The commune voted in 1844 to adopt the principles of Association and thereafter called itself the Brook Farm Phalanx. It began to discuss the intricate workings of Groups and Series and to allocate work according to Fourier's precepts. Although *The Harbinger* expounded Fourier's doctrines and the commune put his theory of labor credits into practice, Fourierism only added new constraints and problems. A Phalanstery, completed on March 2, 1846, burned the very night its erection was being celebrated, a fate suffered with slight variation only a few years later by the North American Phalanx. After this depressing event Brook Farm was never the same. Its lands were sold at auction in April 1849, and the experiment to combine the thinker and worker came to an untimely end.

The 1840s and 1850s were alive with other communal schemes. The community of Skaneateles, founded in 1843 at Community Place and Mottville, New York, adopted an antireligious, antigovernment stance which was trumpeted in its controversial journal, the *Communist.* Skaneateles' tenure of three years was substantial compared to Fruitlands, an Ohio commune which stressed vegetarianism and dietary reform and which lasted only through the summer of 1843. Josiah

Warren's village of Modern Times, built in 1851 at a site on Long Island, was an attempt to create a community where people could exchange labor notes instead of money and where cooperation would replace competitive capitalism. These and other communes based on practical or utopian ideas continued to be founded throughout the two decades preceding the Civil War. They exemplified the blend of naivety and idealism which characterized American reform thinking in the days when the nation was still young and developing.

THE ONEIDA COMMUNITY

Almost all the communes mentioned thus far were either founded by European immigrants or by Americans inspired by European religious and social ideas. This was not the case, however, with the Oneida Community, a society of native Americans who followed the teachings of John Humphrey Noyes. The Oneida Community was remarkable in many respects. It maintained a successful experiment in communism for thirty-three years. It produced a wide variety of manufactured goods for which it gained both fame and profit. It developed a social system based on multilateral sexual relations, planned parenthood, and mutual criticism. It reared its children in isolation from their parents, but in the care of responsible, devoted adults. Even when it was dissolved in 1881, the Oneida Community left its mark. One of its most successful business enterprises, the manufacture of silver tableware, was continued on a joint-stock basis. Oneida Community Limited is still a thriving company today.

John Humphrey Noyes was born in Brattleboro, Vermont in 1811. His father was a well-to-do congressman who could afford to provide his son with an excellent education. Young John studied first in local schools, then Dartmouth College, and after graduating prepared for the ministry at Andover and later Yale Theological School. It was during his stay at Yale that Noyes experienced a religious awakening. Stirred by a revivalist preacher, he began to reflect on "new views on the way of salvation, which took the name of Perfectionism."

Put simply, John Humphrey Noyes became convinced that Christ's second coming had already occurred; that as a consequence of this it was possible for men and women to achieve perfection, a state which he described as the total cessation of sin. Mankind's present task, Noyes asserted, was to build a church founded on the doctrine of salvation from sin which would duplicate the approaching Kingdom of Heaven. This could best be achieved in communities of sympathetic believers.

Noyes expanded his religious ideas to include the twin concepts of communism and complex marriage. The first held that communal

ownership of property was the way of the primitive church and was
the best system to eliminate greed and competition. The second
maintained that communism should extend to persons as well as
property; marriage should be eliminated and replaced by multilateral
sexual relations in which procreation would be carefully regulated by
the community. Noyes maintained that complex marriage was not
only justified on economic and scientific grounds but had religious
sanction as well. He believed that monogamous marriage was ap-
plicable to man in his *fallen state* whereas complex marriage was appropriate to his *perfected state.* "Exclusiveness, jealousy, quarreling
have no place in the marriage supper of the Lamb. In a holy community, there is no more reason why sexual intercourse should be restrained by law, than why eating and drinking should be—and there
is as little occasion for shame in the one case as in the other."[38]

Having articulated these unconventional ideas, Noyes set out to
put them into practice. By the mid-1830s he was back at his ancestral
home in Putney, Vermont preaching his doctrines of Perfectionism
and gathering about him a small group of converts. In 1840 Noyes, his
wife of two years, and a few families of the same religious faith
founded the Putney Association, a commune devoted to living the
gospel of salvation from sin.

> Our establishment, such as it is, exists in the midst of an or-
> dinary village, and differs not in its relation to the community
> around from a manufacturing corporation or any such other
> ordinary association. A few families of the same religious faith,
> without any formal scheme or written laws, have agreed to re-
> gard themselves as one family, and their relations to one another
> are regulated as far as possible by this idea. The special object of
> the association is not to make money, nor to exemplify the per-
> fection of social life, but to support the publication of the gospel
> of salvation from sin, by papers, books, tracts, etc.[39]

In 1844 the commune formally adopted communism and complex
marriage; two years later the practice of Male Continence was introduced as the best means of avoiding unwanted pregnancies. Noyes'
doctrines scandalized the small Putney community and upon the advice of his brother-in-law he decided to move the commune to a more
isolated region. In 1848 Noyes purchased a tract of land which was

[38] Constance Noyes Robertson, *Oneida Community, The Breakup, 1876–
1881* (Syracuse, N.Y., 1972), p. 2.
[39] Holloway, *Heavens on Earth,* pp. 183–184.

once part of the Oneida Indian reservation in upstate New York. On January 1, 1849 the community announced in its first *Annual Report* that it was safely settled on 160 acres which included a farmhouse, a log hut, a sawmill and some outbuildings, and that it already numbered fifty-eight adults and twenty-nine children.

The Oneida Community grew with remarkable rapidity. In 1850, it had 172 members; in 1851, 205. When Nordhoff visited it in 1874 the community numbered 283 persons; 238 living in Oneida and 45 residing at Wallingford, Connecticut, a smaller commune begun in 1850. The community was able to grow and prosper because of Noyes' keen sense of communitarian economics.

> Judging by our own experience we incline to think that this fondness for land, which has been the habit of Socialists, had much to do with their failures. Farming is . . . the kind of labor in which there is . . . the largest chance for disputes and discords in such complex bodies as Associations. Moreover the lust for land leads off into the wilderness, "out west," or into by-places, far away from railroads and markets; whereas Socialism, if it is really ahead of civilization, ought to keep near the centers of business, and at the front of the general march of improvement. . . . Almost any kind of a factory would be better than a farm for a Community nursery.[40]

Under Noyes' guidance Oneida flourished. The commune began to manufacture steel traps, sewing silk, traveling bags, silk ribbon, mop handles and strawberry boxes. It also raised small fruits for canning, built rustic furniture, and in 1877 began to manufacture the silver tableware for which it became famous. The commune's sawmill provided all its required lumber; its foundry and machine shop designed and manufactured all the machines and tools used in the community. From an investment of a few thousand dollars made in 1848, the community's worth grew to $500,000 in 1880. Between 1857 and 1865 alone, its net earnings amounted to just under $155,000.[41]

All this activity was made possible by efficient administration. Twenty-one standing committees and forty-eight administrative departments were responsible for all aspects of community life. Every Sunday department heads gathered at a Business Board where all the details of production and distribution were discussed. Accurate book-

---

[40] Bestor, "The Transit of Communitarian Socialism to America," *Backwoods Utopias*, pp. 263–264.
[41] Robertson, *Oneida Community*, p. 11.

keeping was maintained, showing profit and loss for each branch of industry and agriculture, and a general Finance Committee monitored all money transactions and set yearly appropriations. The only activity which was permitted to run a deficit was the commune's printing offices which published two newspapers, the *Circula*, from 1855 to 1876, and the *American Socialist*, from 1876–1879. Since publication and dissemination of Perfectionist ideas was considered a central objective of community life, the newspapers were offered at cost to those who could pay, and free to those who could not. Noyes requested wealthy subscribers to pay more than the two dollars yearly subscription to help make ends meet.

The focus of Oneida's daily activities was a large brick structure called the Mansion House. There the commune had its living quarters, dining hall, library, meeting rooms and small natural history museum. A separate building housed the community's children, watched over by a committee and department just like any of the other community's activities. During the day people were busy with their various activities; at night the group gathered to listen to committee reports, discuss common concerns, listen to a talk by Noyes or some visiting lecturer, or amuse themselves with music, theatricals, or other recreation. On the whole Oneida was one of the most relaxed and pleasant of the American communes. No harsh laws restricted social behavior or prescribed what one could read or think. The community, for example, at one time became interested in spiritualism and held seances to determine whether the activity had any merit or meaning. Noyes approved this particular excursion into the occult. Had he disapproved, however, the seances would not have been outlawed but merely frowned upon and considered spiritually unsound.

One area of Oneida life, however, was carefully regulated: relations between the sexes. Noyes was aware of the passions and feelings involved in his system of complex marriage and therefore he insisted that his ideas be followed accurately and faithfully. "Complex marriage meant, in theory, that any man and woman might freely cohabit within the limits of the community. In practice, however, there was less freedom than might have been expected. The partners in this new form of relationship were obliged to obtain each others' consent, 'not by private conversation or courtship, but through the intervention of some third person or persons.' "[42] To avoid unwanted pregnancies the young of both sexes were encouraged to associate sexually with older persons who had mastered some of the techniques of birth control, (i.e. self control). They were discouraged, however, from developing

---

[42] Holloway, *Heavens on Earth*, p. 186.

romantic attachments with their sexual partners which Noyes called "selfish" or "special" love. As Noyes said on one occasion:

> Charles, as you know, is in the situation of one who is by and by to become a father. Under these circumstances, he has fallen under the too common temptation of selfish love, and a desire to wait upon and cultivate an exclusive intimacy with the woman who was to bear a child through him. This is insidious temptation, very apt to attack people under such circumstances; but it must nevertheless be struggled against.[43]

Exclusiveness and possessiveness, he believed, had no place in a community where all persons were supposed to love each other equally.

Related to complex marriage was Noyes' concept of stirpiculture, an attempt to produce children of superior intellect and physical endowment. In 1869 Noyes and a committee of elders helped pair off twenty-four men and twenty women who they believed would produce superior offspring. Within the next ten years sixty-two children were born from these unions. This attempt at selective breeding was administered carefully by Noyes who made sure that those chosen for stirpiculture would not be targets of envy and hostility. Every male in the community was allowed one opportunity to father a child although, as Noyes' son Pierrepont observed, "aside from the preferred 'stirps,' they had *only* one."[44] This attempt to maintain equality, at least in a psychological sense, seemed to work well and the community followed the precept of stirpiculture until 1879. In that year, however, outside criticism and Noyes' forced exile in Canada made continuation of stirpiculture and complex marriage unworkable. Both were abandoned, the latter after thirty-three years, ending one of the most controversial aspects of the Oneida experiment.

One Oneida institution which helped the community deal with interpersonal problems as well as provide spiritual and emotional guidance was mutual criticism, a fundamental component of Noyes' philosophy. Mutual criticism was a procedure designed to enhance self-knowledge. Individuals volunteered to appear before the entire community or a select committee to hear their faults enumerated or their weaknesses exposed. During the course of this proceeding the person in question would sit quietly without responding as committee members spoke. Mutual criticism was not intended to humiliate mem-

---

[43] Nordhoff, *Communistic Societies,* p. 292.

[44] Pierrepont Noyes, *My Father's House, An Oneida Boyhood* (New York, 1937), p. 10.

bers of the community but rather to make them aware of how others perceived them and what aspects of their behavior were considered objectionable. At the end of these sessions Noyes usually offered suggestions for personal and spiritual improvement which blended criticism with emotional support. There is no evidence that mutual criticism was damaging or harmful. Everyone at one time or another submitted to the ordeal, and the sessions were carried on in the spirit of helping persons who were troubled by some spiritual quandary or personal problem.

Mutual criticism was the principal mechanism by which the Oneida commune eased tensions and hostilities. For Noyes, however, it was more than a psychological safety-valve. He used it to urge his flock to greater soul-searching and spiritual mindedness. He believed it could instill and reinforce the community values of cooperation and brotherly love. Noyes also believed that mutual criticism could be used as therapy for illness originating in neurosis or anxiety. Several individuals stated that after submitting to criticism their health improved, having recognized the emotional and psychological dimension of their illness. The mixture of spiritual exhortation, encounter and psychological analysis contained in mutual criticism evidently helped the community on many levels.

After more than three decades of successful community life, the Oneida community began to experience internal problems and external pressures which ultimately forced the commune to disband. Internally the problems arose as John Humphrey Noyes approached old age and the issue of who would succeed him arose. Noyes' choice for community leader was his son Theodore, whose own spiritual quest had brought him through the by-ways of Spiritualism, Positivism and ultimately Agnosticism. In 1876, however, while still professing Perfectionism, Theodore was accepted as Oneida's leader, a position, it turned out, he was not qualified by temperment to fill. He closely associated himself with Ann Hobart, a strong-minded spiritualist and writing medium who dominated him and influenced all his important decisions. Theodore made enemies by deferring to "Mother Ann," governing autocratically and attempting to keep track of each member's hours of work and sexual liaisons. Within six months Theodore was forced to step down as leader, discredited as much by his poor financial direction as his overbearing manner. Although John Humphrey Noyes assumed the commune's leadership once again, he never gave up the hope that Theodore would be accepted back at some future time. This evidence of special love was all too apparent within the community and created an anti-Noyes sentiment which had not existed before.

There were other internal problems, however, which stimulated discontent during the 1870s. A clique formed around a recent arrival, James Towner, which sought to change the management of the Children's House and to gain greater control over the commune's property and financial affairs. A spirit of unrest manifested itself among the younger generation who were spiritually and intellectually removed from the earnest Perfectionism and Communism of their parents. Breakdowns in work discipline, in the rules governing sexual behavior and a general lack of respect for community norms also emerged. In retrospect, it is clear that no one factor triggered Oneida's downfall. Several factors, working together, caused its demise.

It was external pressure, however, which posed the most serious threat to community life, pressure which drove Noyes into exile at a time when his leadership and counsel were urgently required. This came in the form of a crusade begun by the Presbyterian Synod of Central New York, led by Professor Mears of Hamilton College, which initiated a sustained volley of criticism directed at Oneida's unconventional social practices. By the summer of 1879 Noyes became convinced that his continued presence at Oneida would do it irreparable harm; on June 23, 1879 he suddenly left the community to take up residence at Niagara Falls, Canada. Noyes continued to direct and influence affairs at Oneida from this distant location, where he was free from arrest and persecution.

After a period of reflection, Noyes sent the community his recommendation that they abandon complex marriage as the most expedient way of ending outside attacks and of saving the community's experiment in communism. Although a group at Oneida fought this suggestion, the community voted to accept Noyes' proposal as the only reasonable course of action. In late August 1879 complex marriage was abandoned, each individual left to choose between celibacy or marriage "after the fashion of the world." Soon after this momentous decision community members began to drift away. Some attempted to found new communes. Others decided to live and work in the outside world. A small group followed Noyes into exile where they continued to maintain contact with the stalwarts at Oneida.

By this time, however, it was apparent that the community's very existence was in jeopardy. A great debate ensued, focusing on how best to maintain, or liquidate the community's resources. Many proposals were put forward, but the one finally adopted ended definitively the experiment in communism. On January 1, 1881 Oneida Community ceased to exist, superseded by a joint stock company named Oneida Community Limited. A complex agreement assigned shares in the new enterprise to members according to their age and tenure in the old community. Noyes, living in exile, consoled himself that the end of community life was somehow part of God's design. He lived on at Niagara Falls until his death in April 1886, surrounded by a small group of faithful Perfectionists.

CONCLUSION

By the third quarter of the nineteenth century the commune movement was in decline, its ideology out of step with the growth of large cities and giant industries and its religious inspiration sapped by the new devotion to science and evolution.

> In the late nineteenth century, it is true, numerous communitarian experiments were talked about and even commenced, and their prospectuses echoed the brave old words about planting seeds of a future universal social order. But such promises had ceased to be credible to any large number of Americans.[45]

From the 1870s on it no longer seemed possible to change society by first creating model communities in microcosm. Reformers turned instead to mass movements such as Populism, Progressivism, Socialism, and Trade Unionism to implement their programs for social and economic improvement. By the 1880s the commune seemed headed the way of the vanishing buffalo, a distinctly American species overtaken by the march of events and technology.

It is of great interest, therefore, to witness the revival of communitarianism in our own era. The revival of the commune movement affirms that communes have an intrinsic appeal for Americans and that communes, at times of particular opportunity or stress, emerge as ways of dealing with social problems and social disillusionment. The revival of the commune movement also affirms that Americans retain many of the millennial, utopian, optimistic, and reformist impulses that characterized their ancestors. One may conclude that Americans have taken seriously "the pursuit of happiness," and that this accounts for their social experimentation and faith in the communal ideal. A complete understanding of the motivation for founding communes, however, will only emerge when the rich history of American communitarianism is fully explored.

Suggestions for Further Reading

A good source for studying present day communes is *The Modern Utopian,* published by the Alternatives Foundation, San Francisco,

---

[45] Bestor, "Patent-Office Models," *Backwoods Utopias,* p. 250.

California. Some useful books on the commune movement include Richard Fairfield, *Communes USA* (1972); Robert Houriet, *Getting Back Together* (1971); Keith Melville, *Communes in the Counter Culture* (1972); Raymond Mungo, *Total Loss Farm* (1970); and Theodore Roszak, *The Making of a Counter Culture* (1969). An article critical of the commune movement is Sonya Rudikoff, "O Pioneers! Reflections on the Whole Earth People," *Commentary* (July, 1972), 62–74. Two works of fiction that have generated discussion about communes are Robert Rimmer's, *The Harrad Experiment* (1966), and B. F. Skinner's *Walden Two* (1948).

There are numerous studies of communes in American history. The definitive work on Owenism in America is Arthur Bestor, *Backwoods Utopias* (second enlarged edition, 1971). Other works include Alice Felt Tyler, *Freedom's Ferment, Phases of American Social History to 1860* (1944); Mark Holloway, *Heavens on Earth, Utopian Communities in America, 1680–1880* (1966); Charles Nordhoff, *The Communistic Societies of the United States* (1875, reprinted, 1965); John Humphrey Noyes, *History of American Socialism* (1870); Edward Deming Andrews, *The People Called Shakers* (1963); and Lindsay Swift, *Brook Farm* (1890). Three studies which offer insights into the Oneida Community are Constance Noyes Robertson, *Oneida Community: An Autobiography, 1851–1876* (1970); and *Oneida Community: The Breakup, 1876–1881* (1972); and Pierrepont Noyes, *My Father's House: An Oneida Boyhood* (1937). Additional suggestions for reading about communitarianism may be found in the bibliographies of Holloway and Bestor.

Cracks in the
Ivy Wall

3

Three Centuries of American
Higher Education

American colleges and universities are emerging from a decade of dissent and controversy marked by some of the most violent struggles in academic history. Buffeted by student unrest, criticized by minority groups, suffering from cutbacks in federal aid and lacking a clear consensus on what constitutes educational reform, institutions of higher education are being forced to reappraise their roles and functions. During the last decade colleges have become the battleground for issues that deeply divide American society: the Indochina War, equality among the races, meaningful democracy, purposeful existence. Complicating these problems is the fact that no one is sure any longer what kind of education is meaningful and "relevant."

At this critical juncture in the history of American higher education it is important to find answers to several perplexing questions. Why are professors, particularly in the universities, still unsure whether their primary responsibility is to teach or to engage in research? Why have students in recent years attacked colleges and universities? What major unsolved problems face the academic community in the 1970s? What can the history of American higher education tell us about our own problems and predicaments?

Before we begin to explore answers to these problems, it is valuable to understand some of the distinguishing characteristics of American higher education.

THE NATURE AND STRUCTURE OF
AMERICAN HIGHER EDUCATION

American colleges and universities vary greatly in size, academic standard, curriculum, and educational philosophy. Unlike European universities, which resemble one another markedly in educational standard, function and purpose, American institutions of higher education run the gamut from giant state and private universities to small religious colleges; from liberal arts colleges with high admission standards to community colleges committed to "open enrollment." This diversity evolved over several centuries of educational experimentation and continues to be an important part of our educational tradition.

American higher education functions on the principles of autonomy and decentralization. In the United States no government agency decides academic policy and no government official is empowered to intercede in the affairs of a college or university as a minister of education might sometimes do in European countries. Money for operations is raised from tuition fees, revenues from endowment and from business and alumni contributions without direct aid from the federal government. Even where state legislatures provide funds for a university system, governance of the university remains in the hands of administrators and faculty.

American higher education is popular rather than elitist in tradition. Between 1900 and 1960, for example, the nation's college population increased from 250,000 to over seven million, an increase of almost 3,000 percent while the population as a whole increased only 100 percent. During the last century more and more students from low-income families and minority groups have gained access to higher education. Black people have not benefited as much as other ethnic groups from this democratizing trend, but there are signs that this exclusion is coming to an end. Overall, it may be said that American higher education reflects the ideals of an open society. This is certainly true when it is compared with higher education in Europe, Asia and Latin America.

American institutions of higher education fall into three categories: universities, colleges and two-year colleges. The university is the largest and most complex of these institutions; it offers both undergraduate and graduate training and administers research institutes, foreign student programs, and hundreds of other projects, services and educational programs. The modern university is best likened to a giant corporation which runs many different companies serving many different markets. It must not only administer its programs efficiently but it must raise money, oversee plant and equipment and balance the ofttimes conflicting interests of its "workers"—faculty and administrators—and its "consumers"—students, community leaders and the public at large.

The college, by contrast, is smaller and administratively less complex than the university. It is usually a four-year institution with no graduate or professional schools. It concentrates on teaching rather than research, and traditionally has been interested in introducing students to broad areas of knowledge. Colleges today are rapidly changing as more aspire to university status and more offer specialized instruction. New experimental colleges are also emerging which emphasize personal experience and psychological development in place of the traditional curriculum and traditional concepts of knowledge.

The third component of American higher education is the two-year college. These modified colleges developed during the 1920s as upward extensions of high schools and as a means of providing brief college training preparatory to graduate and professional study. Junior colleges grew from 52 in 1920 to 890 in 1968. Today they serve farm community and city alike, and offer a broad spectrum of courses in academic and nonacademic subjects.

Statistics offer a capsule view of higher education, showing where it is presently and where it is going. In 1972, for example, there were 2,606 institutions of higher education in the United States of which 159 were universities, 1,513 were four-year colleges and 934 were two-year colleges. Collectively, these schools enrolled almost nine million students; 6,804,309 attended public-supported colleges and universities, and 2,144,335 attended private-supported institutions. Five million, two-hundred thousand of these students were men and 3,741,639 were women. They were taught by 620,000 faculty members, and their schools spend nineteen billion dollars for their education.[1]

Looking toward the future, one scholar forecasts that by 1980 there will be twelve million students in colleges and universities, a 103 percent increase over 1965 enrollments.[2] For the same period (1965–1980) the number of BAs awarded will jump ninety percent, MAs 119 percent, and Ph.Ds 157 percent. These estimates, made in 1968, seem inflated in light of the fact that colleges and universities

---

[1] U.S. Department of Health, Educaton and Welfare, *Digest of Educational Statistics, 1972* (Washington, 1973), Higher Education, *passim*.

[2] Sidney G. Tickton, "The Magnitude of American Higher Education in 1980," in Alvin Eurich, *Campus 1980* (New York, 1968), p. 18.

experienced declining enrollments and financial reversals in the mid-1970s. Should enrollments again increase they are not likely to rise as fast as the above figures suggest.

TEACHING VS. SCHOLARSHIP

At different times in our educational history, professors have faced different problems. During the nineteenth century professors were asked to teach four or five courses, put in long hours, and work without adequate library or laboratory resources. Before college teachers gained full professional status (during the decade after 1900) their problems were lack of prestige, lack of adequate compensation, and lack of real power within their institutions. While these problems still exist to some degree, another problem in recent years has generated considerable anxiety: the professor's confusion as to whether he is primarily a teacher or a scholar.

This problem, as we shall see, has its roots in the development of the American university. It goes back to the demands made by early university presidents that their faculty imitate European professors who devoted most of their time to research and publication. From the original demand that university professors be research scholars the idea emerged that all college teachers should be judged by their scholarly productions. This meant that a professor's success depended upon how many articles or books he could write.

By the 1950s and 1960s publication was so important a yardstick in judging the merits of college teachers that critics of higher education began analyzing the "publish or perish" syndrome. This syndrome followed a consistent pattern. A young professor, anxious to advance in his profession, devoted most of his time to research and writing. The majority of ambitious professors neglected their teaching and their students as the pressure to publish increased. A professor who failed to publish, or took too long to publish, was either not promoted or not given tenure by the better universities and colleges. Jacques Barzun, the ex-provost of Columbia University summed up the consequences of this problem in 1968: "The student sees and resents that teaching is no longer the central concern of the university nor its members."[3]

One should not gain the impression that the publish or perish syndrome has destroyed good teaching on every college campus. Good and effective teachers still abound in many colleges and even

---

[3] Jacques Barzun, The American University (New York, 1968), p. 69.

in universities where the pressure to publish is considerable; but as a general rule, many college professors feel torn between two obligations: teaching and scholarship. Why should this continue to be so? Why can't college professors concentrate on teaching?

One reason is that there are strong arguments favoring the professor as scholar. Research enhances man's ability to control and better his world. Progress depends upon new knowledge and more understanding of man and the physical environment. If college teachers neglect research they will have little to teach their students that is new and pioneering. Universities will cease to be places where intellectuals explore the unknown and will lose their importance and vitality.

Another argument favoring the professor as scholar involves a negative assumption: college teachers *must* publish because this is the only way their colleagues can judge their professional abilities. A published article or book is tangible evidence that a professor has spent time in research and writing. Assuming that the quality of what he writes is taken into account, scholarly publication presents itself as the best yardstick for judging a teacher's professional competence. Publication, of course, measures only one part of a professor's function, but because there is no agreed upon measure of what constitutes good teaching, publication remains the only criteria by which college teachers are judged.

Much of the tension arising from the teaching vs. scholarship problem may be traced to the professional training of college teachers; to the Ph.D. In our universities, this degree is earned only by those who excel in research and scholarship. Virtually no training is offered in the arts of teaching, evaluating students, or creating interesting curricula. As a result of this one-sided training, graduate Ph.D.'s are encouraged to regard research and publication positively and teaching negatively. Those who enjoy teaching confront the problem of having to devote a great deal of time to scholarly pursuits.

Within the last five years a few of the better known American universities have begun to grapple with this problem so that some of the ambiguity in the professor's role can be eliminated. Some graduate schools offer courses in the teaching arts; others are offering new degrees designed to develop teachers, not scholars. Unfortunately, the student who chooses to pursue a Doctor of Arts or some other degree that emphasizes teaching, still must make a career in an academic world where the research-oriented Ph.D. retains its prestige and dominance.

The teaching vs. scholarship problem has inevitably created dissension and resentment within the academic community. Students are aware that professors are reluctant to spend time with them because they feel they should be writing an article or book. University administrators and public officials—despite their desire to have prestigious scholars—are also beginning to feel that they are not getting enough teaching from professors who teach only a few hours a week so that they can pursue their scholarly interests. Clearly, adequate recognition to both teaching and scholarship is required to resolve this conflict.

STUDENT DISCONTENTS

Many students are aware that their interests suffer when scholarship and publication take precedence over teaching; many have demanded a reordering of priorities within universities and colleges. A small minority of students, politically aware and activist, believe that institutions of higher education share the blame for many of the social and economic problems that exist in American society. In recent years they have declared war on the university hoping to destroy activities they . regard as evil and to turn their colleges and universities into socially "relevant" institutions.

Between 1964 and 1970 the many crises confronting the nation were reflected in campus events. Every major university and many colleges experienced sit-ins, building occupations and demonstrations. The Free Speech Movement which paralyzed the Berkeley campus of the University of California in the fall of 1964 was a paradigm of things to come. On that occasion the administration imposed restrictions on students who wished to use the campus to advocate political action, and the struggle escalated into a massive student strike. The events at Berkeley, widely publicized in the press and on television, brought home to Americans the fact that students were joining forces to protest the power, connections and organization of the university.

Following the events at Berkeley students began to organize. Protest meetings against the war in Vietnam became common in 1967 and 1968. Students began to speak out against racial barriers in housing and employment, against the university's ties to the Pentagon and on such issues as the hiring and firing of faculty for political reasons. In 1968 Columbia University was closed down by riots stemming from student opposition to defense-related research and the university's insensitive attitude toward people living in the local community. The same year San Francisco State University and Cornell University suffered from student uprisings; at Cornell a racial incident convinced black students they should arm themselves with rifles for self-protection. Nineteen sixty-nine witnessed a rising tide of campus disruptions but 1970 was the year of tragedy. On May 4, 1970 National

Guardsmen, called to break up an antiwar rally at Kent State University, panicked and fired on the assembled throng. Four students were killed. A few weeks later state policemen killed two students at Jackson State College in Mississippi.

Student recourse to open rebellion was a manifestation of grave discontent; after the Columbia riots several formal groups set out to determine why students had become so hostile to "the system." The National Commission on the Causes and Prevention of Violence[4] gave the following historical assessment of the causes of campus unrest:

1. When students entered the struggle for racial equality in the South in the late 1950s and early 1960s they were fired by high idealism. When they were jailed and beaten by southern authorities and when the federal government seemed hesitant to correct deep wrongs, students became angry and alienated.

2. Students who studied the origins of poverty in the classroom and who entered the "war on poverty" in the ghettos and Appalachia grew skeptical about the government's commitment to eliminate poverty in America. They saw poverty programs snarled in red tape, and bureaucracies which lacked empathy with the poor. They began to interpret these failures as a form of deception.

3. The strike at Berkeley and Clark Kerr's characterization of the university as "Multiversity"—the servant of industry and government—gave fuel to those who viewed this institution as spiritually bankrupt, undemocratic and hostile to humane values.[5]

4. The war in Indochina presented a major dilemma for faculty and students. Many viewed the war as immoral, illegal, imperialistic and alien to the American tradition.

5. Student immunity from the draft dissipated as the war in Vietnam escalated. Students agonized over serving their country or following the dictates of conscience.

6. Revelation that universities worked hand in hand with the Department of Defense, the Central Intelligence Agency and other federal agencies made the university seem culpable in

---

[4] Jerome Skolnick et al., *The Politics of Protest* (New York, 1969).

[5] In the *Uses of the University* (1964), Clark Kerr, then President of the University of California, observed that the modern university had lost its sense of shared values and traditions. It was, he said, not one community but several diverse communities, devoted increasingly to serving the needs of industry and the state.

the eyes of students. Many of these activities were considered to be inconsistent with academic values.

7. The issues of race, poverty and urban decay began to preoccupy students. Many reasoned that the war in Indochina drained money away from programs at home and they questioned whether the government sincerely meant to solve these problems.

8. Black students became alienated from governmental and educational institutions as self-consciousness and self-respect developed. Many black students began to consider American society racist, oppressive and exploitative in character.

Concurring in this assessment, the Cox Commission which investigated the Columbia riots of 1968 had this to say.

The ability, social consciousness and conscience, political sensitivity, and honest realism of today's students are a prime cause of student disturbances. As one student observed during our investigation, today's students take seriously the ideals taught in the schools and churches, and often at home, and then they see a system that denies its ideals in its actual life. Racial injustice and the war in Vietnam stand out as prime illustrations of our society's deviation from its professed ideals and of the slowness with which the system reforms itself. That they seemingly can do so little to correct the wrongs through conventional political discourse tends to produce in the most idealistic and energetic students a strong sense of frustration.[6]

By no means do these two appraisals exhaust the list of causes of student discontent. To them one could add the shock of the Robert Kennedy and Martin Luther King assassinations, the belief that the 1968 Democratic National Convention was boss-run and politically corrupt, the feeling of impotence as the Nixon administration widened the war in Indochina, the anger at big depersonalized educational institutions. Central to the causes of student activism too, has been the desire to "restructure" the universiy to make it responsive to student and minority groups and elements in local communities. Demands for greater student power, increased black student enrollments, community action programs and curricula dealing with social problems have been voiced in many university protests.[7]

---

[6] The Cox Commission Report, *Crisis at Columbia* (New York, 1968), p. 4.

[7] Seymour M. Lipset offers perceptive comments in "American Student Activism," in G. Weaver and J. Weaver, *The University and Revolution* (New York, 1969), pp. 19–41.

It is too early to determine how student activism will affect the future course of American higher education. Evidence to date suggests that universities and colleges have responded to student rebellion and hostility in a number of positive ways. Many institutions have altered their constitutions and administrative arrangements to include students in the decision making process. At those institutions student activism has markedly decreased. Some institutions have followed the advice of antiwar students and professors and have severed all their connections with the Pentagon and related government agencies. Some universities have broken ROTC contracts, banned secret research projects and developed a climate of openness and trust within the academic community.

Reexamination of goals and operations has also led many colleges and universities to develop courses that are problem and action oriented, that stress experimental teaching and learning, and that deal with subjects such as poverty, race and economics in new and unconventional ways. Much of this reform and revitalization has resulted from the student unrest of the 1960s. Whether or not this reforming zeal will continue into the 1970s and 1980s, and to what degree, remains to be seen.

UNSOLVED PROBLEMS

Many of the problems which exploded colleges and universities in the 1960s are still with us in the 1970s. Among academic problems, three stand out for the amount of controversy and discussion they have generated. They are: 1) the problem of developing a relationship between universities and the federal government and large corporations that does not compromise academic freedom and autonomy; 2) the problem of determining how much students should participate in governing colleges and universities; and 3) the problem of creating a "relevant" curriculum.

FEDERAL MONEY AND ACADEMIC INDEPENDENCE

In the early 1970s a professor engaged in biomedical research, a scholar interested in studying population growth, or a scientist unlocking the secrets of animal communication would, in all likelihood, have his research funded by the federal government. He would prepare an elaborate research proposal, consult with the business office of his university, and, if his project merited, visit Washington for discussions with government officials. Research grants totaled one and a half billion dollars in 1969 with an additional 394 million dollars go-

ing to university-affiliated research institutes.[8] The largest granting
agencies were the Department of Health, Education and Welfare and
the Department of Defense. The National Science Foundation, the
Atomic Energy Commission, the Department of Agriculture and the
Space Administration also made sizable numbers of grants.

The figures cited above do not constitute the total federal program
in higher education. One must also include federal giving for graduate fellowships, loans for building dormitories and student centers,
and payments to G.I.'s returned from Vietnam. Together, these grants
and payments fund a large part of university budgets, guaranteeing
large enrollments, big salaries and excellent research facilities. Federal
grants for research presently account for roughly 75 percent of all
university expenditures for research and 15 percent of total university
budgets. This, of course, applies to the largest universities, which in a
real sense have become "federal grant universities."

The benefits derived from federal funding have been considerable.
Universities have been able to compete with industry to attract the
best talent, and students have been able to borrow money for their
education from government-financed low-interest loans. Federal expenditures have created new centers of learning, opened up new
fields of study and created more opportunities for college teachers,
primarily in the natural sciences. Although the government has been
more interested in defense-oriented research than strengthening education per se, many disciplines have felt the impact of federal grants.
Sociologists, political scientists and historians have received grants to
study problems only marginally associated with national security.

Federal subsidies, however, have also had negative effects. Federal
funds have gone largely to a few, already strong universities and have
flowed more amply to the sciences than the social sciences and hu-
manities. Money has gone to strengthen graduate education at the
expense of undergraduate education, and federal grants have induced
professors to neglect many teaching functions. Some professors who
have their research supported by the federal government develop
more loyalty to the agency which supplies their funds than to the
university where they teach. This situation has created serious conflicts
of interest.

As more and more universities rely on federal subsidies to fill in
part of their budgets, government interference in academic life becomes a problem. One analyst has pointed out that government interference may evolve merely from the pressures of formal regulations
and red tape "which can frustrate and devitalize much intellectual

[8] *Digest of Educational Statistics, 1972*, p. 129.

effort."[9] Another danger, he asserts, "is not so much of the government 'buying up' . . . leading scholars . . . but, rather, of the goals of universities being shaped by the needs of the nation rather than the needs of science, of scholarship, and of man."[10] This latter problem surfaced dramatically in 1968 when students at the Massachusetts Institute of Technology and Columbia University demanded that their institutions sever relations with M.I.T.'s Instrumentation Laboratory and the consortium known as the Institute for Defense Analysis, both funded by the Department of Defense. Students made the claim that scholars were devoting too much time to projects given high priority by the government and that government support for these organizations introduced government influence and control.

So far, professors across the nation do not seem unduly alarmed by the specter of government interference and control. They point out that state legislatures have meddled in university affairs far more than the federal government and most seem to favor continued government support. Some professors and administrators, however, believe that reliance on government money will ultimately lead to outright political control. Those who taught during the McCarthy era (1950–1954) remember the visits of F.B.I. agents and the elaborate security clearances required to perform "classified research."[11] Others point to recent "disclaimer affidavits" which were attached to National Defense Loans.[12] These scholars assert that dependence on government inevitably limits academic freedom. They contend that the price the university will pay for handsome subsidies will be an imposed conformity and suppression of unpopular ideas.

The university's relationship with large corporations also raises important questions. University presidents now sit on the boards of directors of major corporations; university laboratories are frequently recipients of corporate grants and are run by professors who are paid consultants for scientific companies. Does this situation compromise the university in any way? Is liaison with business incompatible with the pursuit of truth?

Unless one condemns capitalism outright, it is safe to say that receiving support from business is not inherently evil. Corporations provide universities with expensive equipment and money which enables professors to carry out sophisticated research of benefit to students

---

[9] Harold Orlans, *The Effects of Federal Programs on Higher Education* (Washington, 1963), pp. 288–289.

[10] *Ibid.*

[11] *Ibid.*, p. 291

[12] These were oaths disclaiming disloyal associations principally aimed at communists.

and society alike. Contacts with industrial corporations enable scholars to leave the campus cloister and to pursue research in settings infused with practical and social concerns.

Intimate relations with business corporations, however, do raise
serious problems involving academic autonomy and the unfettered
pursuit of truth. Critics argue that when a university receives a large
grant of money from a corporation the university will inevitably serve
the interests of that corporation in some way. They assert that it is
wrong for university presidents to spend time advising corporations
how to make money and that it is wrong to accept money for research
which will ultimately have commercial value. They also point out that
an engineering professor who acts as a consultant for an automobile
manufacturer is unlikely to criticize the safety of that company's
products and that a professor who receives large consulting fees from
an oil company will be reluctant to use the university laboratory to
study oil pollution. The validity of these allegations cannot be discussed here. It should be apparent, however, that when institutions
of higher education develop ties with big business serious problems
arise involving conflicts of interest, favoritism and compromised
objectivity.

STUDENT POWER: HOW MUCH?

At campuses across the nation students are asking for a greater voice
in educational affairs. Frequently heard are demands that students be
represented on discipline, cirriculum, and policy-making committees,
and that they share in the decisions involving hiring and firing of
faculty. Students have also asked to participate in making budgetary
decisions and for representation on boards of trustees. Years ago these
proposals would have seemed preposterous, but recent campus unrest and radical changes in educational philosophy have made professors and administrators sensitive to student demands.

Advocates of student power argue that students are exploited;
they have no formal voice in what they are taught, how they are
taught, where they may live, and how they are disciplined. They point
out that colleges and universities do not reflect the values and procedures of a democratic society and that students are discriminated
against because they pay "tuition without representation." The solution to student exploration, they assert, is to give students real power
within colleges and universities. They believe that once students participate in the decisions that affect their lives they will be more responsible, positive and constructive members of college communities.

Student power raises serious issues and problems. Student demands challenge the assumptions and administrative procedures sanctioned by academic tradition; student power creates fears among administrators and professors that their spheres of influence will be invaded and their status will decline. Notwithstanding these political and psychological factors, one must deal with student power on its merits. Are the assumptions of student power advocates logical and correct? Are the demands reasonable?

Charles Frankel, a Columbia University philosophy professor and author of *Education and the Barricades* finds the weakest link in the student power argument to be the assumption that institutions of higher education are democracies.[13] He points out that colleges and universities are not democracies and can never be democracies because they are communities based upon skill, not rights; they are hierarchies of different degrees of competence. Students should not demand participation in university government as a right, he maintains, just as porters should not demand a voice in running hospitals because they do not have the knowledge and competence of trained administrators. Frankel points out, however, that it may make perfect *educational good sense* to have students participate in campus governance and educational policy-making, as long as the arguments do not rest on the assumption that students have an inherent right to such participation. He writes:

> While universities are democratic organizations in the sense that individuals have a broad array of personal rights within them, and that there is a play of opinion inside them which has a massive effect on their evolution, they are not democratic organizations in the sense that majority rule applies to them. For within a university there are acceptable procedures by which people can be graded in accordance with their competence, and grading people this way is essential to the conduct of the university's special business. The egalitarian ideal does not apply across the board in universities any more than it does in any other field where *skill* is the essence of the issue. . . . If there is a case to be made for student participation in the higher reaches of university government, it is a case that is not based upon *rights,* but upon considerations of good educational and administrative practice.[14]

---

[13] Charles Frankel, *Education and the Barricades* (New York, 1968), chapter 4.
[14] *Ibid.*, p. 50.

Frankel is a philosopher and justly focuses on the logic of basic assumption. Jacques Barzun, another Columbia professor, has also written about the student power issue and he finds fault with student power advocates on practical grounds.[15] He maintains that students cannot effectively participate in campus governance because they do not have the time to devote to complex tasks. He believes, for example, that students have neither the time nor the skill to make up a budget, which requires hundreds of hours of study and consideration. He also believes that students cannot judge the merits of faculty members because they do not yet understand all the criteria for judging academic achievement. Barzun maintains that because student generations change in style and opinion, because students are present at college for four or fewer years, and because they have no vested interest in academic freedom or the continued success of their academic institutions, students should not participate in many administrative tasks.

While the debate over student power continues, many colleges have already acted to change the status of their students. Some have created representative bodies such as senates and academic councils to which students in substantial numbers, are elected. Some universities have invited students to participate in disciplinary proceedings involving their peers, and discussions involving curriculum revision. Many colleges and universities now allow students to evaluate their instructor's performance in the classroom and to express their opinion of a given course and its required readings. A very small number of colleges and universities have allowed students to participate in choosing new teaching faculty and to recommend whether professors should be rehired or given tenure.

It remains to be seen whether student power, either won as a right or extended out of educational good sense, will bring about the desired consensus and peace that most members of university communities desire. As mentioned earlier, there is evidence that on campuses where students participate in making important decisions there is less tension and more good feeling. Student power, however, has a long way to go before it is accepted as intellectually justified and politically acceptable.

WHAT IS RELEVANT?

Student power advocates, as well as students generally, have been saying for some time that they want to study subjects that are relevant. Some believe that a subject is relevant if it has something personal to

---

[15] Barzun, *University, passim.*

say to them, something that touches their lives. Others talk of relevance in political terms; learning how to change society or expose inequities and corruption. Most students believe that something is relevant if it can be made to relate to present day issues and concerns. Thus, history should deal with problems and teach lessons; economics should be taught as an instrument for change, and sociology should deal with life in the communities from which students are drawn.

One of the problems facing educators in the 1970s is dealing with the claims of students and professors who believe that curriculums must be revamped and revitalized by using relevance as a yardstick. Because there is no unanimity of opinion concerning the meaning of relevance, however, a great deal of misunderstanding and distortion has grown up around this concept. Too often relevance is equated with something that is exciting or something with immediate emotional appeal. A course is deemed irrelevant if it deals with the past or with a language or an artistic medium that appears to have no direct bearing on contemporary issues, tastes or concerns. Inexact definition of what is relevant has led to a mounting anti-intellectualism in colleges and universities and a rejection of much of the liberal arts curriculum.

In the final analysis a definition of what is relevant emerges from one's educational philosophy. Those who believe that excitement, stimulation and heightened motivation are the true test of a subject's relevance will open the academic gates wide for any subject that meets these criteria. They will welcome all kinds of innovation in methods and topics as long as students respond favorably to what they are studying.

Those educators, however, who believe that relevance is something that one creates in one's mind, something that one imposes on a given subject, will be less ready to throw out many time-honored subjects that are currently called irrelevant. They will insist, for example, that art history or French or Latin have relevance to students when students take the facts and discipline learned in these courses and *make them relevant* to their lives. Relevance, in this sense, is not something that is perceived immediately, but rather something that grows with intellectual maturity and with age. It is a relationship drawn in the mind that may become apparent only after a person has many different emotional and intellectual experences.

NEW DIRECTION

A brief word remains to be said about some of the most recent developments in American higher education. The shock waves that hit college and university campuses in the late 1960s, cutbacks in federal aid to education in the early 1970s, and a decline in enrollments in some private institutions, has forced the higher education community to reappraise many of its basic premises and programs. The most notable result of this reappraisal has been a willingness to experiment with new courses and new educational formats which give students more diversity and flexibility in their college programs.

One of the most recent developments has been the "college without walls," a college (Empire State College, SUNY) founded on the principle that students can profit from pursuing independent study under the guidance of tutors, without any requirement that they attend formal classes. Another development has been the adult-education college which permits students to receive credits for "life" or "learning" experiences, which are an integral part of a regular degree program. The creation of minicourses that run three to five weeks, the appearance of weekend colleges, where working people can attend without conflicts in their schedules, and the emergence of all kinds of interdisciplinary courses and independent study programs attests to the fact that institutions of higher education are responding in positive ways to the criticisms leveled at them during the 1960s.

Notwithstanding these important innovations, colleges are experiencing new tensions and frustrations. The feverish growth of the 1960s seems to be at an end and with it much of the federal money that fueled this growth. One consequence of this has been a determined effort to cut and balance budgets and work out a list of educational priorities. College professors have been hard hit in this trimming and reorganization and are responding to budget cuts, firings, and attacks on tenure by forming unions and engaging in collective bargaining. Hard hit too are students who must pay large increases in tuition at a time when a college degree no longer guarantees high-paid employment. Some educators believe that the newest development on the higher education horizon will be the creation of student unions, which will bargain for their members in matters of tuition, curriculum design, and teacher accountability. What can be said with certainty is that all the old assumptions in higher education are crumbling and that new educational programs and power arrangements are in the making.

THE COLONIAL COLLEGE

The era of the colonial college, to which we now turn, knew very few of the problems we have discussed, for before the American Revolution there were only nine colleges in existence and they enrolled only a handful of students. In the beginnings of our society, however,

American higher education did face the problem of defining itself within a new environment. England's Oxford and Cambridge were uprooted and an attempt was made to recreate them in a frontier society with no traditions and no history.

The first colleges in the English colonies were founded primarily to create a trained ministry; literacy meant knowledge of the Bible and this knowledge was considered essential for survival. Harvard College was founded in 1636 by those "dreading to leave an illiterate ministry . . . when our present ministers shall be in the dust," and it was followed by William and Mary (1693), Yale (1701), Princeton (1746), King's College (Columbia, 1754), the College of Philadelphia (Pennsylvania, 1755), the College of Rhode Island (Brown, 1764), Queens (Rutgers, 1766) and Dartmouth (1769). The religious orientation of these colleges showed its influence in the government of the college, the curriculum it offered and in its general educational assumptions. Ethics and religion, strong moral guidance, and discipline of the intellect took precedence over scholarship, or what we today would call the search for truth. Congregationalists, Presbyterians, Anglicans and Dutch Reformed all agreed: knowledge of God and his laws superseded all other concerns.

The colonial colleges, from the outset, were governed from above; ministers and prominent men in the community sat on boards of control and delegated authority to a president who was usually a minister himself. The president chose his faculty, determined what should be taught, supervised admissions and student discipline and taught several classes. Since he was answerable only to the board or corporation, he had a free hand in academic and administrative matters and was feared by faculty and students alike. Unlike the distant educator-bureaucrat of later years, his presence and personality dominated the college. He taught all seniors "moral philosophy," knew students by their first names and, like the patriarchs of old, carefully supervised the manners and morals of his flock. In the small "log cabin" colleges on the frontier, founded after the Revolution, it was not uncommon for the president to provide food from his garden or help in building the college halls. From his meager salary he even occasionally provided student loans.

Being governed from above was a fact of life for a faculty who were few in number and who served at the president's will. Unlike their European counterparts who exercised substantial control in their institutions, American professors lacked power and prestige, in part because scholarship was not revered in a society devoted to the mechanical and the practical. In many instances, college professors were not properly trained nor were they asked to be creative in the way they taught. Teaching was done by the recitation method and students were graded every day on what they had read or memorized the previous day. Professors were empowered to flog a student, box his ears, or impose other forms of discipline, methods accepted widely until the middle of the eighteenth century. There is little doubt that students found their lessons dull and their professors ofttimes callous. The record of student pranks, practical jokes, and misbehavior attests to the dreariness and paternalism which permeated the colonial college classroom. .

Students in colonial times had little choice in what they studied: the curriculum was imported from England where, since the Renaissance, it had trained men to be literate and conversant with the great thinkers of the past. Latin, Greek, Hebrew (the language of the Old Testament), rhetoric, and logic were studied the first year and repeated the second with the addition of natural philosophy, an early precursor of physics. The third year saw a repeat of these subjects with the addition of a course in moral philosophy. As seniors, students reviewed their Greek and Latin, studied more natural philosophy and took a smattering of mathematics.[16] No student studied a modern language other than English, and none ever studied a technical subject. These were not introduced until the mid-eighteenth century.

Memorizing passages from Homer or Virgil, pouring over the Hebrew alphabet, was something less than stimulating, and the lack of extracurricular activities and emotional outlets other than churchgoing led to youthful rebellion. In 1807 Princeton expelled 125 students for rioting, roughly 60 percent of its total enrollment.[17] At Hobart students rolled red-hot cannon balls down a dormitory corridor, while Harvard students (in 1817) broke all the college crockery.[18] Students who were drawn into politics during the Revolution helped oust several college presidents. In may 1775 President Cooper of King's College (Columbia) left office by jumping over the back fence for fear of the mob (held at bay by Alexander Hamilton, class of 1774), and five years later Harvard's president Samuel Langton was told by his students that he was thoroughly despised. Upon their demand, he resigned.[19]

Riots and disruptions, while breaking the monotony of study, did little to change the fundamentals of college life; youthful rebellion was sporadic and rarely aimed at constructive educational reform. As

---

[16] Frederick Rudolph, *The American College and University* (New York, 1962), pp. 25–26.

[17] Russel B. Nye, *The Cultural Life of the New Nation* (New York, 1963), p. 186.

[18] *Ibid.*

[19] Rudolph, *American College,* pp. 33 and 39.

the eighteenth century progressed, however, the colleges began to feel pressure to revise the curriculum to make it more modern and more relevant to the times. Eighteenth-century European philosophers were studying politics and psychology. Newtonian science was gaining popularity, and technology was being viewed as a new religion. It wasn't long before these influences crossed the Atlantic.

The colonial colleges, however, responded only halfheartedly to changing times. Some, like Harvard and Yale in the 1730s and 1740s, introduced courses in mathematics and astronomy. At King's College in 1754, and later at the College of Philadelphia, students were introduced to surveying, geography, navigation, and greater emphasis was placed on English and English literature. Although some botany, physics, and chemistry was taught in the colleges before the Revolution, science remained a secondary concern. A few students squinted through telescopes or studied trajectories. The vast majority remained ignorant of science and its ways.

Although colonial society felt certain democratic stirrings, the colonial college remained basically an aristocratic institution. For the most part, its students came from the affluent: wealthy Boston merchants sent their sons to Harvard or Yale, the sons of the planter aristocracy applied to William and Mary, and the established families in the Middle Colonies attended the College of Philadelphia, Queens or Kings College in New York. Because the average farmer had little cash and needed the labor of his sons, and because higher education did not train people for practical work, the colleges did not feel pressure to open admissions. Not until the Revolution came and a democratizing trend began to be felt were voices heard calling for higher education open to the citizenry. As late as 1771 Harvard graduated only 63 students, and in 1776 it had only 3000 living alumni.[20] As the commencement orator said in the 1670s: without Harvard the rulers would be ruled by the uneducated mechanics, cobblers and tailors. Such a situation was unthinkable in early America.[21]

THE COLLEGIATE ERA

Nine colleges were founded in America before the Revolution. By contrast, close to 900 were founded before the Civil War although 700 of these failed.[22] This staggering increase reflected dynamic

---

[20] *Ibid.,* p. 22.
[21] *Ibid.,* pp. 6–7.
[22] *Ibid.,* p. 47.

changes in America's society and economy. After independence the states began to vie with one another in creating academic institutions. the frontier opened up, and men hoped the sons of rugged woodsmen would seek higher education. The strongest promoters of the college movement were Baptist, Congregationalist, Presbyterian and Catholic missionaries who competed in sponsoring colleges and seminaries. Once they enlisted a president and built a few classrooms, a college was considered in full swing. These were, however, precarious foundations upon which to build. In Missouri, between 1790 and 1860, 65 out of 77 colleges went under for lack of support and lack of students.[23]

The colleges founded after the Revolution modeled themselves after their colonial predecessors, largely because their presidents and faculty were graduates of these institutions. With little variation they continued to offer the classical curriculum and the stress on character building and religiousity was maintained. During the early years of the Republic the idea of what a college should be became firmly fixed. Colleges existed to provide society with leaders who were morally upright, self-reliant and religiously sound. They existed to foster liberal culture: a knowledege of the classics, the Bible, the English language and the rudiments of mathematics. It was widely believed that quartering boys in dormitories helped promote good character because there mutual respect, companionship and self discipline were emphasized. Geographically, the best place for all this growing and learning was the countryside, away from the hubbub, distractions and vices of the city.[24] Jefferson had often said that the land was a source of virtue and that Americans would be safe from corruption if they stayed close to the soil. College founders adhered to this agrarian ideal. Quite consciously they contributed to the isolation of students and professors from the realities of everyday life.

There were, however, questions raised about this conception of college life and study. The country was growing, and canals and roads were being built. A nationally conscious people were beginning to expand, and the pressure for more democracy was building. Where did the colleges fit in to all of this? Would they respond to the need for engineers, trained agriculturalists, scientists and mechanics? Would they give up the emphasis on Greek and Latin and become more "relevant" to the society? Would they drop their elitism and become democratic?

---

[23] George P. Schmidt, *The Liberal Arts College* (New Brunswick, N.J., 1957), p. 11.
[24] Rudolph, *American College,* pp. 95–97.

During the 1820s and 1830s a few individuals suggested changes. At the University of Nashville, President Philip Lindsley spoke in favor of creating a college which would educate the farmer, the mechanic, the manufacturer and the merchant. At Harvard, George Ticknor, professor of Spanish and French, suggested creating advanced studies and giving students more choice in choosing courses. The president of the University of Vermont proposed dropping the Greek and Latin requirements for students pursuing nonclassical studies, and at Amherst College in 1826 a short-lived "parallel" course was introduced which allowed students to study modern languages, English, history, certain sciences, architecture, bridge design and applied chemistry. At Union College in 1827 president Eliphalet Nott introduced scientific courses and modern languages, and the University of Virginia in 1825 Thomas Jefferson founded a school unlike any other in existence.[25] The university had eight schools: ancient languages, modern languages, mathematics, natural philosophy, natural history, anatomy and medicine, moral philosophy, and law. Each student chose his field of specialization (although he followed a prescribed curriculum in his school), pursued his work at his own pace and received a degree after a rigorous oral and written examination. Jefferson believed that college students were mature individuals; this was a radical departure from contemporary paternalistic thinking.

The tradition that the college must stress the classics and build the individual's character worked against the reformers of the 1820s. Their voices were heard only locally. The Amherst and Nashville experiments failed, and the religious-oriented colleges, which made up the majority of institutions of higher education, rejected their ideas. The introduction of more science into the curriculum, however, made some headway. As early as 1804 Benjamin Silliman began to teach chemistry and natural history at Yale, thus becoming the mentor of many future professors. At Amherst, Williams, Harvard, Lafayette, Union and Wesleyan serious scientific study was begun, although too frequently this work was developed in small scientific societies which offered no credit toward a degree. The technology that was so urgently desired by the practical, industry-minded Americans was not pursued. Except for the United States Military Academy at West Point founded in 1802, and the Rensselaer Polytechnic Institute founded in 1824, no college offered meaningful technological study.

It was not until the 1840s and the 1850s that science found a permanent place in the college curriculum, but even then it was

---

[25] John S. Brubacher and Willis Rudy, *Higher Education in Transition*, rev. ed. (New York, 1968), pp. 99–102.

either offered as a parallel course of study without a B.A. or separated from the college and taught in separate scientific schools. In 1847 Harvard and Yale developed scientific courses leading respectively to a Bachelor of Science and Bachelor of Philosophy degree. In 1852 Yale's Department of Philosophy and Arts added instruction in civil engineering, and soon after the Yale Scientific School was set up. During the 1850s, separate scientific schools or departments were created in over thirty colleges and universities.[26] Even at this late date, however, scientific students were considered second class. Admission standards were lower for those pursuing scientific work, and their degree was considered inferior to the Bachelor of Arts. The older colleges stuck by the classics while the country cried out for bridge builders and engineers.

The college's response to the democratic trend was similar to its sluggish and half-hearted response to science. During the 1820s America was moving towards becoming a people's republic. Andrew Jackson, an unlettered frontiersmen, became president in 1828, and everywhere there was a leveling sentiment. Jacksonian democracy was really a demand for economic opportunity, and this demand took the form of an attack against privilege. Jackson's ascendency to the presidency meant that the little man could make it, even though the true Jackson was a man of some means when he entered the White House. Visitors from abroad during this period sensed that everyone wanted to be everyone else's equal. This climate of opinion created problems for the colleges and their friends.

By 1828 many people thought the colleges were too aristocratic. Their enrollments were still limited, their students generally came from the wealthy families, and the courses they offered were associated with England, the gentlemen's life and with leisure. Some of the colleges responded to the democratic striving; they stopped ranking students and offered scholarships to the needy. Some lowered costs and introduced more practical courses.[27] To the average individual, however, the colleges still seemed committed to elitism. As a result, state legislatures, once the friends of the colleges, began to channel money to the public elementary schools where all the people could be educated. In the process of losing state support, many quasi-public institutions were forced to become fully private in character.

By the 1830s it was clear that the colleges were out of tune with the aspirations of America's citizens. Despite this, there was no general movement to reform the curriculum, to make the colleges more

[26] Rudolph, *American College*, pp. 231–233.
[27] *Ibid.*, p. 205.

democratic or to provide students with more freedom of study during the decades before the Civil War. In 1850, Francis Wayland, the president of Brown University summed up why the colleges were experiencing declining enrollments and hostility: they had not adapted to the democratic, aggressive, practical society in which they functioned. The Greek and Latin scholar could not help tame the American continent. The student could not chose his course of study.[28] From 1850 to 1855 Wayland attempted to make Brown a model of reform. Courses in applied science were stressed, students were permitted to elect their courses, and professors gave lectures to groups in the neighboring community. For a few years the Brown experiment looked promising but soon it faltered. Too many people feared a lowering of standards and enrollments fell off. Wayland resigned in 1855. The American college would not have a reformer of his stature until Charles Eliot appeared at Harvard four years after the end of the Civil War.

TRANSITION

The America that emerged from the Civil War was a nation transformed. The triumph of the North meant more than a victory for republicanism and nationalism; it meant enhanced importance for commerce and industry, new emphasis on urban values and culture, and confirmation, for many, of the ideals of an open, progressive society. The colleges of America, perceiving these trends, responded with innovative, relevant programs. Old colleges altered their curricula, new universities were created, and a spirit of scholarship and academic excellence began to replace the collegiate emphasis or morals and behavior. Many new courses were created and new professional schools began to flourish. By 1890 it was clear that higher education spoke for more people than at any time in its history, and that it was moving with the times.

The federal government was instrumental in this metamorphosis. In 1857 Congressman Justin Smith Morrill of Vermont introduced a bill to create in every state at least one college "where the leading object shall be, without excluding other scientific or classical studies, to teach such branches of learning as are related to agriculture and the mechanic arts."[29] Morrill argued that American colleges were too

---

[28] *Ibid.*, pp. 237–240 and Wayland's Report to the Brown Corporation quoted in Richard Hofstadter and Wilson Smith, *American Higher Education: A Documentary History* (Chicago, 1961), vol. II, pp. 478–487.

[29] Rudolph, *American College*, p. 252.

devoted to European concepts of education. They had hitherto excluded the very courses that were appropriate to the American environment: scientific agriculture and industrial technology. Morrill was only saying what President Wayland of Brown had already said. The colleges must adapt or risk slowly fading away.

In 1862, with the Civil War underway and with the South's negative votes nullified, the Morrill Act was passed. It provided for the federal government to give 30,000 acres of land to each state for each representative and senator representing that state in 1860. This land, in turn, was to be sold by the states and the bulk of the money received was to support a college or university. The land-grant program was immediately successful. Some states used their money to create entirely new Agricultural and Mechanical (A and M) colleges. Others used their money to support existing institutions which would add courses in technology and agriculture. In 1887 the Hatch Act provided federal funds for agricultural experiment stations, and in 1890 a second Morrill Act created yearly subsidies to the land-grant institutions. The Morrill Act of 1862 was not the first federal involvement in higher education, but it was certainly the most significant. The new colleges provided the farmer and workingman with courses relevant to their lives. They were democratic and practical in their orientation, and they set the standard for future educational and curricula reforms.

Closely related to the land grant movement was the growth of state universities in the West. State universities had two distinct origins: 1) they developed in the southern states and in Vermont shortly after the Revolution to fill an important educational vacuum, and 2) they were created in 1787 and after when the Confederation government agreed to give the Ohio Company two townships of land to support a university. This agreement set an important precedent. After the Ohio agreement, every state entering the Union was given two townships (roughly 46,000 acres) of public lands to dispose of as they wished. The money from the sale of this property was committed to supporting higher education.

The state universities in the West broke new educational ground. At the University of Michigan in 1852, President Henry Tappen began a campaign to create a university "made for studying every branch of knowleddge in full, for carrying forward all scientific investigation: where study may be extended without limits, where the mind may be cultivated according to its wants . . . "[30] Although Tappen's plans proved to be premature, Michigan became a powerful educational institution under James B. Angell who took office in 1870. At Min-

---

[30] Brubacher and Rudy, *Higher Education*, p. 158.

nesota and Wisconsin, at Illinois and Michigan State, universities quite different from the old eastern colleges slowly developed. These universities opened their doors to the people; they offered courses that were useful and meaningful; they sponsored coeducation and service courses for the community. They also strengthened secondary education by certifying those high schools that offered acceptable college preparatory work. The public schools in turn fed the state universities, insuring the continued development of their democratic character.

One university which was neither a state university nor strictly a land grant institution was Cornell, an institution which clearly reflected the new trend in educational thinking. Cornell was created in 1865 when the New York State legislature voted to subsidize a university with land-grant funds and when Ezra Cornell, a wealthy stockholder in Western Union, donated his own half-million dollars toward the endowment. Cornell's first president was Andrew D. White, a man who had visited all the great European universities and dreamed of creating one which combined their best features in America. What White created, however, was uniquely American. It was nonsectarian; it was closely linked to the public school system; it maintained parity between the classics and the sciences; it admitted women and it promoted agricultural and mechanical studies. When Cornell opened it boasted four hundred entering freshmen. The Cornell idea was obviously attractive, and the experiment at Lake Cayuga was carefully watched by a new breed of educators.

One of the most distinguished of this new breed was Charles William Eliot, a Harvard graduate, professor of mathematics and chemistry at M.I.T., and newly elected president of Harvard in 1869. Eliot was only 35 when he assumed the Harvard presidency, and his youth and modern scientific outlook helped him identify what was wrong with Harvard College. In his inaugural address he spoke to this problem:

> Only a few years ago, all students who graduated at this College passed through one uniform curriculum. Every man studied the same subjects in the same proportions, without regard to his natural bent or preference. The individual student had no choice of either subjects or teachers.[31]

To Eliot the prescribed curriculum, the sameness of studies, was stifling student interest in learning. He challenged the belief that Latin and Greek, rhetoric and mathematics developed separate parts (facul-

---

[31] Hofstadter and Smith, *American Higher Education*, p. 608.

ties, they were called) of the mind and maintained that mental discipline could be achieved in many fields of study. Instead of slavishly following a set pattern of courses for each college class, Eliot suggested that Harvard adopt an elective system, one which would allow a true freedom of choice.

> The elective system fosters scholarship, because it gives free play to natural preferences and inborn aptitudes, makes possible enthusiasm for a chosen work, relieves the professor and the ardent disciple of the presence of a body of students who are compelled to an unwelcome task, and enlarges instruction by substituting many and various lessons given to small, lively classes, for a few lessons many times repeated to different sections of a numerous class.[32]

Despite opposition from the Harvard Board of Overseers, Eliot succeeded in introducing the elective system. Within a few years seniors were relieved of taking required courses. In 1879 juniors and in 1884 sophomores were allowed to elect their courses. By 1897 the only required course at Harvard was a year of freshman rhetoric.[33] The college grew tremendously during this period attesting to Eliot's sound educational decision. He continued to maintain, until he retired in 1909, that the elective system solved the problem of motivation; it asked students to find out what they wanted to study and then required them to pursue their unique interests. No longer would a student have to study material considered educationally important forty or sixty years before his time.

The elective idea was loudly praised and loudly condemned. President McCosh of Princeton took Eliot to task in 1885 when he said that the elective system was ruining higher education by substituting freedom for sound educational guidelines and discipline. The president of Williams College and Syracuse University attacked election as inappropriate for college students; they believed it forced students to specialize too early and that it destroyed the common liberal education that all college students should receive. Despite these serious attacks, the elective system took root elsewhere. By 1900 all but the small liberal arts colleges and conservative Catholic institutions allowed students some element of choice in their studies. It was clear to many that the elective principle gave new vitality to the college curriculum and helped erase the old dreariness from the col-

---

[32] *Ibid.,* p. 610.
[33] Rudolph, *American College,* p. 294.

lege classroom. It was an important step in transforming the American college into a modern, up-to-date institution.

The dreariness of the college classroom was also enlivened by the presence of a new group of scholars: women. Women had long been denied higher education; their place, proverbially, was in the kitchen and there, it was thought, advanced knowledge was not required. But the uniqueness of the American environment soon changed these traditional notions. Particularly in the West, women took their place beside men enduring the hardships of the frontier; in the public schools they participated as equals. Thus it was, in Ohio at Oberlin College in 1837, that the first women freshmen were admitted to pursue a Bachelor of Arts degree. The University of Iowa followed suit in 1855 and soon after the land-grant colleges and the state universities of the West allowed women full equality in formal college training.

Frontier conditions, however, had long ceased to exist in the tradition-oriented East, and it was not until the 1860s that women gained access to higher education. In 1859 Matthew Vassar, a wealthy beer manufacturer, founded a woman's college that took his name. In 1875 Wellesley was founded, and in the same year Sophia Smith's fortune went to a new woman's college at Northhampton, Massachusetts. These colleges were not coeducational, but they offered courses on the same level with the men's colleges of the time. It was not necessary for women to pursue only studies that led to domestic accomplishment or cultural refinement. If the men at Harvard and Princeton studied Greek and mathematics, women could too.

Cornell, in every other way a pace setter, became the first major college in the East to introduce coeducation. Thereafter, the old time colleges began to recognize the right of women to be educated. At Harvard, Columbia and other all-male institutions a compromise arrangement was worked out. Separate annex schools were created where professors could give courses to the ladies; by the 1890s these annexes—Radcliffe and Barnard among them—became full-fledged institutions. By 1900, 71 percent of all American colleges were coeducational.[34] Women had gained their foothold in the classroom. Soon they would seek the same foothold where the votes were being counted.

The presence of women in the colleges did not alter many traditional attitudes. Women did not follow men into the scientific laboratories, or study to become engineers, doctors, or lawyers. Most stuck to the liberal arts courses and trained to become teachers, social

---

[34] *Ibid.*, p. 322.

workers or intelligent housewives. The colleges opened up new possibilities for women, but the society at large still constrained them. Coeducation did not mean complete equality. Even in America, the land
of equality, sexual distinctions were not obliterated.

The distinction of color was even harder to erase; during the post-
Civil War era Negroes gained their first taste of formal education but
on all levels it was decidedly inferior by traditional standards.

Prior to the Civil War few Negroes benefited from education on
any level. In the South, slavery depended on obedience and ignorance, and literacy for blacks was feared by every white slaveholder.
In the North, the situation was hardly better. Some black people
attended the common schools. A tiny minority entered academies
which graced their portals with collegiate titles. By 1860 there were
only 28 Negro college graduates in America.[35] This, in a nation which
had four and a half million black people.

At the end of the Civil War the first attempts were made to educate and train the ex-slaves. In the forefront of this movement was the
Freedmen's Bureau, which set up elementary schools and training
centers throughout the southern states.[36] The Bureau also helped
found the first Negro institutions of higher education. Howard University, which was founded in 1867, was named after the Bureau's
chief, General Oliver O. Howard, and Fisk University, founded by
the American Missionary Association in the same year, was named
after General Clifton B. Fisk, assistant commissioner of the Bureau for
Kentucky and Tennessee. The Hampton Institute, St. Augustine College, Storer College and Biddle Memorial Institute also received aid
from the Bureau. The great majority of Negro colleges founded during
this period, however, received the bulk of their support from Christian missionary societies.[37] The Baptist Home Missionary Society of
New York founded Augusta Institute (Morehouse College) in 1867,
Virginia Union University (1865), Shaw University in North Carolina
(1865) and Benedict College in South Carolina (1870). The American
Missionary Society founded Atlanta University in Georgia (1865), Talladega College in Alabama (1867), Fisk in Nashville and Tougaloo
University in Mississippi (1869). These missionary societies and several
which were entirely black organizations were also responsible for
staffing hundreds of rural elementary schools.

In 1870 the educational program of the Freedmen's Bureau was

---

[35] Brubacher and Rudy, *Higher Education,* p. 77.

[36] Dwight O. Holmes, *The Evolution of the Negro College* (New York,
1934), *passim.*

[37] *Ibid.,* and Dwight O. Holmes, "Seventy Years of the Negro College:
1860–1930," *Phylon,* X, no. 4, pp. 307–313.

terminated because of lack of congressional support; as the South returned to white rule, higher education for black people suffered serious setbacks. Southerners who feared the equality implicit in sound educational institutions burned down college buildings and, in one instance, killed a Negro college president (Talladega College, 1870). As Republican reconstruction governments were extinguished throughout the South, educational funds provided by state legislatures dried up. As a result of the white resurgence, few of the Negro colleges developed into full-fledged institutions of higher education. Most of them taught reading and writing and concentrated on religious training. Hampton Institute and Tuskeegee under Booker T. Washington concentrated on vocational training. Even the Morrill Act of 1890 which prohibited discrimination in tax-supported colleges— the South evaded by creating "separate but equal" colleges for black people—did little to advance Negro higher education. Seventeen southern states set up land-grant institutions for blacks, but a 1917 study by the Phelps Stokes Fund showed that only twelve students enrolled in these colleges were receiving college-level training as it was known in the North.[38] No amount of northern pressure or benevolence could mitigate southern reluctance to educate the freedmen. In retrospect, it seems that only a massive federal program could have given southern blacks, as well as their semiliterate white neighbors, a sound educational system.

Despite some gains made during the last quarter of the nineteenth century, higher education among Negroes advanced slowly. The central problem of this period was what kind of education would best prepare the freedmen for self-advancement (southerners preferred subservience) and most people, either willfully or resignedly, accepted Booker T. Washington's solution. Education, he said, should stress mechanical, industrial, craft and agricultural knowledge. Black people would benefit from having a skill to sell and by developing habits and attitudes that appealed to white employers. Although Washington's program was bitterly attacked by the Atlanta University professor W.E.B. Du Bois (he thought it degrading and self-limiting), the Tuskegee idea won adherents among whites and blacks. To Negroes it was perhaps only a temporary strategy; for the majority of whites, however, vocationalism was an attractive "final solution." Thus, it was not until well after World War I that black educational institutions abandoned their vocational orientation. The grip of Washington's ideas had to be broken before southern black institutions could develop high-quality educational programs.

---

[38] Brubacher and Rudy, *Higher Education*, p. 79.

THE UNIVERSITY ERA

The post-Civil War period, as we have seen, was an era of transition. The old-time college began the long process of adapting to an increasingly industrialized America, and new institutions were created to meet the demand for trained agriculturalists and engineers. The elective principle caught fire; women entered the college classroom and Negroes received their first formal educational training. An equally significant development during this period was the emergence of graduate education. Across the country colleges transformed themselves into universities. The era of high scholarship arrived.

During the nineteenth century 10,000 Americans crossed the Atlantic to study in European universities. The majority of these students went to Germany where they were impressed by the breadth and depth of German scholarship. There, students were permitted to study whatever subjects they pleased; they were permitted to travel from university to university to study under illustrious teachers, and the methods and goals of study they encountered were different from those at home. Formal lectures were given; small seminars and tutorials required independent study and high standards of performance. The German professor guided his pupils in research, rigorously and with scientific detachment. There were no dormitories; no class or chapel attendance was required, and there were no class recitations. The German university student was considered a mature, aspiring scholar.

American educators who studied abroad returned to the United States convinced that Americans should emulate the German universities. Obviously, the colleges did not answer the need for advanced study, and even though Yale and Harvard had started scientific schools, where could one receive advanced training in history, philosophy, literature, linguistics or chemistry, physics and medicine? Andrew White tried to bring the German university idea to Cornell; Charles Eliot would ultimately bring it to Harvard. But it was Daniel Coit Gilman who built the first German-style university in Baltimore, Maryland. The railroad magnate Johns Hopkins supplied the money, and Gilman provided the ideas and organizing genius.

The Johns Hopkins University opened in 1876 and everything about it was unique. First, it was a faculty-centered institution and it was primarily a graduate school. Second, the emphasis was placed on research and experimentation, with money going to establish libraries, laboratories and graduate fellowships rather than buildings and gardens. Formal lectures were given; small seminars delved into specialized fields of research, and students studied closely with their teachers in the scientific laboratories. The scholar's freedom to teach what interested him and the student's freedom to follow his special interests were also integral parts of the Johns Hopkins program. There was little about Johns Hopkins that one could identify with the old-time college.

Johns Hopkins quickly became a model for the older liberal arts colleges to follow. Charles Eliot, who had helped Gilman plan the Baltimore experiment, began to expand Harvard's embryonic graduate school until it rivaled and surpassed Hopkins in faculty renown. Yale, which had pioneered in scientific education in the 1840s, moved more slowly, but by the 1880s it too had a graduate school and was committed to advanced specialized study. In 1880 John W. Burgess, a Columbia professor deeply imbued with German university ideals helped set up a graduate department of political science which ultimately blossomed into the Columbia Graduate Faculties. Princeton also began to create graduate departments; in 1896 it changed its name to Princeton University.

Several entirely new universities were founded in the closing decades of the nineteenth century and they also followed the Hopkins example. In 1889 G. Stanley Hall, a former Hopkins professor of psychology, became the first president of Clark University at Worcester, Massachusetts; in the same year the Catholic University of America in Washington D.C. opened its doors. Dwarfing all of these institutions, however, was the University of Chicago which was favored by a two-million dollar gift from John D. Rockefeller and supporting funds from the Chicago business community. At Chicago president William Rainey Harper not only created a college and graduate school but he set up a university extension for the community, a university press, fine libraries, laboratories and a museum. Learning of discontent at Clark he "raided" the faculty, and with Rockefeller's ample funds encouraged scores of leading scholars to make the journey west. When Chicago opened in 1892, 120 faculty, prepared to teach in twenty-seven fields, were available to instruct 594 students.[39] The dynamism, fine organization, and the productivity of the faculty made Chicago the western Hopkins, a paradigm of the new university. All this pleased the oil tycoon whose Baptist upbringing convinced him his benefaction was implementing God's will.

The emergence of universities which emphasized scholarly research, scientific studies and graduate education dramatically altered the style and structure of American higher education. A new development was the requirement that would-be college teachers have a Ph.D., warranting that they had undergone rigorous training in schol-

---

[39] *Ibid.*, p. 188.

arship. The Ph.D. was hardly known in America before the 1870s, but after John Hopkins began to train doctoral students other graduate institutions followed suit. Universities devoted to research and seeking prestige made the Ph.D. mandatory for all senior positions and made it known that promotion would be based upon what a man published and not on how well he taught. One fine professor at Harvard had to wait eighteen years before his promotion came through, and other teachers who did not "produce" failed to succeed. The Ph.D. degree also created distinctions among teachers where few had existed before. A hierarchy beginning with the lecturer or instructor and ascending to the assistant, associate and full professor came into existence. This led to increased competition and snobbism. Chairmen came to rule like petty dictators, seeking to build up their departments in numbers and prestige.

Structurally, more radical changes took place. As knowledge advanced, departments began to split up, creating more specialized disciplines and interdepartmental competition. It was no longer sufficient to have a department of Political Economy, for example, because separate departments of economics, political science and sociology were required. As institutions grew in size, making them run smoothly became more difficult, and a new breed of nonacademic managers, called administrators, rose to the helm. The president now withdrew to raise money and plan the university's expansion. In time, he would know his administrators better than he knew his faculty.

Increasingly, the larger universities took on the characteristics of industrial corporations.[40] They emphasized scholarly output; and they prized the aggressive professor who had new ideas, new methods and a following in his discipline. Moreover, boards of trustees came to be dominated by industrialists and financiers. Their wealth and contacts were important assets, but their presence created new problems. Frequently they were out of touch with academic ideals and values and they tended to place high priority on efficient management. As a result, the gap betwen those who taught and those who governed widened. Trustees also tended to be conservative and took a dim view of professors who spoke out to change the system.

ENTERING THE MAINSTREAM

As new universities were founded and the older liberal arts colleges acquired university status, they gradually oriented themselves toward

---

[40] Rudolph, *American College*, p. 438.

serving the community beyond the campus. Service, in the sense of training ministers, teachers, doctors and lawyers had always been a function of the colleges, but as American society became more complex, more urbanized and industrialized, the academic community became aware of broader responsibilities. During the early twentieth century this awareness brought the university into the mainstream of American life.

This new awareness was apparent at the University of Wisconsin. As a state-supported institution, Wisconsin had been chartered to improve agriculture, industry and inform the citizenry. In 1904, when Charles R. Van Hise became president, Wisconsin embarked on a multitude of programs to fulfill this mandate. Working closely with Governor Robert La Follette, a crusading reformer, Van Hise brought the university to the people by creating extension and correspondence courses, setting up a Bureau of General Welfare which answered questions on technical subjects, and by encouraging university professors to undertake research on problems confronting the farmers and manufacturers. Wisconsin professors also helped draft legislation regulating railroads and banks and served on public commissions which sought solutions to state and city problems. Wisconsin became so closely tied to La Follette's reform program that it was accused by some of meddling in state politics. Reformers, however, applauded the university's involvement in community affairs.

The "Wisconsin idea" was soon copied by many of the other state universities of the West. They set up extension programs, created courses that were relevant to their students and undertook research which would help solve state problems and promote the state's economy. The idea of service spread rapidly to the eastern universities and even to the small colleges. Students entered the industrial slums to set up settlement houses and provide relief for the poor.[41] Others helped organize social-action programs and sponsored lectures for newly arrived immigrants. Although the service idea waned during the 1920s, it was revived again during the depression and grew to a ground swell in the 1960s. Knowledge of, and service to, the community, became a distinct goal of American higher education as the twentieth century progressed.

A different kind of service was promoted by the city universities which grew in size and prominence during the early 1900s. The City College of New York, founded in 1847, became a leader in free higher education for the masses, offering thousands of immigrants a chance to train for a profession. City College created the first night

---

[41] *Ibid.*, Chapter 17.

college in 1909 and set up courses for social workers, nurses and civil service employees. In the late nineteenth and early twentieth century, city colleges and universities began to do for the urban centers what the older land-grant institutions had done for the agricultural west. They opened their doors to the average citizen and taught courses that led to professional careers and social advancement. Wisconsin university scientists helped the Wisconsin dairy industry. The city colleges helped many of the urban poor.

In order truly to enter the mainstream of American society the colleges and universities had to divest themselves of the last traces of elitism; this they did during the late nineteenth and early twentieth centuries with astounding swiftness. In 1870 there were 50,000 students in American colleges; by 1920 there were nearly 600,000 and by 1970, 7 million students were enrolled! In 1870 1.68 percent of young people aged 18–21 went to college; by 1946 22.1 percent of this age group were enrolled and by 1967 46.6 percent were in college.[42] Burgeoning enrollments swelled the state and municipal universities, but a new institution, the two-year college, accelerated the democratizing trend. In the academic year 1900–1901 there were eight junior colleges in the United States with roughly a hundred students in each. By 1959–60 there were 816,000 students enrolled in 663 junior colleges.[43]

Greater democracy in college enrollments inevitably helped more Negroes gain access to higher education. Since Reconstruction, the South produced the largest number of Negro college graduates, and in this section their numbers steadily advanced. In 1876 only 137 black students graduated from Negro colleges; by 1900 this number rose to 1,883. By the 1920s Negro colleges were graduating several thousand students each year, and between 1939 and 1952 almost 70,000 black students won their degrees.[44] Numbers, however, do not tell a complete story. In 1950 only 14.4 percent of southern black youngsters completed high school and only 4 percent went on to college. As late as 1968 a major study of Negro colleges concluded that many were academically poor and unselective.[45] Private Negro colleges lacked funds and facilities, and southern states spent less on Negro public schools and public-supported black colleges. Moreover, until 1954 segregation in education was strictly enforced. One must

---

[42] *Digest of Educational Statistics, 1968,* p. 68.

[43] James W. Reynolds, *The Junior College* (New York, 1965), p. 10.

[44] Henry A. Bullock, *A History of Negro Education in the South from 1619 to the Present* (Cambridge, Mass., 1967), pp. 173–174.

[45] A. J. Jaffe et al., *Negro Higher Education in the 1960s* (New York, 1968), Conclusions.

conclude that higher education did not fully enter the mainstream where Negroes were concerned.

THE FEDERAL GOVERNMENT AND HIGHER EDUCATION

Without money from the federal government, it is unlikely that American colleges and universities could have grown as fast and as large as they did after 1900. The traditional notion that government had no business interfering in educational matters was replaced during the twentieth century by an attitude which favored government aid to education. This, of course, was not entirely new, since the government, through land-grant legislation, had supported higher education indirectly for some time. What was new, however, was the broad range of educational programs the government came to support and the magnitude of this support.

Two world wars and a third "cold war" had a great deal to do with getting government into the business of education. During World War I hundreds of colleges received subsidies to set up military training for students (already required in land-grant institutions), and after the war the Reserve Officers Training Corps (ROTC) came into being. Between the wars, the government gave the universities money for cancer research, new agricultural training stations and assisted students with scholarships through the National Youth Administration (1935–1943). World War II, however, brought the government and the universities into an unprecedented partnership. With federal funds the universities undertook vital research; biologists, cartographers, cryptographers, language specialists, chemists and nuclear physicists turned their attention to winning the war. The atom bomb was created by university scientists, radar was perfected and new weapons were devised. At the war's end the government was providing the bulk of support for science research in the universities. In 1944 it also assumed the burden of paying tuition for college-bound GI's.

National defense, and not educational interests per se, continued to be the primary motive for government aid to higher education during the 1950s and 1960s. In 1957 the Russians launched their famous Sputnik, awakening Americans to the fact that they had lagged behind in scientific research and education. As a result, the following year the National Defense Education Act was passed; it provided states with money to support the teaching of science in the public schools and it made student loans and scholarships available for college and graduate students. In 1963 a Higher Education Facilities Act authorized grants for the construction of classrooms, libraries and laboratories, and in 1965 new legislation expanded all of these programs. By

1970 hardly anyone questioned the right or wisdom of government support for higher education. A cautious few feared that academic autonomy would be compromised, but most educators welcomed government subsidies.

Government aid to higher education swelled enrollments and permitted financially weak institutions to improve their educational facilities; it created massive science research programs and promoted the training of mathematicians, teachers, and foreign language experts. Federal involvement in higher education, however, created serious problems. Colleges became dependent on continued federal support; science and medical research was advanced or retarded by budgetary (political) considerations in Washington; the whole apparatus of higher education came under the influence of those far from the campus. When student disruptions hit the colleges in the late 1960s more than a few congressmen hoped to stifle dissent by withholding much-needed federal funds. The century-old relationship between the colleges and the government began to show signs of tension and stress.

CONCLUSION

The diversity of higher education in the United States has permitted it to embrace many different ideas and philosophies. At times elitist, and at times democratic, tradition-minded yet anxious to be modern and relevant, it has never been without an inner dynamic for change and self-reform. In every period of American history educators and students have grappled with the problems of campus governance, curricula relevance, student activism and the questions raised by democratic enrollment. Our era is not alone in attempting to define what the college and university should be and what constitutes a meaningful higher educational experience.

Suggestions for Further Reading

An invaluable resource for studying the problems and prospects of American Higher Education is the *Carnegie Commission on Higher Education Series* published by the McGraw-Hill Book Company. When completed, the Series will number about 80 titles.

Books that discuss the contemporary university and its problems are Jacques Barzun, *The American University* (1968); Clark Kerr, *The Uses of the University* (1964); Alvin Eurich, *Campus 1980* (1968); and Gary Weaver and James H. Weaver, eds., *The University and Revolution*

(1969). Statistics on higher education may be found in *Digest of Educational Statistics* which is published annually.

There are a number of good books on student unrest. Among these are: Jerry Avorn et. al., *Up Against the Ivy Wall* (1968); The Cox Commission Report, *Crisis at Columbia* (1968); Charles Frankel, *Education and the Barricades* (1968); Seymour M. Lipset and Sheldon S. Wolin, eds., *The Berkeley Student Revolt: Facts and Interpretations* (1965); Seymour M. Lipset, ed., *Student Politics* (1967); and Jerome H. Skolnick et al., *The Politics of Protest, A Task Force Report Submitted to the National Commission on the Causes and Prevention of Violence* (1969).

For the relationship between the federal government and institutions of higher education one may consult The American Assembly, Columbia University, *The Federal Government and Higher Education* (1960), and Harold Orlans, *The Effects of Federal Programs on Higher Education: A Study of 36 Universities and Colleges* (1963).

The best general study of the history of higher education is Frederick Rudolph, *The American College and University* (1962). Good also are John S. Brubacher and Willis Rudy, *Higher Education in Transition,* rev., (1968); Richard Hofstadter and C. Dewitt Hardy, *The Development and Scope of Higher Education in the United States* (1952); and Richard Storr, *The Beginnings of Graduate Education in America* (1953). An excellent documentary history is Richard Hofstadter and Wilson Smith, eds., *American Higher Education: A Documentary History,* 2 vols., (1961). An in-depth treatment of the evolution of academic freedom is Richard Hofstadter and Walter P. Metzger, *The Development of Academic Freedom in the United States* (1955).

There are scores of studies of individual colleges and universities. They are uneven in quality. Among the best that are relevant to this chapter are Carl Becker, *Cornell University: Founders and Founding* (1943); Samuel Eliot Morison, *Three Centuries of Harvard 1636–1936* (1936); Hugh Hawkins, *Pioneer: A History of the Johns Hopkins University 1874–1889* (1960); and Merle Curti and Vernon Carstensen, *The University of Wisconsin: A History, 1848–1925* (2 vols., 1949). Two fine studies of Negro colleges are Dwight Oliver Holmes, *The Evolution of the Negro College* (1934) and Henry Allen Bullock, *A History of Negro Education in the South from 1619 to the Present* (1967).

The role of the federal government in financing higher education is discussed in Alice Rivlin, *The Role of the Federal Government in Financing Higher Education* (1961). Also see, E. D. Ross, *Democracy's College* (1942) on land-grant institutions, and Richard G. Axt, *The Federal Government and Financing Higher Education* (1952).

Founding Women

4

Women as a Force in American History

Among the many "liberation" movements that surraced during the 1960s, Women's Liberation was the least expected and the most lightly regarded. American social awareness during these years extended itself, albeit sluggishly and unwillingly, to black people, Puerto Rican immigrants, Mexican Americans, Indians, prisoners, narcotics addicts, migrant workers and juvenile delinquents, but for a variety of reasons not to women. A majority of Americans, including women themselves, felt that women had no special problems related to their sex; the few that believed these problems existed also believed they could be worked out in the context of long-term social change. In sum, the idea that women had something to be liberated from was not taken very seriously.

A few people dissented from this view, however, and sometime after 1965 their voices joined to create a strident chorus. Women did have problems, these people said; problems deep, pervasive and damaging. The political rights gained by women in the nineteenth and twentieth centuries had not significantly changed the unequal status of women either socially or economically. Women were still exploited, controlled, humiliated, stifled and programmed for failure in a male-run society. The problem was compounded by the fact that many women would not admit to themselves that the problem of sex inequality existed or that it applied to them.

These sweeping denunciations were made by women who, living in a revolutionary age, slowly became touched by the revolutionary vision. They came piecemeal at first, in books and articles written by unhappy, frustrated women, but the interpretations and insights they elucidated began to reach into the consciousness of women everywhere and in all walks of life. In the fullest meaning of the word, a woman's movement was born during the late 1960s, a movement that was small and disorganized, politically fragile and with no agreed-upon leader, but nevertheless a genuine social movement. What bound it together was a common feeling that women in America had unrealized potential, and that they were spectators not participants in the important activities of national life.

Men and women, grappling with the problems we have mentioned, also became aware that Women's Liberation had a history, hitherto largely ignored or presented in the most cursory way in history books and texts. Aside from the tales of the suffrage leaders, few books could be found which adequately treated the story of women in America. At what point had the Jeffersonian ideal of equality been sidetracked? Why had the long struggle for political equality that culminated in the Nineteenth Amendment not provided full social and economic equality? Were there spokesmen for equality between the sexes in our history and what did they say? These and other questions began to be answered in the late 1960s, answered in ways that reached popular audiences and college students and not merely specialists and researchers.

THE SPECTRUM OF CONCERN

It is impossible to chronicle the successes and failures of the contemporary Women's Liberation movement because it is so recent and diverse a phenomenon. Women liberationists do and do not favor a constitutional amendment guaranteeing equal rights; they do and do not support the idea of lesbian love; they do and do not belong to formal organizations pressing for equal rights and opportunities; they disagree on the methods and techniques to be employed in the struggle for self-realization and autonomy. Despite the wide spectrum of views and feelings, however, there is elemental agreement regarding the plight of women in American society: women are second-class citizens; Americans have accepted and internalized the myth of female inferiority; until women become conscious of their oppression and do something about it they will remain prisoners of sex.

From scores of books and magazine articles, from manifestos, fact sheets and propaganda leaflets it is nevertheless possible to piece together the essence of contemporary Women's Liberation. A central insight is that American society denies women the opportunity to realize themselves as individuals and as human beings. This process begins at birth when female and male infants are treated differently because parents believe females have different natures, abilities and life-roles. It continues into childhood where the assertive, action-oriented, creative tasks are assigned to males while females are encouraged to be passive, delicate and decorative. During adolesence a girl finds she must conform to the societal goal of finding, marrying and pleasing a man; this goal is best achieved by not competing with men, by quelling desires for self-assertion and excellence in work and by eliminating thoughts of finding a career. During the early adult years the burden of being a woman continues as wives find themselves locked into household tasks and living their lives for and through their husbands and children. For the working woman, both single and married, being a woman means working in unrewarding, routine jobs, being paid less than men in similar employment and knowing that the most interesting and challenging jobs are reserved for men.

Such criticism deserves close scrutiny to ascertain both the truth of the assertions and the reasons why these conditions persist. The reports of the President's Commission on the Status of Women and of the Department of Labor's Women's Bureau affirm their validity.[1] Consider, for example, the following facts:

—Women constitute 37 percent of the American labor force, some 30 million in number.

—Roughly 82 percent of women workers work in nonprofessional, nonmanagerial positions.

—Women constitute 97.5 percent of all people working in private households, 72.2 percent of all waitresses, cooks and bartenders, 98.2 percent of all stenographers, typists, and secretaries, 69.9 percent of all clerical workers and 61 percent of nurses and auxiliary medical personnel.

—In 1970 women year-round, full-time workers had a median wage salary income of $5,323 which was 60 percent of that of men ($8,966).

—The income gap between men and women full-time workers has widened in recent years.

—Women constitute about 43 percent of entering college freshmen although they are 51 percent of the population.

---

[1] *American Women, Report of the President's Commission on the Status of Women, 1963.* U.S. Department of Labor, Women's Bureau, *Women Workers, 1969.* Also, "Gap Widens in Equal Pay," *The New York Times,* February 18, 1972, p. 40.

—Women are earning only 1 in 3 of the B.A.s and M.A.s awarded by American institutions of higher learning, and only 1 in 10 of the Ph.D.s These ratios compare unfavorably with the 1930s when women received 2 out of 5 B.A.s and 1 out of 7 Ph.D.s.

—Although college administrations profess complete equality in hiring and promotion, only 9 percent of the professorial ranks are filled with women.

—Women at all income levels suffer from a lack of readily available, professionally run, day-care centers.

VARIED INTERPRETATIONS

When we consider why these inequalities continue to exist we move from fact to interpretation. Some women in the movement believe that women remain in inferior roles because men consciously and deliberately refuse to share the reigns of power. These women identify the enemy simply as men and advocate extreme doctrines to eradicate inequality between the sexes: suspicion of all men, lesbianism, female capitalism, a new sexism.

Others share the belief in deliberate sexism but extend their analysis and recommend less radical strategies for reform. They believe, for example, that many men would accept greater equality between the sexes if they could divest themselves of prejudices and hangups, if they could break through to a broader definition of masculinity and feminity and really empathize with women's human needs. Women they argue, share the blame for sexism because they continue to reflect and reinforce male-fashioned ideas about themselves. Redress will thus come from conquering ignorance and not from some artificial and impractical separation of the sexes.

Before becoming activists many women have had to discover in a very personal way the objective reasons for their predicament. For some, this discovery has been solitary: accomplished through reading and rigorous social analysis. For others it has come only through group discussions and encounter groups, the so-called consciousness-raising sessions.[2] At these sessions women who have experienced discrimination, or personal unhappiness due to their sex, begin to share their experiences and to analyze and interpret these experiences in social

---

[2] Vivian Gornick, "Consciousness," *The New York Times Magazine,* January 10, 1971.

and political terms rather than personal terms. Thus, unhappiness in the role of housewife, or lack of success in promotion or some other career goal, is not considered a *priori* to be some personal problem or insufficiency but rather is looked at through the lens of sexism. In many cases women have discovered that sexism rather than some personal failing is the core of their problem.

Once women have reached a stage where they begin to define themselves and their goals from within, and see that society sets up strong barriers to self-fulfillment, the hard work of women's liberation begins. So far the main thrust of the woman's movement has been to fight ignorance and challenge male supremacy and the double standard wherever it exists. Holding demonstrations, sit-ins and marches has gained visibility via the mass media. Pressure has been brought to bear to eliminate sex discrimination in employment and to expose biases against women in newspapers and magazines. Women's Liberation has encouraged television stations to hire more women for broadcast assignments. Women have supported legislation for abortion reform and for the creation of day-care centers.

With Women's Liberation in its infancy it is difficult to tell how far into the minds of men and women it has reached, how much consciousness raising it has done outside the encounter groups and rap sessions. It is interesting to speculate, however, what it would be like if women did liberate themselves and to envision a society in which men no longer held their biases and preconceptions about women's nature and abilities. Some of the work currently being done by Women's Liberation groups gives us a clue to what this society would be like.

It would certainly be one in which male and female children were free to develop as people without worrying whether specific acts or ideas were masculine or feminine. Active girls would not be called tom boys; artistic boys would not be called sissies. The whole panoply of toys and games would lose their sexual characteristics and associations. The Women's Liberation movement is helping to bring about this reorientation by encouraging toy manufacturers, book publishers and producers of television programs to eliminate sexual stereotyping in their programs and products.

Similarly, this liberated society would be one in which women did not win men solely by their sexiness and reluctance to compete. It would be one in which men shared many duties in the home, in the rearing of children, in cooking and cleaning, and all the details of domestic life. It would be one in which women did not have to make artificial choices between careers or marriage and motherhood but rather one in which women would be able to leave the home with relative ease. It would also be a world in which women were not denied good jobs or promotions because they were women and one in which women could take on all the demanding jobs now dominated by men. More women would be doctors, judges, corporation presidents, congresswomen and senators, if they had the drive, ability and commitment.

All this speculation sounds fanciful and premature considering the values and attitudes of our present society. Nevertheless, this is the vision of Women's Liberation. In a widely celebrated book, that many consider the catalyst of the woman's movement, Betty Friedan pointed out what has hitherto been the unpleasant side affects of sexism: women who feel empty and bored living in affluent suburbia; women who put a college education to use only in reading detergent labels; women who feel resentment, anger, a sense of being nonpeople and of living for and through others.[3] Friedan tied the drive to consume material possessions, to remain forever young, marital unhappiness, and psychosomatic illness among women to a value system that prizes the homemaker and mother and stigmatizes the woman who is an active participant in the world of business and government. Women, she claimed, were the victims of a dehumanizing "feminine mystique."

The distance between the present male-dominated world and the one envisioned by Friedan and other feminists continues to be great, which leads us to the conclusion that a lot of education and hard work must take place before attitudes and behavior are changed. There are, however, several forces working for Women's Liberation. Technology is increasingly freeing more and more women from housekeeping tasks and forcing them to consider alternatives to leisure and boredom. New contraceptive methods permit women to space, limit or eliminate conception. New federal legislation is in the process of creating more day-care facilities for middle class as well as poor families. States and cities are beginning to enforce laws which permit women to gain redress for discrimination in employment.

There are, however, continuing problems for feminists to face. In the absence of one overriding goal such as suffrage reform, women have not joined the liberation movement in large numbers. The movement so far has not shown evidence of developing strong, well-financed organizations that can "get out the vote" or bring sufficient pressure to bear on corporations or politicians. Too few women's organizations employ full-time staffs to enlist support, marshal facts and monitor the progress of the movement.

For all this, Women's Liberation is gaining strength from the gen-

---

[3] Betty Friedan, *The Feminine Mystique* (New York, 1963).

eral movement for social reform begun in the 1960s. It is influencing the thinking of women, particularly young women. It seems certain that it will win additional freedoms for women in the future. But how much it will alter fixed prejudices and stereotypes about the nature of women, and thereby unlock women's potential for full participation in our society, is at this point unknown.

WOMEN IN THE NEW WORLD

The women who arrived in the New World during the earliest years of colonization may have had liberation on their minds, but it was escape from poverty, religious persecution, class rigidities and spinsterhood that defined this liberation. They came to America for a multitude of reasons but few thought that their personal freedom *as women* would be enhanced. As a matter of fact, many of the first women settlers had already sold their freedom before taking ship, having agreed to work for a master or family for a fixed term. All of the black women who came to America came so under compulsion, in chains and under inhuman conditions of passage. America held out promise to many women, but it was the promise of more food, better living conditions and the chance to marry an independent land owner that provided the motivation for the long Atlantic voyage.

Nevertheless, in sharing the hardships of early settlement, women experienced new freedoms and a new equality with men. They suffered the long winters together, worked side by side in the fields, hunted, fought Indians and helped build homes and churches. Life was too primitive and survival too important for artificial distinctions to take hold. Women were primarily co-workers, "helpmeets," in the language of the day. They were valued not for fragility or gentility but for positive virtues: friendship, fortitude, self-reliance, intelligence, religious conviction, business acumen.

The historian Page Smith has pointed out that there were many areas of life in which colonial women were treated as the equals of men. Relations between husbands and wives, as expressed in contemporary letters and poetry, show a surprising warmth, directness and openness. In New England men and women were treated the same for breaches of the code governing sexual behavior. In the world of work women faced few restrictions.

> Most frequently [women] took over a dead husband's or father's business, and we find them acting as shopkeepers (in very considerable numbers), teachers, blacksmiths, hunters, lawyers, innkeepers, silversmiths, tinworkers, shoemakers, shipwrights, tan-

ners, gunsmiths, barbers, and butchers. Eleven women ran printing presses, and ten of these published newspapers in America before 1776.[4]

In addition, women worked as midwives and healers.

We must not conclude, however, that colonial women were regarded as the true equals of men. Women's abilities and accomplishments were valued in the frontier environment, but the old prejudices and customs persisted. Englishmen brought with them the notion that women had no rights by law, that they were subordinate to their husbands, that men, not women, should run the society. "Married women could not sign contracts; they had no title to their own earnings, to property even when it was their own by inheritance or dower, or to their children in case of legal separation. Divorce, when granted at all by the courts or by legislative action, was given only for the most flagrant abuses; adultery, desertion and nonsupport, and extreme cruelty."[5]

The education women received also reflected their subordinate status. While young men went to school to achieve mastery in mathematics, natural science, Greek, Latin and rhetoric, women, when they went to school at all, studied reading, spelling, music, drawing, and occasionally French.

> Daughters of poor parents were fortunate if they were taught to read and write by a parent or wandering tutor; girls of wealthier families received a hardly better (but more polite) education from a tutor, a dame school, a church school, or a girl's seminary. In New England, girls were admitted to grammar schools at "separate hours" (sometimes from five to seven in the morning) to study reading, writing and spelling. There were also, during the eighteenth century, a number of private girls' schools; some 200 of them existed between 1722 and 1776. Nevertheless, perhaps 50 to 70 per cent of all women in the eighteenth century were either illiterate or barely literate.[6]

This was the situation in the towns and cities along the eastern seaboard. Women's opportunities to receive an education sharply declined as one moved westward.

---

[4] Page Smith, *Daughters of the Promised Land* (Boston, 1970), p. 54.

[5] Eleanor Flexner, *Century of Struggle* (Cambridge, Mass. The Belknap Press of Harvard University Press, 1959; Reprinted by Atheneum Publishers, 1971), p. 8.

[6] Russel B. Nye, *The Cultural Life of the New Nation* (New York, 1963), pp. 167–168.

In religion too women suffered from the double standard. The Quakers alone accepted the equality of women; the other Protestant sects refused to ordain women ministers, have them preach or hold any church office. In Puritan New England ministers never ceased reminding women of the original sin of Eve and the burdens they must inevitably bear.

The case of Ann Hutchinson illustrates how severely the Puritan community could act when it felt threatened by a bright and spirited woman.

Ann Hutchinson arrived in the Massachusetts Bay Colony in 1634 filled with religious passion. She began holding meetings in her home in which sermons were discussed and interpreted. A powerful and articulate woman, she drew large numbers of women as well as men to her weekly sessions until their numbers became a source of embarrassment to the colony's leaders and clergy. She embraced doctrines that were threatening and controversial—she asserted that many of the prominent Puritans believed they were saved but in fact they were not—and she was ultimately brought to trial. Her prosecutors, among them Governor John Winthrop, sought in every possible way to prove her a heretic, until she finally broke under questioning and admitted to a special conversation with God. Banished, she wandered first to Rhode Island and then to New York where she and her family were killed by Indians.

There is little doubt that Ann Hutchinson's "crime" was more threatening because it was perpetrated by a woman. Roger Williams, an equally passionate and obstinate personality, was also banished from Massachusetts Bay, but he was exiled only after most of the Puritans refused to listen any longer to his ultra-purist ideas. The fact that women were special targets of discrimination is amply demonstrated by the Salem witch trials in which mass hysteria resulted in the hanging of 19 women in 1692. One must conclude that America's early civil and religious leaders believed women were equal with men in receiving God's love, but that they held very distinct (and therefore unequal) stations in life. Certainly, God did not intend for women to preach His doctrines.

EARLY DISSENT

As the eighteenth century drew to a close a few women in England and America began to speak out against the subordination of women. The spirit of revolution was in the air when Abigail Adams wrote her husband that "If particular care and attention is not paid to the ladies [in the laws of the new nation] we are determined to foment a rebellion, and will not hold ourselves bound by any laws in which we have no voice or representation."[7] From England, in 1792, came the spirited writings of Mary Wollstonecraft who attacked every assumption of male superiority in *A Vindication of the Rights of Women*. Wollstonecraft's book was the first full-scale tract dealing with the customs and prejudices which kept women in "slavish dependence." She defined the entire spectrum of male supremacy and female trivialization and attempted to convince her readers that it was "time to effect a revolution in female manners—time to restore to them their lost dignity—and make them, as a part of the human species, labour by reforming themselves to reform the world."[8] Wollstonecraft's book was received by men as the rantings of an unhappy woman. Many women, however, were moved and radicalized by her writings.

In America, Judith Stevens Murray also penned a cogent argument in defense of women's equality. It first appeared as "On the Equality of the Sexes" in the *Massachusetts Magazine* in the Spring of 1790.

In her essay Mrs. Murray held up for ridicule the popular myths and assumptions of her day; that Eve's sin was greater than Adam's; that Biblical tradition confirmed the inferiority of women; that men were superior because they are physically stronger. Women, she asserted, were not deficient in reason; they matched men in memory and would equal them in wisdom and judgment if they were not denied an education.

> Will it be said that the judgment of a male of two years old, is more sage than that of a female of the same age? I believe the reverse is generally observed to be true. But from that period what partiality! how is the one exalted, and the other depressed, by the contrary modes of education which are adopted! the one is taught to aspire, and the other is early confined and limited.[9]

Being confined and limited, Murray maintained, made women experience a "mortifying consciousness of inferiority, which embitters every enjoyment." As for the intellectual rewards of being a housewife, she writes:

> Should it still be vociferated, 'Your domestick employments are sufficient'—I would calmly ask, is it reasonable, that a candidate

---

[7] Quoted in Andrew Sinclair, *The Emancipation of the American Woman* (New York, 1965), p. 30.

[8] Quoted in Smith, *Daughters*, p. 98.

[9] Aileen Kraditor, ed., *Up From the Pedestal: Selected Writings in the History of American Feminism* (Chicago, 1968), p. 32.

for immortality, for the joys of heaven, an intelligent being, who
is to spend an eternity in contemplating the works of Deity,
should at present be so degraded, as to be allowed no other
ideas, than those which are suggested by the mechanism of a
pudding, or the sewing the seams of a garment?[10]

Murray concluded:" . . . ye lordly, ye haughty sex, our souls are by
nature *equal* to yours. . . . for *equality only*, we wish to contend."[11]

"WOMEN'S SPHERE": THE EARLY NINETEENTH CENTURY

It is not a coincidence that the writings of Mary Wollstonecraft and
Judith Murray appeared during the last decade of the eighteenth century. The ideals of the American and French Revolutions had generated
widespread philosophical speculation, and it was not likely that relations between the sexes would escape critical scrutiny. The industrial
revolution was beginning to alter family and social relations, particularly in England where large numbers of women left the sanctuary of
the home to work in factories. Along the eastern seaboard of the
United States a new urban middle class was developing a style of life
based on wealth, leisure and a blending of foreign and domestic notions of sophistication and gentility. The remarkable fact is that while
Wollstonecraft and Murray were leveling their guns at existing inequities new and more powerful inequities began to emerge. The
early nineteenth century witnessed further restrictions on females and
an articulation of theories that precisely defined women's sphere.

The shift in attitudes towards women that began to crystalize during the early nineteenth century was marked by a tendency to re-
strict women's sphere of activity, place them in distinctly subordinate
roles, emphasize their fragility and dependence and deemphasize
their sexuality. These attitudes applied almost exclusively at first to
members of the urban middle class who wanted to mark themselves
off from frontiersmen and factory workers and who wanted to show
society that they had "arrived." The sure sign of this was to have
women who did not work outside the home, who dressed fashionably,
who limited their energies to childrearing, housework and churchwork
and who acted with gentility and grace. Small as the urban middle class
was, its values were the values of those who had attained wealth and
success and for that reason they took tenacious hold on the popular

[10] *Ibid.*, p. 34.
[11] *Ibid.*, pp. 34–35.

consciousness. The ideal of "True Womanhood" that the middle class espoused became the model for women of all classes to respect and emulate.

Barbara Welter has studied the magazine stories and ladies books of the early nineteenth century and has come up with a composite portrait of the "True Woman."[12] As portrayed in countless stories and anecdotes she was a vessel of piety, born with a religious nature which it was her duty to cultivate. Religion was considered a proper activity for women because it fostered moral conduct in the home and thereby contributed to the reformation of the general society. Women were believed to be especially sensitive to religious and moral strictures, the guardians of all that was good. If men broke the moral code it was because their nature's were susceptible to temptation; it was a woman's duty to bring her husband back to correct behavior.

The ideal woman was also portrayed as pure and chaste, avoiding any thought or deed connected with sex or lust. Magazine stories dealt with the curse of premarital intercourse with tiresome regularity and in each instance emphasized how the unfortunate heroine faced personal misfortune. Reinforcing the belief that women must regard sex as dangerous were innumerable books on conduct that instructed young women in correct behavior. These, for example, told girls to avoid sitting with anyone in close quarters, to avoid sitting with one's legs crossed, to avoid reading novels, and to abhor "solitary vice." The girl or woman who denied her sexual impulses was held up for veneration in the popular literature of the day.

Passivity and submissiveness to men were also virtues extolled in the ladies magazines. "True feminine genius is ever timid, doubtful, and clingingly dependent; a perpetual childhood."[13] "A really sensible woman feels her dependence. She does what she can, but she is conscious of inferiority, and therefore grateful for support."[14] Statements like these from magazine and pulpit bombarded young women from early childhood and were reinforced in middle-class families in word and deed. The "True Woman" avoided being aggressive, self-reliant, and effective in life. The incredible extent to which this model of behavior was accepted is reflected in nineteenth century fashion. Corsets restrained women's bodies; long skirts made free movement impossible. It is not surprising that when the women's movement began, dress reform was one of its high priorities. The corset made passivity and submissiveness physical realities.

---

[12] Barbara Welter, "The Cult of True Womanhood, 1820-1860," *American Quarterly* 18 (1966): 151–174.

[13] *Ibid.*, p. 135.

[14] *Ibid.*

Another virtue prized in the women's magazine was domesticity. The home was presented as the proper and only sphere for a woman. There she could reign supreme and develop her potential as wife and mother. She must organize the home's activities and supervise servants. She must create an atmosphere of warmth and relaxation— a haven away from the bustle of the "real world." She should guide her children, promote piety, and nurse the sick. It was widely assumed that housekeeping adequately challenged a woman's intellect. A well known woman writer asserted: "The science of housekeeping affords exercise for the judgment and energy, ready recollection, and patient self-possession, that are the characteristics of a superior mind."[15]

Piety, purity, passivity and domesticity; these in sum were the ideal characteristics of the nineteenth-century woman. Corollary to these four "virtues" were innumerable restrictions which women encountered in everyday life. Women were not allowed to speak in public meetings; they were not supposed to have political opinions; they were, of course, not allowed to vote. Women were not permitted to develop close male friendships; they were not allowed to express themselves physically; they were denied the pleasure of feeling their own bodies either in sexual relations or in aggressive sport. Women avoided mention of bodily functions; they even avoided visiting a doctor if their ailment required physical examination. These and other restrictions, too numerous to mention, were part of a gentlewoman's life in nineteenth-century America. In light of this it is not difficult to see why the women's rights movement began in pre-Civil War America.

THE BEGINNINGS OF THE WOMEN'S RIGHTS MOVEMENT

The picture we have just described of a passive, restricted, domesticated woman was the model for middle class women to emulate in early nineteenth-century America. If few women rebelled against this norm it was because all the respected organs and institutions of society gave it support and because women had few opportunities to gather to discuss their mutual problems and predicaments. This situation could not last for long, however; even the lady of good breeding was allowed some public vent for her energies and this she found in church and charity work and ultimately in a variety of reform activities. In the North, abolitionism captured the imagination and elicited the sympathy of many women. In the antislavery movement women discovered the evils of the Southern caste system and soon

---

[15] *Ibid.*, p. 137.

came to perceive that their situation was not unlike that of the black man and woman who suffered in bondage.

The reform movements of the 1830s and 1840s provided new opportunities for female involvement; these were decades when Americans tried to live "the pursuit of happiness" by abolishing slavery, building utopian communities, opening wider the doors of education, creating better prisons, revitalizing religious feeling. Primarily in the North and West, middle-class women began to form clubs and associations, sometimes affiliated with the church, sometimes as informal groups for reading or discussion. Women during these years created the first Female Anti-Slavery Societies, which numbered more than a hundred by 1840; they began to familiarize themselves with public issues; they even began to petition state legislatures and the United States Congress. This flowering of female activism was in no way a woman's movement. But when women were ridiculed and criticized for abandoning their proper sphere, they became conscious of their inferior status. This awareness crystalized in the late 1840s into a demand for equal rights.

The lives of Sarah and Angelina Grimké illustrate the formidable barriers to self-expression women had to face in the 1830s. They were born in South Carolina, Sarah in 1792 and Angelina in 1805. Their father was rich and respected, and they grew up with all the comforts and lack of responsibility of the plantation upper class. But instead of learning to accept the slave system as a necessary prop to their station in life, the sisters recoiled at its horrors. Sarah tried to teach one of her servants to read; she was repelled by the brutality of the work house where slaves were sent to be punished. Angelina, too, could not be convinced that blacks were best kept in bondage and that frequent punishment instilled proper discipline. Convinced that no amount of reason could persuade Southerners that slavery was evil, the sisters came North to breathe the air of freedom.

In the North, however, the sisters could not forget the conditions in the South, and they were slowly drawn into the embryonic abolitionist movement. The sisters read the abolitionist press. A letter written by Angelina was printed by William Lloyd Garrison in his newspaper, The Liberator. Before long the sisters made the acquaintance of numerous abolitionist agitators including the famous orator Theodore Weld. In 1836 Sarah and Angelina and 38 men met under the leadership of Weld to train as antislavery agents. The next year they began speaking in public on the evils of the slave system.

As antislavery agents the Grimké sisters were pioneers, not only because they were among the first of their sex to become active in the abolitionist movement, but because they braved criticism, ridicule and riot to speak their conscience in public. This was a novelty in 1837 for it was considered improper for a woman to speak publicly, to chair a public meeting or to address mixed audiences. Undaunted, the sisters carried out a 23-week tour of New England in which they spoke before 88 meetings in 67 towns to 40,500 people.[16] Women and men came to hear them even though press and pulpit denounced their proceedings and castigated them as agitators, frustrated spinsters, and promoters of racial "amalgamation." The sister's final triumph was an appearance before a Committee of the Legislature of the State of Massachusetts in February, 1838. There they spoke about their experiences in the South and catalogued the sins of their countrymen.

> I [Angelina] stand before you as a southerner, exiled from the land of my birth by the sound of the lash and the piteous cry of the slave. I stand before you as a repentant slaveholder. I stand before you as a moral being and as a moral being I feel that I owe it to the suffering slave and to the deluded master, to my country and to the world to do all that I can to overturn a system of complicated crimes, built upon the broken hearts and prostrate bodies of my countrymen in chains and cemented by the blood, sweat and tears of my sisters in bonds.[17]

Had the Grimké sisters speaking tour on behalf of abolitionism been their sole accomplishment their achievement would have been considerable. But caught in the vortex of reform feeling, the sisters went beyond pleading for the slave and brought into the open the subjection of women. Sarah, in particular, was sensitive to the problems of being a women for from childhood to womanhood she encountered restrictions and humiliations. As a girl in the South she had watched her brothers advance into the professions while she received an inferior education. As a young woman in the North she joined the Quakers only to find that Quaker women were carefully supervised and more restricted than men. On their speaking tours the sisters faced constant ridicule for transcending their "proper sphere." These experiences brought Sarah to the realization that women and the slave had much in common. Her response to this was to speak and write about the condition of her sex.

In July, 1837 Sarah Grimké wrote a now famous series of letters entitled *Letters on the Equality of the Sexes* which appeared in the New England *Spectator* and were reprinted in *The Liberator*. They

---

[16] Gerda Lerner, *The Grimké Sisters from South Carolina: Rebels Against Slavery* (Boston, 1967), p. 227.
[17] Quoted in Lerner, *Grimké Sisters*, p. 8.

were a response to a "Pastoral Letter of the General Association of Massachusetts to the Congregational Churches under their care" which denounced agitators and women "who so far forget themselves as to itinerate in the character of public lecturers and teachers." Sarah's response to this was to review the long history of woman's subjection to man, to point out that the Bible was sexist because written and interpreted by men, to claim for women all the rights and prerogatives of men and to assert boldly," . . . whatsoever it is morally right for a man to do, it is morally right for a woman to do." Women, she maintained, must abandon their dependence, their vanity and obsession with personal attractiveness and become involved and active in the great issues of the day. Only in this way would they be able to gain self-respect and the respect of men.

Angelina Grimké also wrote on feminist themes. Her arguments appeared in a series of *Letters to Catherine Beecher,* a well-known educator who had written against organizing women for abolitionism. The letters, later reprinted as a pamphlet, primarily dealt with refuting Beecher's contention that gradualism and colonization were the best solutions to slavery. Angelina pointed out that both these expedients were founded on racism and that they would harm the free Negroes of the North. In the last two letters of her series, Angelina attacked Beecher's statements that women were subordinate to men and that women should confine themselves to persuading men to act responsibly and morally. This was not enough, Angelina asserted, for women have a right and a duty to petition, to speak in public and to agitate for reform.

> Now, I believe it is woman's right to have a voice in all the laws and regulations by which she is to be governed, whether in Church or State: and that the present arrangements of society, on these points, are a *violation of human rights, a rank usurpation of power,* a violent seizure and confiscation of what is sacredly and inalienably hers . . . If Ecclesiastical and Civil governments are ordained of God, *then* I contend that woman has just as much right to sit in solemn counsel in Conventions, Conferences, Associations and General assemblies, as man—just as much right to sit upon the throne of England, or in the Presidential Chair of the United States.[18]

With these words Angelina Grimké summed up the political goals of thousands of future feminists.

---

[18] Quoted in Kraditor, *Up From the Pedestal,* p. 65.

SENECA FALLS: 1848

In her letters to Catherine Beecher, Angelina Grimké had written, "The discussion of the rights of the slave has opened the way for the discussion of other rights." So it was for many other women who became active in the abolitionist movement. Once women began to analyze and criticize the slave's condition, it was natural that they would apply the same techniques of analysis and insights to their own condition. Once they began to organize and petition for black enfranchisement, it was only a matter of time before they would organize and petition on their own behalf.

Feminism was born with abolitionism and *within* abolitionism: when women activists realized that the movement's male leaders feared the cause would be tainted by discussing women's rights or ridiculed because women acted too assertively. The Grimkés had been made aware of this when they were asked to eliminate public statements regarding women's rights; Lucretia Mott and several American female delegates to the World Anti-Slavery Convention, held in London in 1840, became aware of their secondary status when they were refused seats at the Convention on the basis of sex. Lucretia Mott and Elizabeth Cady Stanton, the young wife of the abolitionist Henry Stanton, discussed this humiliating decision at the time of the convention and determined to work to eliminate discrimination based on sex. They planned together to hold their own convention back in America that would address itself directly to the issue of women's rights. Eight years passed, however, before this plan materialized.

The Seneca Falls Convention of July, 1848 was a small meeting compared to many abolitionist meetings of the day, but it was dynamic, controversial and unprecedented. The germ of the idea for such a meeting dated from the conversations of Mrs. Mott and Elizabeth Stanton in 1840, but it was given impetus by the experiences of Mrs. Stanton during the intervening eight years. She had moved with her husband and family of young children to Seneca Falls in the Finger Lakes region of New York. There she found no relief from the drudgery of childbearing and housekeeping, no opportunity to express herself intellectually:

> The general discontent I felt with woman's portion as wife, mother, housekeeper, physician, and spiritual guide, the chaotic condition into which everything fell without her constant supervision, and the wearied, anxious look of the majority of women, impressed me with the strong feeling that some active measures should be taken to remedy the wrongs of society in general and of women in particular. My experiences at the World Anti-

Slavery Convention, all I had read of the legal status of women, and the oppression I saw everywhere, together swept across my soul, intensified now by many personal experiences. It seemed as if all the elements had conspired to impel me to some onward step. I could not see what to do or where to begin—my only thought was a public meeting for protest and discussion.[19]

The result of this conviction was put into motion when Mrs. Mott visited her sister's family near Seneca Falls in July, 1848 and she and Mrs. Stanton were reunited. Together with Mrs. Mott's sister and two women friends they decided to issue a call for a meeting which they advertised in the *Seneca County Courier.*

Woman's Rights Convention—A Convention to discuss the social, civil and religious rights of woman will be held in the Wesleyan Chapel, Seneca Falls, New York, . . . the 19th and 20th of July current. . . . During the first day the meeting will be held exclusively for women, who are earnestly invited to attend. The public generally are invited to be present on the second day, when Lucretia Mott of Philadelphia and other ladies and gentlemen will address the convention.

Despite the novelty of the idea, despite the competing demands of farm work, women from the surrounding area responded to this advertisement by crowding into the little chapel in Seneca Falls to follow the proceedings. For two days Mrs. Stanton, the Mott's, the Negro abolitionist Frederick Douglass, and other feminist sympathizers spoke about the problems confronting women. On the second day, Mrs. Stanton read her Declaration of Principles, an acerbic document patterned after the Declaration of Independence.

We hold these truths to be self-evident: that all men and women are created equal. . . .
The history of mankind is a history of repeated injuries and usurpations on the part of man toward woman, having in direct object the establishment of an absolute tyranny over her. To prove this, let facts be submitted to a candid world.[20]

There followed a long list of grievances:

---

[19] Quoted in Flexner, *Struggle,* pp. 73–74.
[20] E. C. Stanton et al., *History of Woman Suffrage* (Rochester, N.Y., 1881), vol. I, pp. 70–71.

He has never permitted her to exercise her inalienable right to the elective franchise.

He has compelled her to submit to laws in the formation of which she had no voice. . . .

He has made her, if married, in the eye of the law, civilly dead.

He has taken from her all right of property, even to the wages she earns. . . .

He has so framed the laws of divorce as to what shall be the proper causes, and in case of separation to whom the guardianship of the children shall be given. . . .

He has monopolized nearly all the profitable employments. . . .

He has denied her the facilities for obtaining a thorough education. . . .[21]

When it came time to pass resolutions, resolution nine was hotly debated and narrowly passed: "Resolved, that it is the duty of the women of this country to secure to themselves their sacred right to the elective franchise." Rather than be present when this resolution was presented, Henry Stanton left town.

The Seneca Falls Manifesto, as the Declaration of Principles is popularly known, summed up the personal unhappiness of Mrs. Stanton. But it spoke for countless women who were too isolated, too frightened, or too inarticulate to speak in their own behalf. The fact that it was only a statement of principles, the fact that it was signed by only 100 men and women, does not detract from its historic significance. It signaled a new stage in the consciousness of American women and it opened the long battle for women's rights.

ENTERING "MAN'S WORLD": EDUCATION AND THE PROFESSIONS

While Mrs. Stanton and her sympathizers were articulating the goals of a woman's movement, quiet changes in woman's status were already taking place. In education and the professions barriers to women slowly began to yield. As these barriers disappeared women gained new perspective, self-confidence and self-respect. Conversely, it became more difficult for men to claim that women were frail and dependent when women proved themselves as teachers, doctors, ministers, writers, public speakers and factory workers.

---

[21] *Ibid.*

Much of the progress won by women in the nineteenth century may be traced to changes in educational outlook during the early part of the century. Until then women received a second class education, partly due to the fact that women were considered intellectually inferior to men. But as American society absorbed the liberating influences of the Revolution and the Enlightenment, and as men recognized that educated women could help them in running a store or a farm, prejudices against formal education for women began to wane. In 1821 Emma Willard opened the Troy Female Academy, the first endowed institution for the education of girls. In 1823, Catherine Beecher founded the Hartford Seminary, and in 1837 Mary Lyon founded Mount Holyoke, a seminary for girls in South Hadley, Massachusetts. These three institutions shared the belief that women could master the traditional male curriculum. Consequently, girls at Troy studied mathematics and physiology, and at South Hadley women took entrance examinations and studied such "male" subjects as rhetoric, geometry, algebra, natural philosophy, logic, geology and moral philosophy. To insure that women would not be defeminized by all this intellectual labor they also studied Music, French and helped cook and clean!

It was not until 1837, however, when Oberlin College in Ohio began offering its full course of study to women, that higher education for women was introduced. But Oberlin's experiment was not enthusiastically endorsed and except for a few examples such as Elmira Female College in New York, higher education for women did not take root until the decades after the Civil War. Then, with the land-grant institutions and states universities of the West leading the way, one college after another opened its doors to women.

First the University of Iowa in 1855 and then the University of Wisconsin in 1863 opened their doors to women, followed by Indiana, Missouri, Michigan, and California. The readiness of the western institutions to adopt coeducation unquestionably derived in part from the fact of western life, where an equality of the sexes was achieved in the ordinary work of the farm. Western woman was not a thing apart. Neither pampered nor fragile, . . . she was a person in her own right who had commanded the respect of her menfolk by assuming responsibility and working hard.[22]

---

[22] Frederick Rudolph, *The American College and University* (New York, 1962), p. 314.

The East lagged behind the West in adopting higher education for women, but here, too, appreciable gains were made. In 1861 Vassar was founded, followed by Smith and Wellesley in 1875. These women's colleges were determined to erase the stigma attached to the older female academies; thus, they applied strict admission standards and offered curricula nearly identical to the best male colleges. In 1872 Cornell admitted women, the first college to offer coeducation in the East. Thereafter, the die was cast. "By 1880 over 30 percent of all American colleges admitted women and in another twenty years 71 percent of all American colleges were coeducational."[23]

College life was tremendously stimulating to the first generation of college educated women; they discovered new knowledge, tested their abilities, shared common experiences and made deep and lasting friendships. A new kind of woman emerged from these institutions, eager to express herself, eager to participate in the work of society, and anxious for economic opportunity and recognition. But the experience of college frustrated many young women because society provided no outlet for their talents. They graduated with skills but found new opportunities to utilize them. They mastered math and botany but found men scornful of women who transcended their "sphere." The tension created between women's aspirations and the obstacles they faced generated deep discontent. This discontent motivated many women to join and sympathize with the emergent feminist movement.

Entering one of the professions was more difficult than obtaining a college education; the former was a direct threat to male monopoly and privilege, the latter only an attempt to gain knowledge and culture. Women found it easiest to gain entrance to those professions in which men had no interest such as teaching and nursing; writing novels or stories for ladies' magazines also provided alternatives because this could be pursued discreetly and in the home. Law, medicine, and the ministry yielded only after women had proved themselves in other areas and then only reluctantly. These professions remained closed during the nineteenth century to all but the most aggressive and determined women.

The trials faced by Elizabeth Blackwell in becoming a doctor illustrate contemporary prejudice. After being rejected by twenty-eight medical schools she was finally accepted by Geneva Medical School in 1846. Once enrolled she had to insist on her right to attend classes in anatomy and dissection. Fighting self-doubt and loneliness, she

---

[23] *Ibid.*, p. 322.

nevertheless managed to graduate at the head of her class; then she traveled in Europe to further her studies.

> When she returned to New York in 1851, she encountered a stone wall. She had great difficulty in finding a place to live or an office to rent. No private patients came to her; she could not gain access to the wards of city hospitals or even the chance to work in a dispensary; and she was shunned by her fellow physicians. A mind eager for further growth and for the exchange of ideas was completely cut off from professional companionship or stimulus.[24]

Although Elizabeth Blackwell succeeded in proving her professional competence—she founded the New York Infirmary with an all-female staff in 1857—many more women succumbed to humiliation and self-doubt in their quest for careers. The stalwarts among them succeeded, but only at a price. Anna Howard Shaw was miserable in theological school and almost starved to death because she was denied the money subsidy offered to men. Women who succeeded in graduating from law school eked out penurious existences because they were denied access to the courts and the comforts of professional and moral support. Women who sought careers in college teaching were consistently passed over in favor of men when it came to promotion or support for research. American society until well into the twentieth century was not prepared to see women assume positions that would challenge the professional hegemony of men.

ENTERING "MAN'S WORLD": THE FACTORY

In one area of working life, however, the factory, women found ready access; and few men objected that this work was too demanding, too difficult or too degrading. Here the scruples dealing with women's nobility, fragility and proper "sphere" were abandoned, first, because it was women of the lower class that were involved, and second, because women provided the only surplus labor at a time when men preferred to strike out West or remain on their farms. The new textile industry that grew up in New England after the War of 1812 beckoned to the young farm girl who had nothing to show for a full day's work on her family's farm. Young women by the thousands were lured to the mills and factories of expanding America with the

---

[24] Flexner, *Struggle*, p. 117.

hope of earning a dowry, putting a brother through school or helping out a struggling family.

By the Civil War there were 270,987 women factory workers in America; by 1870 there were 323,370.[25] As the tide of "New Immigrants" swept over the United States during the 1880s and 1890s women became an increasingly large part of the total working force. "The 2,647,000 gainfully employed in 1880 grew to 4,005,500 ten years later, from 15.2 percent to 17.2 percent of the total working labor force."[26] By the end of the century women factory workers dominated clothing manufacture; they made cigars, shaped hats, printed newspapers and produced shoes, paper boxes and carpets. Most women worked for meager pay and worked long hours, unprotected from the hazards of machine accidents, poor ventilation and overcrowding. None knew the benefits of sick leave, maternity leave or protective legislation in handling and carrying.

Through their fortitude and backbreaking labor, working women showed the capabilities of their sex as much as their middle-class counterparts. They destroyed once and for all the idea that women could not do the work of men; they disabused men of the notion that women were helpless when they organized on their own and struck for higher wages. Working women were not drawn into the women's rights and suffrage movements, however, because their reality was the reality of the factory, and until conditions there could be improved all other issues, be they women's property rights, the vote, or liberalized divorce laws seemed academic and remote. The women's movement was overwhelmingly white, middle and upper class for a reason. Working women, preoccupied with the struggle for survival, simply could not identify with the concerns of their wealthier, bettereducated sisters.

ORGANIZING FOR SUFFRAGE: 1848–1869

When Elizabeth Cady Stanton read her Statement of Principles in 1848 she foresaw that the road to their realization would be long and sparsely traveled. Within a few years, however, she found she was joined by other women fired by her example and rhetoric. Lucy Stone, an Oberlin graduate, began speaking for women's rights in the late 1840s. Newcomers like Ernestine Rose and Abby Kelly Foster, and old-time abolitionists like Lucretia Mott, actively joined the move-

---

[25] *Ibid.,* p. 131.
[26] *Ibid.,* p. 193.

ment shortly afterwards. In 1850 Elizabeth Stanton met Susan B. Anthony, a Rochester Quaker interested in abolitionism and temperance reform. The two women developed a warm and unique friendship and forged a working alliance for women's rights that lasted over half a century.

For Stanton and Anthony the immediate task in 1850 was to bring the cause of women before the American people. They were delighted to see that women's rights conventions began to be held in towns and villages patterned after the meeting at Seneca Falls. They were even more pleased by the appearance of newspapers that championed the women's cause such as Amelia Bloomer's *The Lily* and Paulina Wright Davis's *The Una*. Educating the public, however, was no easy task in a society where activist women were ridiculed and maligned. Undeterred, Stanton and Anthony took every opportunity to petition, speak, debate and write on women's behalf. Anthony traveled the length and breadth of New York in the mid-1850s to gather petitions for constitutional reform. Stanton wrote articles and speeches from her home where for many years she was tied down by family responsibilities. She recalls:

> Miss Anthony and I wrote addresses for temperance, anti-slavery, educational, and woman's rights conventions. Here we forged resolutions, protests, appeals, petitions, agricultural reports, and constitutional arguments; for we made it a matter of conscience to accept every invitation to speak on every question, in order to maintain woman's rights to do so.[27]

The first few decades of the women's rights movement were exhilarating but also disappointing years. Feminists had many grievances but found it difficult to sort out priorities or effect meaningful change. Susan Anthony narrowed her interests to three concerns: women's right to control their earnings; women's right to keep children in divorce proceedings, and women's right to vote. But other issues crowded in. Dress reform gained national recognition when Amelia Bloomer advocated that women rid themselves of hoops and long skirts in favor of pantaloons and short skirts. The propriety of women petitioning and speaking before legislatures was also much debated during the 1840s and 1850s. With so many issues and so few resources at their disposal feminists, understandably, made slow progress toward realizing their goals.

Small gains, however, were made. In 1854 the Massachusetts Legis-

---

[27] Elizabeth C. Stanton, *Eighty Years and More* (New York, 1898), p. 164.

lature passed a Married Women's Property Law which gave women control over their own earnings. In 1860 New York passed its own women's property act which gave women the right to collect wages, sue in court and have property rights similar to those applying to men. Although Susan Anthony campaigned extensively in New York State to see this bill enacted, its passage did not hinge on her efforts. The law was enacted because wealthy citizens wanted to pass on their property through their daughters if no male heir existed. It was not passed to protect women per se.

The Civil War dominated the thoughts of all Americans in the 1860s, and many women's rights advocates hailed it as a welcome event. Here, they argued, was an opportunity for women to prove themselves as patriots and as active participants in the life of the nation. Many threw themselves into the struggle by serving as nurses; others visited hospitals to cheer the soldiers or served on committees to aid the war effort in any way they could. Many more stayed home to maintain a farm or a store for a husband or kinsman.

When the war ended, however, feminists were shocked to find their patriotism had counted for naught. The Fifteenth Admendment gave the vote to newlyfreed male slaves, but women were deliberately excluded from receiving the franchise. In vain the leaders of the woman's movement turned to their abolitionist friends who replied that "this was the Negroes' hour." Stanton and Anthony were deeply hurt and angered that illiterate black males could now vote, but not the most esteemed and educated woman. From this point on they vowed never to make political alliances or friends with any group or individual that that did not put women's interests first.

The Civil War thus brought severe disappointment to many hopeful women. Perhaps fortuitously, this disappointment encouraged feminists to adopt a new political realism and to think in terms of developing sound organization and rational strategies. An illustration of this new political orientation was their participation in the state referendum in Kansas in 1867 where the voters were asked to take the word "male" out of the voting qualifications. Feminists such as Stanton, Anthony, Lucy Stone and Olympia Brown decided to travel to Kansas and to canvass the state to win votes for suffrage. Although the voters turned down the amendment, the speaking tours of these women gave them fresh insights and practical experience in the political arena.

Searching about for a vehicle to reach a wider audience for their views, Stanton and Anthony launched a newspaper dedicated to furthering women's rights in January, 1868. The brainchild and financial backer of this new venture was an eccentric speculator named George Francis Train who set the operation in motion by telling the two women he would furnish them with a newspaper during the Kansas campaign. Delighted to have a friend and sponsor, the two women set to work; the product of their effort was a small tabloid called *The Revolution,* which made its appearance on January 8, 1868.

The Revolution fulfilled an important function at a time when few organs or institutions spoke for women. It was hardhitting and factual; it was comprehensive in its coverage of women's activities and problems; and it was not so biased that it was afraid to print the objections of nay sayers and foes. *The Revolution* was filled with news of conferences and congresses, of pending legislation and with statistics dealing with women and work. It serialized the books of famous feminists and ran articles about women in other societies, cultures and eras. Stanton and Anthony saw *The Revolution* as a means of raising the consciousness of American women and of galvanizing them into action. The masthead of their periodical expressed their enthusiasm and confidence:

The Revolution Will Advocate:

1. In Politics—Educated Suffrage, Irrespective of Sex or Color; Equal Pay to Women for Equal Work; Eight Hours Labor; Abolition of Standing Armies and Party Despotism. Down with Politicians—Up with the People!

No doubt *The Revolution* would have continued to be the voice and spirit of radical feminism had it not failed to pay its way. Problems began as soon as George Train left for England and his patronage fell off. Stanton and Anthony tried to raise money through advertising and personal contributions but these were never enough to carry the paper. After two years they faced reality and sold out. Thereafter, they had to rely on a hostile press to carry and disseminate their controversial views.

THE NATIONAL AMERICAN WOMAN SUFFRAGE ASSOCIATION (NAWSA)

In 1869 when *The Revolution* was still flourishing, Stanton and Anthony took another bold step towards marshalling support for women's rights and suffrage; they decided to found an organization devoted solely to the woman's cause and open only to women. The immediate reason for this decision was the refusal of the abolitionist Equal Rights Association to endorse Mrs. Stanton's resolution calling for a woman suffrage amendment. More fundamental, perhaps, was Stanton's and Anthony's desire to lead an organized crusade for women which would not defer to men and which would concern itself with the broad spectrum of issues and problems confronting women.

The National Woman Suffrage Association which Stanton and Anthony founded in May, 1869 was not born without a fight and without important dissenters. Many women did not sympathize with the National's stand on divorce and religious questions and disliked the organization's concern for working- and lower-class women. Thus at the same time that the National was seeking new members and formulating policy, a group of women led by Lucy Stone and the well-known minister Henry Ward Beecher founded a rival organization, the American Woman Suffrage Association, which established headquarters in Boston. This organization found supporters among the new class of professional women and among women who believed the suffrage issue should not be associated with broader, more radical reforms. The American also favored fighting for suffrage on the local and state level, whereas the National supported change through a constitutional amendment.

The American and National organized support in their separate constituencies and remained hostile to one another for twenty-one years. By 1887, however, leaders of the two organizations realized that the suffrage issue transcended their personal and ideological differences and talks were initiated to effect a reconciliation. Resolution came in 1890 when the two organizations merged and took the name National American Woman Suffrage Association. Mrs. Stanton became the NAWSA's first president; Miss Anthony was chosen vice president at large and Lucy Stone became chairman of the executive committee. Thereafter the woman's movement spoke with one voice on major issues until another break occurred in 1914. On this occasion it was the NAWSA that was accused of being too conservative. In 1914 a group of militants broke with the NAWSA and formed the Congressional Union.

SUFFRAGE GAINS AND LOSSES: 1870–1914

The last decades of the nineteenth century were frustrating years for suffragists. Although they had finally begun to organize and win more female converts to their cause, they made scant headway in influencing elected officials or winning vital state referenda. During the 1870s it seemed for a moment that a legal technicality might win women the vote when the president of the Missouri Woman Suffrage Association, Virginia Minor, brought suit against the St. Louis Election Registrar for refusing to accept her ballot. The case went to the

Supreme Court in 1874, but the Court's unanimous decision reaffirmed the right of the states to determine which class of citizens may or may not vote. Susan B. Anthony also had her day in court when she was arrested and brought to trial for voting in the 1872 presidential election. The judge was openly biased; he charged the jury to bring in a guilty verdict and ended up fining Miss Anthony $100. She refused to pay the fine but was never sent to jail because her incarceration would have given her automatic grounds for an appeal.

For some time suffragists were aware that there were two means by which they might gain the vote. The first was to put pressure on congressmen and senators to get them to pass an admendment to the constitution. This path was exceedingly difficult because an amendment required a 2/3 vote in the Congress and ratification by 3/4 of the state legislatures. As early as 1868 a federal amendment was proposed in Congress but hardly won a hearing. In 1878 Senator A. A. Sargent of California, a friend of Susan Anthony, introduced a similar amendment—the famous Anthony Amendment—which read "The right of citizens of the United States to vote shall not be denied or abridged by the United States or by any state on account of sex." On this occasion the woman suffrage amendment received a committee hearing but little more.

Within a few years, however, woman suffrage sentiment began to reach the ears of recalcitrant legislators, and Select Committees on Woman Suffrage were appointed in both houses of Congress. By the mid-1880s these committees were urging congressional action, but in 1886–1887, when the Anthony amendment finally went to the Senate, it was decisively voted down. "The vote, sixteen in favor to thirty-four opposed, with twenty-six absent, put seven more senators on record favoring suffrage than had voted for it in the District of Columbia in 1866. A geographical breakdown of the tally showed that the South was solidly in opposition. . . . "[28]

Recognizing the difficulty of the federal amendment route, suffragists determined to fight in the individual states by means of popular referenda or by means of legislative action which would permit women to vote for presidential electors. This method, however, also presented obstacles because it was first necessary to petition to get the referendum on the ballot and then necessary to campaign effectively to get out the vote. Fifty-six state referenda campaigns took place between 1867 and 1918 but few were successful before 1910. Two victories during the early years, however—Colorado in 1893 and Idaho in 1896—gave suffragists just enough hope to sustain their

---

[28] Flexner, *Struggle*, p. 175.

organization and enthusiasm. Their failures also taught them vital lessons in strategy and political tactics.

Each of the state campaigns presented different problems for the national and state suffrage organizations. Suffrage was frequently associated with prohibition in the minds of men; consequently women faced hostility from liquor interests, saloon keepers and most drinking men. In many states the entrenched political machines opposed women's suffrage for fear that the "ethical" vote would put them out of office. But prejudice more than anything else was women's worst enemy because it was deep-seated and irrational. Too many men silently agreed with Senator Vest of Missouri when he said:

> For my part I want when I go to my home—when I turn from the arena where man contends with man for what we call the prizes of this paltry world—I want to go back, not to the embrace of some female ward politician, but to the earnest loving look and touch of a true woman. I want to go back to the jurisdiction of the wife, the mother; and instead of a lecture upon finance or the tariff, or upon the construction of the Constitution, I want those blessed loving details of domestic life and domestic love.[29]

To counter this prejudice suffragists began to alter their arguments as to why they should be given the vote. The old argument that justice and natural rights demanded that women vote was gradually displaced by arguments based on expediency. Women should vote because it would make them better citizens, they said. Women should vote because only the ballot would provide them with equal protection as workers, wage earners and housewives. Moreover, women could help in drafting legislation which affected their daily lives— food inspection, sweatshop sanitation, street cleaning and public school education.[30] Women worked in the professions and in factories. It was now proper to give them a fair say in the state legislatures and Congress.

Antiforeign and antiblack prejudice also became an important part of the suffragist argument as many northern women joined southern women in declaring the superior worth of the Anglo-Saxon race. The argument that white native women outnumbered black men and illiterate foreigners, and that giving white women the vote would insure white supremacy, was all too popular in race-conscious America in the

---

[29] Quoted in Flexner, *Struggle,* p. 175.
[30] Aileen S. Kraditor, *The Ideas of the Woman Suffrage Movement 1890– 1920* (New York, 1965), p. 68.

1890s; the paradox that suffrage was born in the abolitionist movement did not seem to bother women bent on getting the vote. As Aileen Kraditor has pointed out, "The woman suffrage movement had ceased to be a campaign *to extend the franchise* to all adult Americans. Instead, one important part of its rationale had become the proposal to *take the vote away from* some Americans—Negroes in the South and naturalized citizens in the North."[31]

As women began to put forward new reasons why they should be given the vote, they also perfected the means to achieve their goal. State organizations recruited new members, solicited contributions, organized petition campaigns, held public meetings, organized speaking tours, and began to use private detectives and poll watchers to insure that elections were not "stolen." These techniques gradually began to pay off. After a period of no state referenda victories from 1896 to 1910 Washington State broke the deadlock by passing a woman's suffrage law in 1910. California, Kansas, Oregon and Arizona were won for suffrage in 1912, Alaska in 1913 and Nevada and Montana in 1914 .

NEW DEVELOPMENTS

After the turn of the century the suffrage movement was strengthened by a number of new developments. The most important of these was the growth of women's organizations and the increasing level of women's educational and professional competence. During the Progressive Era—after 1896—women became active in many areas of reform work. Francis Willard organized the Women's Christian Temperance Union (1876) and during the 1890s forged it into a mighty alliance of women determined to wipe out alcoholism. The WCTU also supported women's suffrage. Wealthy and middle-class women helped organize the first settlement houses in immigrant, working-class neighborhoods and learned at firsthand the problems of the poor and politically impotent. They also became active in such organizations as the Consumers League (founded in 1899), which attempted to improve working conditions for women, and the National Women's Trade Union League, which worked toward the same goal.

A group of women drawn from these various organizations succeeded in 1908 in getting Congress to undertake the first full-scale study of women's working conditions. The investigation, which took

---

[31] *Ibid.*, p. 137.

four years to complete, culminated in the publishing of a nineteen volume study of women's work which documented, for the first time, the harsh and unhealthy conditions in female employment. The Consumers League also retained Louis D. Brandeis in 1906 to fight a now-famous case in behalf of women working in Oregon laundries. Brandeis won the case and set a precedent by detailing the hardships of the laundresses rather than stressing complicated legal points.

Another important development during these years was the emergence of new leaders in the suffrage movement, women dedicated to fighting the long struggle and to applying sound techniques of organization. The most notable of these women on the national level was Carrie Chapman Catt who took over the presidency of the National American Woman Suffrage Association from Susan Anthony in 1900. Mrs. Catt began to mold the NAWSA into a full-time working organization but cut short her work to involve herself in the international suffrage movement in 1904. She was followed in the presidency from 1904 to 1915 by the less able, but equally dedicated, Anna Howard Shaw. Mrs. Catt returned to the presidency in 1915, however, and reorganized and strengthened the NAWSA and devised a "game plan" for victory. She insisted on total loyalty to the cause, a full-time staff and carefully thought out plans for organizing, galvanizing and recruiting new members. In 1917 she committed a substantial personal inheritance to the suffrage fight.

WINNING THE NINETEENTH AMENDMENT: 1914–1920

Although suffragists could count 13 states in the suffrage column in 1914, it was painfully obvious that winning the vote by means of conducting state referenda was costly, enervating, and too frequently doomed to failure. Campaigns in New York, Massachusetts, Pennsylvania and New Jersey in 1915 confirmed this; women were well-organized, well-financed and highly motivated but failed in each case to overcome the opposition. Nevertheless, the National American Woman Suffrage Association was reluctant to accept an alternative strategy, believing that opposition in the Congress was still too great to put time, money and energy into a federal lobby. Congressional committees had not reported favorably on the Anthony amendment since 1896, and there was no indication that attitudes had changed substantially since then. Mrs. Catt believed that going the federal route was premature. Thus, the NAWSA continued doggedly to support state referenda.

A new component in the politics of suffrage began to develop after 1912, however: the emergence of a group of younger women fired by the example of British suffragists who had gone over to militant tactics in their struggle to obtain the vote. This group, headed by Alice Paul and Lucy Burns, at first worked within the NAWSA, taking over the job of lobbying for a federal amendment in 1912. Zealous, imaginative and dedicated to fighting the suffrage battle on the federal level, Alice Paul and her colleagues began to organize parades, pilgrimages, and petition campaigns designed to convince congressmen and the President that women were determined and organized enough to make their politician's lives uneasy and tenuous.

In 1914 Miss Paul's tactics aroused the concern of the more conservative NAWSA's leadership and an open split occurred. Thereafter, Paul and her followers began independent action as the Congressional Union, an organization devoted to winning the vote by prodding Congress to pass a federal amendment and one determined to follow the British example of holding the party in power responsible for withholding suffrage support. This policy inevitably led the Congressional Union toward militant tactics. It announced its intention to defeat the Democrats in the Congressional election of 1914; it campaigned against President Wilson in 1916 and formed a National Woman's Party to realize this goal. When these strategies failed, Woman's Party members made headlines by picketing the White House and by withholding support for the United States during World War I. These activities made them many enemies and the government reacted harshly. Women pickets were arrested, placed in jail and maltreated when they failed to cooperate. Several were force fed when they went on hunger strikes.

The militancy of the Woman's Party had an effect on the NAWSA. Mrs. Catt, who reassumed the presidency in 1915, did not agree with fighting the party in power or picketing the White House and vilifying the President, but she soon realized that getting a federal amendment through Congress was not as hopeless as she had once thought. Congress had been prodded by the defeat of several Democrats in 1914 to vote once again on the Anthony Amendment, and even though it was voted down, hope for its eventual passage was rekindled. Consequently, Mrs. Catt tried to use her personal influence to win President Wilson over to the suffrage idea. She also strengthened the NAWSA lobby in Washington and evolved a plan that involved simultaneous pressure on the state and federal levels. Although she insisted that women should support the war effort, she never modified her strong suffrage stand. Women had been misled during the Civil War into thinking that patriotism and patriotism alone would soon guarantee them the vote.

American entry into World War I in 1917 affected the suffrage movement in a number of ways. Women were called upon to shoulder the burdens of men called to the front; they entered factories in record numbers and proved their technical competence, physical strength and patriotism. Women served as nurses, sold Liberty Bonds, taught classes in food conservation and kitchen gardening. Politically active women such as Dr. Shaw and Mrs. Catt served on the Women's Committee of the Council for National Defense. The NAWSA even ran an overseas hospital in France.[32]

Suffrage leaders perceived correctly that the best strategy was to maintain a patriotic posture while pressing their political demands. They also recognized that practical politics and the necessity for ideological consistency would eventually win them support in the White House. President Wilson did not support women's suffrage when he was elected in 1912, but by 1916 he recognized the desirability of ·posing as a woman's advocate. It also became increasingly difficult for him to talk about making the world safe for democracy when the United States disenfranchised half of its adult population. By 1917 he openly favored giving the vote to women and by the summer of 1918 used his personal influence to get the woman suffrage amendment passed in the Senate. Wilson, like many other politicians, was a late convert to women's suffrage. He did not help the women's movement in any spectacular way, but his support during the final political battles was warmly appreciated by the NAWSA's leadership.

Major gains in state suffrage contests in 1917 put congressmen and senators on notice that the nation was moving towards support for women's suffrage. In January, 1917 North Dakota granted women the vote by legislative action; Ohio, Indiana, Rhode Island, Nebraska and Michigan followed suit. On March 6, Arkansas legislators voted for women's suffrage, "the first historic breach in the Solid South."[33] More impressive and decisive, however, were the results of the New York State referenda where the suffrage vote margin tallied more than 100,000. This powerful state with its large congressional voting block was now committed to suffrage for the first time. It was clear in which direction the nation was moving.

On January 10, 1918 the Woman Suffrage Amendment was brought up in the House of Representatives. After a dramatic role call vote in which four representatives arrived from sick-beds—one on a stretcher—the House voted by exactly two thirds to pass the Anthony Amendment. Leaders of the suffrage movement who were hopeful of an early victory in the Senate, however, were deeply disappointed. There, an entrenched opposition kept the amendment from being

---

[32] Flexner, *Struggle*, p. 289.
[33] *Ibid.*, p. 290.

called up for a full year and a half; when it was called up it was twice defeated; once by two votes and again by one vote. It was not until new congressional elections were held and three more states voted for women's suffrage that the Senate voted for the amendment.

Notwithstanding this conclusive victory it still took another 14 months for suffrage battles to be waged successfully in 36 state legislatures. On August 26, 1920 the last technical obstacle to suffrage was erased when Tennessee certified that its legislators had in fact voted favorably on the Nineteenth Admendment. The 72-year fight to grant women the vote was finally over.

THE VOTE IS NOT ENOUGH

In the aftermath of their suffrage victory many feminists were hopeful that women would emerge as a force in local and national politics and use their newly won power to redress the inequalities of the past. Almost from the beginning, however, there were bitter disappointments; women voted in almost equal numbers as men but no true "women's vote" emerged; women were given symbolic or unimportant positions in the party hierarchies and kept from positions where decisions were made. When it became clear that politicians had little to fear from women voting as a bloc, women and women's concerns were again systematically ignored. Women activists found no issue, except perhaps the passage of child labor laws, that bound women together once suffrage was won.

A great deal did change in the decade after women began to vote but few of these changes may be attributed to women's new political role. Women continued to enter new professions and increase their numbers in the labor force. The number of college degrees granted to women jumped from 18,029 in 1920 to 55,266 ten years later.[34] Women began to experience a relaxation in the code governing their personal behavior; family supervision of unmarried women diminished; women experienced new freedoms in dress, sexual conduct, language and travel. During the 1920s thousands of new laborsaving devices appeared on the market which held out a promise (although not the reality) that the number of hours spent in housekeeping would be reduced.

Whether these changes constituted real progress, however, was doubted by many women who observed the harsh facts of social and

---

[34] U.S. Bureau of the Census, *Historical Statistics of the United States, Colonial Times to 1957* (Washington, D.C., 1960), pp. 211–212.

economic life. Women were still barred from many of the professions; they still earned less than men working at the same job; they still constituted the principal labor pool for unskilled and semiskilled jobs. When one considers that contemporary opinion held up the unmarried career woman for scorn and pity, that married women had no institutional arrangements to help them if they wanted to work, and that academic psychology continued to stress women's unique biology, social role and motivation, it is little wonder that feminists challenged the assumption that progress was being made. Never had the old axiom seemed more appropriate to women's status than after the passage of the Nineteenth Amendment: the more things changed, the more things stayed the same.

Charlotte Perkins Gilman, the author of several trenchant works dealing with women, had correctly prophesied that the vote would not solve women's social and economic problems. In *Women and Economics* (1898) and *The Home Its Work and Influence* (1903) Mrs. Gilman analyzed why women were held in bondage and suggested the means by which they might gain their freedom. Women, she maintained, were subservient to men because men produced the wealth while women merely "received it at their hands." After centuries of living this way women became culturally conditioned to do only one thing: attract men. "From the odalisque with the most bracelets to the debutant with the most bouquets, the relation still holds good, woman's economic profit comes through the power of sex-attraction."[35] The way out of this degrading condition, Gilman maintained, was to free women from the prison of the home and enable them to participate in the world of work. Of course, this would require a radical transformation of the home. Gilman called for establishing professionally supervised kitchens serving large housing complexes, the creation of day-care facilities to allow women to work and the introduction of paid, skilled workers in all areas of housekeeping and maintenance. She reiterated her thesis again and again. Until women broke their "sexuo-economic" dependence they would never experience freedom and equality. The vote was not enough.

That the vote was not enough became more and more apparent as the memory of suffrage battles waned and as a new generation of women reached maturity. In the 1940s and 1950s statistics indicated a deterioration of woman's status since the 1920s; fewer women were entering the professions; fewer women were receiving graduate degrees; median annual full-time earnings for women continued to be

---

[35] Quoted in Carl Degler, "Charlotte Perkins Gilman on the Theory and Practice of Feminism," *American Quarterly* 8 (Spring 1956): 23.

substantially less than men's; women had failed to break into the inner sanctum of big corporations, unions and political parties. As if to compensate for this regressive trend, popular opinion (manipulated by the mass media) began once again to stress the delights of home-making, childrearing and husband-pleasing, reviving a cult of domesticity that reigned supreme throughout the nineteenth century. This emphasis on the home and motherhood, however, could hardly parade as something new and, as the evidence of women's frustration surfaced, the new domesticity was unmasked and renamed the "feminine mystique." By the early 1960s socially aware women were ready for a new and more meaningful feminism.

Had Susan B. Anthony or Elizabeth Cady Stanton been alive during the mid-twentieth century none of these developments would have come as a surprise. They were convinced from the outset that only a true social revolution would eliminate the prejudice and barriers faced by women. They were convinced that real change would only come about when the sexes rethought their respective roles in marriage, child rearing and work. The feminists of the 1960s and 1970s inherited Anthony's and Stanton's insistence on rigorous social analysis, on seeking fundamental solutions and on viewing women's problems in the broadest possible context. That is why the perceptions of these early feminists still form the basis of a serious women's movement.

Suggestions for Further Reading

Any analysis of the role of women in contemporary society must begin with Betty Friedan's *The Feminine Mystique* (1963). Since publication of this book many attempts have been made to deal with women in America and Women's Liberation. Among these are: Leslie B. Tanner, ed., *Voices From Women's Liberation* (1971); Robin Morgan, ed., *Sisterhood is Powerful. . . .* (1970); Joanne Cooke, et al., *New Women: A Motive Anthology on Women's Liberation* (1970); Elsie Adams and Mary Briscoe, *Up Against the Wall, Mother: A Women's Liberation Reader* (1971); Deborah Babcox and Madeline Belkin, *Liberation Now* (1971); Miriam Schneir, ed., *Feminism* (1971); Caroline Bird, *Born Female* (1971); and Vivian Gornick and Barbara Moran, ed., *Woman in a Sexist Society* (1971). Three books that became best sellers were Kate Millett's *Sexual Politics* (1971); Germaine Greer's *The Female Eunuch* (1971); and Norman Mailer's *Prisoner of Sex* (1971). For facts and statistics as well as valuable analysis consult Robert Smuts, *Women and Work in America* (1959); Mabel Newcomer, *A Century of Higher Education for Women* (1959); U.S. President's Commission on the Status of Women, *American Women* (1963); and *Women Workers, U.S. Bureau of Labor, Woman's Bureau* (1969).

There are very few histories of women in America that are comprehensive and objective. The best is Eleanor Flexner, *Century of Struggle* (1959, reprinted 1971). Others include William O'Neill, *Everyone Was Brave* (1969); Andrew Sinclair, *The Emancipation of the American Woman* (1966); Page Smith, *Daughters of the Promised Land* (1970); Robert Riegel, *American Women* and *American Feminists* (1970 and 1963); and William O'Neill, ed., *The Woman Movement* (1971). An excellent article is Barbara Welter, "The Cult of True Womanhood, 1820–1860," *American Quarterly*, XVIII (1966), 151–174. A good anthology is Aileen Kraditor, ed., *Up From the Pedestal: Selected Writings in the History of American Feminism* (1968). A fine pictorial essay is Oliver Jensen, *The Revolt of American Women* (1952).

On suffrage the outstanding work, written by the suffrage cadres, is Elizabeth Cady Stanton et al. *History of Woman Suffrage,* (six volumes, 1881–1922) recently reprinted. Also consult Aileen Kraditor, *The Ideas of the Woman Suffrage Movement, 1890–1920* (1965); Inez Hayes Irwin, *The Story of the Woman's Party* (1921); Elizabeth C. Stanton, *Eighty Years and More;* and Ida Husted Harper's three-volume biography of Susan B. Anthony. William H. Chafe covers the fifty years since the suffrage battles in *The American Woman: Her Changing Social, Economic, and Political Roles, 1920–1970* (1972).

Specialized studies include: Gerda Lerner, *The Grimké Sisters from South Carolina: Rebels Against Slavery* (1967); Mary E. Massey, *Bonnet Brigades: American Women and the Civil War* (1966); Eleanor R. Hays, *Lucy Stone,* William L. O'Neill, *Divorce in the Progressive Era* (1967); David Kennedy, *Birth Control in America, The Career of Margaret Sanger* (1970); Jane Addams, *Twenty Years at Hull House* (1910); and Carl Degler, "Charlotte Perkins Gilman on the Theory and Practice of Feminism," *American Quarterly*, VIII (Spring, 1956), 21–39. Two classics are Mary Wollstonecraft, *Vindication of the Rights of Woman* and Charlotte P. Gilman, *Women and Economics* both recently reprinted.

Newspapers and magazines written by or published for women are valuable sources for the historian. They are all listed in Frank Luther Mott's *A History of American Magazines* (5 vols., reprinted, 1966–1968.).

Urban Habitats

5

The Rise and Significance
of the American City

Many Americans still think of wilderness, the frontier and the farm when they think of our national origins. So much of our history is filled with references to the Far West, the Great Plains and the cowboys that the port city, the factory town, the railroad center and the slum tenement seem to have little to say about where we came from and how we were shaped as a people. Only after we have learned about Daniel Boone, Lewis and Clark and Jefferson's vision of a nation of farmers, do we learn about Philadelphia and Detroit, Chicago and New York. These seem to appear full grown with their slums and vice, their factories and their immigrant inhabitants.

The fact is, of course, that Americans from the beginning lived and worked in cities, and cities were dynamic forces in American life and

thought. City people forged our political ideals as much as the country gentry and helped make our revolution. City people financed our economic development. Cities on the frontier provided markets, communication, transportation and cultural institutions which determined whether or not a region would survive and prosper. Cities were the home of the mercantile aristocracy, American workers, black slaves, freedmen, displaced farmers and millions of immigrants.

Today urban history has come to maturity, and for the first time Americans are becoming aware of the important contribution cities have made to their history. Professional historians are writing comparative and interpretive histories of our cities. They are attempting to study the developmental phases of cities to determine what they have shared in common and in what respects they have been unique. They are interested in how cities grew and prospered, how social divisions showed themselves in housing patterns and employment, and how cities met or did not meet the needs of their expanding populations. They are focusing particular attention on urban social problems to see, for example, why racial segregation, crime and poverty became common features of city life.

THE STATE OF AMERICAN CITIES

Before tracing the rise and significance of American cities, it is useful to have an overview of the state of our cities today. There is broad consensus among scholars and students of the city that life is difficult, often dangerous and unsatisfying for the great masses who reside in our central cities. A major exponent of this point of view is the Commission of the Cities in the 1970s, which attempted to evaluate whether conditions in American cities had improved or deteriorated since the urban riots of 1967. It's conclusions are disquieting.

> Our basic finding is that, despite the widely accepted Kerner finding that one major cause of ghetto disorders of the 1960s was the shameful conditions of life in the cities, most of the changes in those conditions since 1968—at least in the cities we visited—have been for the worse.
> * Housing is still the national scandal it was then
> * Schools are more tedious and turbulent
> * The rates of crime and unemployment and disease and heroin addiction are higher
> * Welfare rolls are larger
> * And, with few exceptions, the relations between minority communities and the police are just as hostile.[1]

Reading through the Commission report, one finds documentary and statistical evidence to suggest that American cities are, indeed, in imminent peril of collapse. The report stresses, for example, the flight of middle class white people from the central city. It details the depth of poverty and joblessness among minority groups. ("In central cities, 7.8 percent of white families are currently below the poverty line, compared with 23.6 percent of black families.") It traces the

---

[1] *The State of the Cities. Report of the Commission on the Cities in the '70's* (New York, 1972), p. 5.

spiraling costs of welfare and the inability of municipalities to shoulder the huge burdens of aiding the poor. Whether the subject is housing, education, crime or health and nutrition, the conclusions of the report read like a grand jury indictment of our national urban policy. Sol Linowitz puts it bluntly:

> One thing is clear: Our society cannot indefinitely endure the tensions created by a nation half-ghetto and half split-level. As we look about us and see the chaos in city after city after city, as we listen to the voices of frustration and anger and despair coming from the citizens who are trapped in those cities, as we read the bleak statistics of our failure to right the wrong of racism, there is danger that the United States may be on the verge of tearing itself apart.[2]

The Commission report, of course, represents only one point of view. But the Kerner report which preceded it, and the large number of books which probed urban problems after 1967, affirm what the Commission has to say. One doesn't need to sift through scholarly materials, however, to arrive at similar conclusions. The daily newspapers, the mass circulation magazines, and public opinion polls on the quality of urban life all accept the premise that contemporary cities are not satisfactory living environments. A Gallup Poll issued on December 17, 1972, for example, showed "that only 13 percent of a cross section of Americans said that the city was an ideal place to live. Even among those who now live in cities, only 20 percent said they preferred city life. That is a striking change since 1966, when a similar survey found that 36 per cent of city residents preferred city life."[3]

There are a few critics, nevertheless, who reject the idea that our cities are in grave danger and who try to prove that things are not as bad as they seem. Edward Banfield, the author, of *The Unheavenly City*, develops this line of argument by trying to show that historically our cities have been much worse off then they are today and that urban problems are considered so critical because people ask more of the cities and their governments than they ever did before. His conclusions—that all cities follow historical patterns of growth and decay; that "the overwhelming majority of city dwellers live more comfortably and conveniently than ever before," and that most of our urban problems can be solved by applying the correct technical solutions—

---

[2] *Ibid.*, p. xi.
[3] *The New York Times,* December 17, 1972.

may not be widely accepted, but they serve to stimulate debate and act as a corrective to the alarmist school of urban thought.[4]

No two urbanologists will agree when discussing the roots of our present urban crisis. One will emphasize the lack of decent housing and the failure of cities to eradicate slums; another will focus on the lack of federal assistance or the absence of regional planning; another will call attention to the burdens imposed by staggering welfare costs. In the final analysis, however, urbanologists know that it is the mix and interrelatedness of factors that causes urban problems.

There are nevertheless two factors that stand out in any discussion of the state of our cities; two factors that frame and influence all others. One is the problem of racism and its blighting effect on city life. The other is the problem of suburban growth which threatens the economic life of the central cities.

RACISM

The Kerner Commission, called to investigate the urban riots of 1967, concluded that racism was a cancer eating at our society and destroying our cities. Among the causes of urban violence it cited pervasive discrimination and segregation in employment; segregation in education and housing; the frustrations of black people who felt powerless to "move the system," and alienation and hostility toward the institutions of law and government controlled by white people.[5]

As we have already seen the Commission on the Cities in the 1970s not only supported the Kerner findings but indicated that racism continues to impose a heavy penalty on city life. Black people are denied decent jobs and housing. Resentment and frustration find vent in crime, drug addiction, and militant political action. Cities divide physically and mentally. An atmosphere of prejudice and mutual distrust dominates the associations and activities of both whites and blacks.

Nowhere is this more apparent than in education and housing, two perennial city problems. Violent confrontations have occurred over busing and the racial "tipping" of schools. Disputes have broken out over community control of schools, curriculum stressing minority viewpoints and over the racial composition of school administrations

---

[4] Edward Banfield, *The Unheavenly City: The Nature and the Future of Our Urban Crisis* (New York, 1968).

[5] *Report of the National Advisory Commission on Civil Disorders* (The Kerner Report, 1968), pp. 1–34.

and staff. Legal and political fights have also flared over construction of low-income housing complexes in white middle class neighborhoods such as at Forest Hills in New York City and in Newark, New Jersey. At the root of these conflicts is the assumption by black people that white society is systematically closing off opportunities for social advancement, while white people fear changes in their communities that might hurt them economically or socially.

There is no adequate way to trace the full impact of racism on urban life but there is little doubt that questions of race influence a great many private and public decisions. It is more than coincidence that minority people swell the ranks of welfare recipients, that black people find it harder than whites of similar abilities to secure decent work, and that the black ghettos are distinguished by the highest crime rates, drug addiction and health and nutritional problems. White reactions to the deterioration of neighborhoods, to school failures and to high crime are also influenced by racial considerations. As central cities lose more and more white people to the suburbs, race tensions heighten for those who remain behind. As cities lose their racial mix, the spectacle of a nation practicing (or condoning) urban apartheid emerges.

THE SUBURBAN EXPLOSION

Large-scale migration from the central cities to the suburbs began shortly after World War II as a result of highway expansion, renewed activity in the building industry and the availability of mortgage money loaned or guaranteed by the Federal Housing Administration and the Veteran's Administration. By the 1950s the nation's economic expansion gave more and more people the opportunity to leave the central cities, and suburb after suburb experienced explosive growth.

The suburbs had many advantages to offer over older congested cities. They had cheap land which was attractive to industries that required horizontal space for factory operations. They had land upon which to build highways and parking plazas. Available space allowed for low density housing. The suburbs, moreover, were new and seemed to provide a safe refuge from the problems cities were experiencing.

Initially, the suburbs did not threaten the life of the central cities because suburbanites commuted to the cities and continued to use their institutions and services. As the number of suburbanites grew, however, a shift in economic forces took place. Restaurants, department stores and a multitude of retail stores emerged in the suburbs.

Banks and small industries followed. It was not long before the suburb; began to rival the cities which had spawned them.

By 1972 more Americans lived in suburbs (37.2 percent) than lived
in cities (34.1 percent) or rural areas (31.4 percent).[6] By this date suburbs outstripped cities economically by providing more jobs than cities, attracting more commuters and by gaining a larger share of every
dollar spent on services and merchandise.

Today it is clear that suburbs contribute to central city problems in
several ways. They attract more and more corporations and industries,
a migration which depletes the tax revenues of the cities. They halt
out-migration from the cities for low income families, especially
minority families, who cannot afford the high suburban rents or the
cost of home ownership. They do not permit city workers to live in
their environs, thus gaining the benefits of labor without the responsibilities of providing homes, schools and other community services.
The cities are left to provide for the old and sick, the indigent and the
working poor, while the suburbs gain from the migration of the middle and upper class.

Not every facet of suburban growth, however, has been without
its problems. Some of the older in-lying suburbs have begun to decay
and these small communities do not have the resources for construction and renewal. Others are experiencing social problems once associated with the central cities: crime, drug addiction, juvenile delinquency, new welfare responsibilities. Those suburbs that have grown
up along highways and that have no core business districts are finding
that there is little community spirit and a restlessness and uprooted-
ness among the young. Moreover, it is difficult for suburbs which have
limited wealth to build cultural institutions that still distinguish the
cities. No suburb has yet built a theater, library or museum that meets
the standards of those in major American cities.

THE URBAN FUTURE

It becomes increasingly apparent as one studies our urban crisis that
for all the studies, surveys and federal, state and municipal programs,
urban problems persist and intensify. It may be that the nation has not
yet made a major commitment to revitalize the cities. It may be that
many programs work at cross purposes and cancel out each others'
benefits. Until we recognize the social character of our urban problems, however, little progress is likely to be made. Urban problems are

---

[6] U.S. Dept. of Commerce, *Pocket Data Book U.S.A. 1971.*

social problems which are intensified by the crowding, competition and heterogeneity of the big city. Racism, for example, will never be eliminated by building better mass transit facilities, better playgrounds or more day-care centers.

This leaves us with a depressing prognosis for our major American cities. Present trends suggest that the cities will continue to decline in importance relative to suburban and rural areas. They will continue to lose their white, affluent populations and have to shoulder more social responsibilities with fewer resources. The only hope for the cities, in fact, is either a radical reordering of priorities on the federal level, which would channel massive aid to the cities, or new regional formulas which would allow cities to incorporate their suburban areas, or gain significantly more power in state legislatures. None of these solutions appear to have much support at present, which leads to the conclusion that our urban crisis will continue into the foreseeable future.

CITIES IN THE WILDERNESS

Before the arrival of European settlers, North America had no urban centers. The Aztec, Maya and Inca built beautiful and complex cities in Central and South America, but North American Indians eschewed urban life. Part of the reason for this was the lack of centralized, bureaucratic government among the North American Indian tribes. Another was the nomadic character of their culture. North American Indians developed attachments to natural phenomena they considered sacred but never to man-made environments.

Europeans brought the idea of the city to North America because since the thirteenth century A.D., as well as in ancient times, cities were the centers of religious and commercial life. When Europeans thought of historic cities they thought of Jerusalem, Alexandria, Athens and Rome. During the Age of Exploration (1450–1650) Versailles, London, Seville, Brussels, Venice, Vienna and Berlin—to name just a few important cities—were seats of government and administrative centers. There the royal palaces, the markets, the great cathedrals, and the homes of the nobility and the wealthy bourgeoisie proclaimed the importance of urban institutions. The majority of Europeans still lived in villages and worked on farms, but cities dominated the cultural, political and economic life of European society.

It was natural then for Spanish, Dutch, French and English immigrants to think in terms of establishing villages and towns in the North American wilderness. A new and hostile environment demanded that the first settlers band together for survival and protection. In addition, many of the early settlers came with the intention of creating religious or commercial "plantations" in the New World. Some of the early charters and instructions given to the English colonists specified that urban communities should be established. In 1681, for example, William Penn instructed his commissioners to sound "on my side of Delaware River, especially Upland, in order to settle a great town."[7] The first governor of the Massachusetts Bay Company, John Winthrop, also searched for a desirable site to begin his religious community, and decided on the well-watered and easy-to-protect harbor which the Puritans named Boston.

During the first century of English settlement in North America a network of towns and villages were established along the Atlantic seaboard which attracted roughly 10 percent of the newly arrived immigrants. These towns were physically small and rigidly governed; they rarely held more than 5,000 people but with constant immigration these towns grew to ten, twenty, and thirty thousand residents by the time of the American Revolution. By today's standards the size of these towns may seem insignificant, but for the eighteenth century they constituted important urban centers. Philadelphia, for example, had 42,444 inhabitants in 1790 and New York had 33,131. No more than 45 cities in the world at this time had populations exceeding 100,000 and only half of these were in Europe.[8]

To grasp the importance of these early urban communities we must realize that they served as the points of arrival, of supply and of orientation for Europeans seeking a start in the New World. It is true that many of these immigrants quickly left the cities to start farming and avoided living in cities, but they relied on these urban centers for communication with their home countries, for articles of manufacture, for political activity, and most of all for marketing their crops. The towns that initially established themselves as trade and shipping centers quickly became more than way stations to the frontier. Boston, New York, Phladelphia, Baltimore and Norfolk were all important shipping centers during the colonial period and all emerged as full-fledged cities during the decades preceding American independence.

The cities of colonial America shared certain common characteristics. They all faced outward toward the Atlantic trade routes and shipbuilding and commerce dominated their economies. They all began as planned communities with attempts made to regulate the size and angle of streets, the disposition of houses, markets and open spaces.

---

[7] Charles Glaab, *The American City. A Documentary History* (Homewood, III., 1963), p. 35.
   [8] *Ibid.*, p. 1.

Their harbor areas were the most densely populated with land values highest at the water's edge. The colonial cities also developed along similar lines socially and politically. Merchants and shipbuilders early established themselves as the leading citizens. This mercantile elite made the decisions by which the majority of town dwellers lived.

COLONIAL PHILADELPHIA

Philadelphia, which has been studied by the historian Sam Bass Warner Jr.,[9] offers perhaps the best example of what a major colonial city was really like. A planned city, Philadelphia was designed on a "gridiron" plan with parallel streets and right-angled streets. Its founder, William Penn, asked his commissioners to:

> Let every house be placed, if the person pleases, in the middle of its plat, as to the breadth of it, that so there may be ground on each side for gardens or orchards or fields, that it may be a green country town, which will never be burnt, and always wholesome. . . .[10]

Although Penn envisioned a "green country town" Philadelphia's rapidly growing population needed homes and shops, and the trees and green open spaces early gave way to factories and warehouses. Typically, the demands of business triumphed over aesthetic and environmental considerations.

Philadelphia was a city of commerce where "the wealthy presided over a municipal regime of little government."[11] The dominant value in this business-oriented society was for each man to make it on his own—a value which Warner terms "privatism." Privatism meant,

> that the individual should seek happiness in personal independence and in the search for wealth; socially, privatism meant that the individual should see his first loyalty as his immediate family, and that a community should be a union of such money-making, accumulating families; politically, privatism meant the community should keep the peace among individual money-makers, and, if possible, help to create an open and thriving set-

---

[9] Sam Bass Warner, Jr., *The Private City: Philadelphia in Three Periods of Its Growth* (Philadelphia, 1968).

[10] Glaab, *The American City*, p. 36.

[11] Sam Bass Warner, Jr., quoted in Paul Kramer and Frederick Holborn, eds., *The City in American Life From Colonial Times to the Present* (New York, 1971), p. 44.

ting where each citizen would have some substantial opportunity to prosper.[12]

With privatism as the dominant value it is easy to see why Philadelphians favored weak government and little community action. Profit seeking and speculation determined where homes and factories would be built. Planning quickly gave way to random building, with crowding and inadequate water and sewer facilities the immediate result. Until well into the nineteenth century Philadelphians were content to let their community develop helter-skelter. The assumption was that "if each man would look to his own prosperity the entire town would prosper."[13]

Philadelphia did prosper as it attracted skilled artisans, shopkeepers, and merchants of many trades. Shops of every description could be found along its streets; owners usually lived above their stores making the family business and residence the same. Warner has shown that while marine trades and merchants clustered around the seafront, the characteristic Philadelphia street housed families engaged in many different occupations and professions. Weavers, tailors, tin and silversmiths, printers, bakers, grocers, and carpenters lived side by side. "The rummage of classes and occupations found in many Philadelphia blocks continued the old tradition of mixed work and residence characteristic of American and English country towns."[14]

The lack of planning and community organization in colonial Philadelphia early showed certain negative effects. Block densities were high, and to accommodate a growing population enterprising builders cut alleys and built houses in their back yards. Streets went unpaved, garbage disposal was slight and polluted wells and human waste collected in the streets creating hazardous conditions of health. Philadelphians attempted to correct the worst of these conditions by creating commissions of local residents to undertake repairs, fight fires, or police the streets, but none of these commissions were very effective during the early years. They did provide training in local leadership, however, which proved valuable as the city's problems grew.

Another characteristic of colonial Philadelphia was the small scale of city life, the close living and interaction of all the residents. The wealthy, of course, had better homes and met to discuss their business in select coffee houses and taverns, but rich, middle class and

---

[12] *Ibid.*, p. 39.
[13] *Ibid.*
[14] *Ibid.*, p. 46.

poor lived and worked closely together and each shared in the life of the city. The life of the streets was intense; there people met and talked, transacted business, or took a stroll to the harbor to see the ships come and go. The era when trolleys, buses and cars would take over city streets still lay in the distant future.

URBAN CONCERNS AND URBAN INFLUENCE

The concerns of the merchants who guided Philadelphia's municipal life were concerns shared by the men of substance and influence in other colonial cities. The chief problem was the omnipresent threat of fire. Without machines to pump water and without men who devoted themselves exclusively to this task, firefighting was difficult and inefficient. Initially, firefighting was carried out by groups of individuals who banded together to fight fires in their locality whenever a signal was given; soon these volunteer companies were organized to protect the harbors and business districts. Firefighting, however, was severely restricted by the voluntary nature of the enterprise. Residential areas lying outside the port and business areas went unprotected until well into the nineteenth century when fire protection became a regular municipal service.

Much the same restrictions applied to the prevention of crime. The night watch, a group of volunteers who patrolled at night, provided some protection against robbery and pilfering when cities were still physically small. These patrols were severely hampered by darkness, however, and were very ineffective. Gradually, merchants found it desirable to pay the night patrols and regulate their activities. Perhaps because cities were small and people knew one another no attempt was made during colonial times to police the city by day.

A third municipal concern was supervision of the poor. The colonial city dealt very inadequately with the poor. Some provided relief out of local taxes or church donations. Almost all required the poor to work at some assigned task to qualify for relief. Some cities tried to discourage immigration by those who could not prove their ability to work and care for themselves. Very early the problems of the poor outstripped the ability of the cities to help them. City fathers, moreover, guided by the ethic of privatism, did not believe it was their responsibility to help those who could not help themselves.

With minor variations the cities of colonial North America shared the same social structure, physical characteristics and mode of life. Their similarities and the power they wielded permits us to speak of a distinct urban influence even though the vast majority of eighteenth-century Americans still lived on farms or in tiny hamlets. This influence made itself felt in many ways. Cities were centers of commodity and financial exchange and decisions made in them affected the livelihood of Americans in rural areas. Cities controlled the flow of goods and people between Europe and America and between East and West and housed the artisans who made the special tools and materials needed throughout the colonies. Urban newspapers influenced public opinion and urban patterns of dress, behavior and morality had a direct effect upon colonial lifestyles.

The urban influence also made itself felt through city institutions that shaped colonial culture. Cities could afford to build well-staffed schools and universities. Of the nine colleges in existence in 1776, five were established in urban centers. Only cities had the population to support newspapers, the first theaters, and clubs and societies devoted to education and civic improvement. Philadelphia had fifty such clubs when the American Revolution broke out. When one considers the meager cultural and social life of the rural communities of America at this time the urban influence stands out clearly.

As a consequence of this associational activity the merchants and better-off artisans of the cities were in a position to exert political influence in far greater proportion to their actual numbers. These city elites wanted to extend their economic influence, they wanted to make their cities the chief marketing centers—in summary, they wanted to rid themselves of their second class colonial status vis-à-vis England and establish their own commercial hegemony. City merchants became politically active after 1763 when England attempted to bring the colonies under stricter control. It was this group who determined to resist English control and work out a new political relationship.

In the decade preceding the American Revolution it was the people of the cities who first organized to resist English control and who formed the Committees of Correspondence and the Sons of Liberty which orchestrated the colonial reaction to English mercantile policy. City newspapers and broadsides circulated in the countryside. News of meetings in Boston, New York, Philadelphia and Williamsburg was carried to villages and farms. Boston's citizens were the first to be shot by British troops, and Boston's merchants carried out the now-famous tea party. It was the Boston silversmith Paul Revere who took the news inland that the British were on the march.

INDEPENDENCE

The American Revolution had a profound effect on all levels of American society. Independence brought with it the problems and responsibilities associated with establishing and winning respect for a new government. But independence also released the latent energies and aspirations of the American people. Mercantilist restrictions that once forced Americans into a dependent agricultural status no longer applied. The revival of the American economy, stimulated by war with Britain (1812–1815), encouraged people to invest in American trade and manufacture and to strike out in new directions. After 1803, when Louisiana was purchased from France, the magnificent trans-Appalachian West was thrown open to exploration and settlement. Urban growth in all sections of the new nation was stimulated by these developments.

A direct product of independence was the planning and construction of an entirely new city designed as a home for the federal government. After considerable wrangling over where this capitol should be built, a site on the Potomac River was chosen and an architect, Major Pierre L'Enfant, was engaged. President Washington and Thomas Jefferson also assisted in designing Washington, D.C. and a black mathematician, Benjamin Banneker, served as a surveyor and engineer. The resulting plan was unlike that of any other contemporary American city and remains unique even today.

Washington, D.C. was meant to be an administrative capitol, and therefore L'Enfant's plan made no provision for areas designed to serve industry and commerce. Following the intent and spirit of the newly written constitution, he gave Washington three main sections; one area for the Congress, one for the executive and a third area for the Supreme Court. Rather than set off Washington's streets in parallels and right angles, so appropriate to a city guided by the demands of commerce, L'Enfant created streets which radiated out from the principal government buildings and squares. He also drew the major roads so that they would provide easy access to the countryside and vice versa. The republican spirit suggested frequent contact between the governors and the governed, and L'Enfant designed Washington to be an open, accessible city.[15]

Washington was not only remarkable in its day for its design— which was closer to the designs of European capitols which incorporated boulevards, plazas and radial street designs—but for the lavish attention given to its principal buildings. A distinguished architect, Benjamin Latrobe, was chosen by Jefferson to supervise public buildings. Latrobe, in turn, engaged a prominent Italian sculptor, to work on the Capitol. The city, which grew slowly during its early years,

---

[15] James Sterling Young, "The Washington Community, 1800–1828." Quoted in Kramer and Holborn, pp. 57–73.

gradually emerged as one of imposing buildings, broad boulevards and green open spaces. One visitor to the Federal City in 1826 observed:

> The capitol, however, which may aptly be called the eighth wonder of the world, eclipses the whole. This stupendous fabric, when seen at a distance, is remarkable for its magnitude, its vast dome rising out of the centre, and its exquisite whiteness. The President's house, like the capitol, rivals the snow in whiteness. . . . the spacious squares and streets, the avenues, adorned with rows of flourishing trees, and all this visible at once; it is not in the power of imagination to conceive a scene so replete with every species of beauty. . . .[16]

Even if one discounts exaggeration, Washington was a unique and beautiful city by contemporary standards. How different, however, were some of the older cities on the Atlantic seaboard, which were being transformed by commerce and manufacturing following the American Revolution. Here merchants, not architects, were triumphant. Here the monotonous gridiron plan spread outward from the original centers, and the green spaces disappeared to make way for factories, warehouses and housing. Even as more and more Americans moved out to populate the virgin frontier, new immigrants swelled the cities and provided the manpower for their expanding economies.

Among the older cities, New York won and maintained preeminent status during the years following American independence. By 1810 it had grown larger than Philadelphia and by 1830 already numbered 202,589 inhabitants. Its spectacular increase in size must be attributed not only to its excellent harbor, but to the ambitions of its merchants who pioneered in many commercial ventures. New York City merchants were the first to establish regular shipping service to Europe and the first to develop an auction system of selling imports which made New York goods cheaper than those found in other ports. New York bankers extended credit to Southern cotton growers and her shipmasters won a large measure of the South's coastal and Atlantic trade. Ethnically the city was always the most heterogeneous of all the original cities and this may explain the openness, diversity and dynamism of its business life.

The benefits derived from the construction of the Erie Canal, completed in 1825, provide an explanation for how New York was able to

---

[16] Glaab, *The American City*, p. 104.

capture two-thirds of the nation's imports and one-third of its exports by 1860. This bold plan, undertaken despite strong criticism, enabled New York to establish a trade route via the Hudson, the Canal and the Great Lakes all the way to the American Middle West. The canal dramatically cut the cost of trade; it permitted the movement of bulky raw and finished materials, and it opened up a vast interior hinterland for development by New York's capitalists. When De Witt Clinton in 1825 asserted that New York would become "the granary of the world, the emporium of commerce, the seat of manufactures, the focus of great moneyed operations, and the concentrating point of vast, disposable and accumulating capital" he was absolutely correct. In his own time, New York was already on the threshold of proving his predictions.

Merchant capitalists in the Atlantic cities watched enviously as New York captured more trade with every passing year. Some, like the merchants of Boston, felt secure enough to go about developing factories and commercial ties with their surrounding countryside without worrying about New York's commanding commercial position. Philadelphia's merchants, however, were worried about their commercial future and determined to establish better ties with their interior areas. A fourteen million dollar canal from Philadelphia to Pittsburgh, employing cable cars to carry goods over mountains, never really solved this problem. Baltimore businessmen took a leap of faith by investing in a railroad which proved to be successful in the 1830s. The Baltimore-Ohio Railroad eventually linked Baltimore with Pittsburgh, Columbus, Ohio and Cleveland, and allowed Baltimore merchants to tap the resources of the Great Lakes area and win some of the trade that New York and Philadelphia could not handle.

While a favorable geographic position was enough to secure a measure of wealth and economic importance for colonial cities, it was no longer sufficient during the years following American independence. Increasingly, the boldness and determination of municipal leaders, the willingness to take risks and commit large sums of money to transportation schemes shaped the economic future of urban communities. City merchants vied for economic control of their hinterlands and inter-city competition was fierce. This rivalry originated in the fight for profits, but, as we shall see, it stimulated civic pride and encouraged cities to compete to improve the living conditions and even the beauty of their respective cities.

THE FACTORY TOWN

During the two decades following the War of 1812 a new kind of urban community began to evolve in the Northeastern states. First in

Massachusetts, and soon after in Connecticut and Rhode Island the factory town made its appearance.

The factory town was largely the creation of Boston capitalists who wanted to invest some of the money they made from shipping profitable commodities to Europe. During the 1820s and 1830s the huge demand for factory-made textiles motivated groups of Boston merchants to build factories along the swift flowing rivers of Massachusetts and Connecticut. As railroads came into common use, these merchant syndicates ventured farther afield until factory towns, built with Boston capital, could be found throughout the length and breadth of New England. While many of these towns began by specializing in textile production, some factories also specialized in the manufacture of furniture, paper products, tools and shoes. The fortunes of these communities were tied to the success and failure of their respective industries. Some grew rapidly only to decay when demand for their products waned or when owners decided to close down unprofitable operations.

The distinctive physical feature of these mill towns was the presence of one or more large factories, frequently built along the bank of a river and serviced by a railroad. Beauty was never considered in building these towns, and usually the local church was the only building with any architectural merit. The homes of the workers consisted of low rows of identical frame dwellings built in clusters near the factories. Parks were nonexistent and life was dreary.

> Mill whistles sounded at six in the morning and six at night, and walking through heavy snow or mud in spring meant that people must live within a mile or two of their work. People crowded into tenements, sometimes ten to twelve families in a house built for two or three. The charming spot just above the dam with a beautiful view of the river and hills became a slum. The newcomers were usually ignorant of the most elementary rules of health and sanitation, and, had they been educated, poverty and lack of facilities would still have made their quarters uncomfortable at best, foul at worst.[17]

This describes the town of Holyoke, Massachusetts during the 1850s but could apply to any of the large mill towns of this era.

These factory towns developed quite differently from the large cities we have already studied. Usually they were run by absentee

---

[17] Constance M. Green, *American Cities in the Growth of the Nation* (New York, 1957), p. 87.

owners who took no interest in the community aside from insuring that profits continued to flow their way. Municipal life was severely impoverished by the lack of individuals with a stake in the town's future. In addition, the industrial character of these communities meant the absence of a middle class who had the education and experience to work for civic improvement. As native Americans sought their fortunes in the movement West, factory towns became filled with immigrants with little knowledge or inclination to participate in civic life.

The factory towns of New England offer an interesting example of towns and cities that failed to achieve important urban status. Despite the success and stability of a few, most suffered from being artificial creations, from being too closely linked to one mode of manufacture, from lacking favorable geographic position, and from being run and manipulated by absentee interests. For most of the nineteenth century these small cities contributed to the phenomenal economic growth of New England only to suffer decline and decay as consumer demands changed and as new technologies and competition emerged at home and abroad.

SOUTHERN CITIES: 1800–1860

In 1800 the South had several important cities along the Atlantic coast. Baltimore, Norfolk and Charleston were already important ports. Richmond, Virginia became an important manufacturing center after the War of 1812 and Savannah, Georgia developed during the same period with the expansion of cotton trade. By contrast with the frenzied commercial activity already characteristic of northern cities, however, southern cities remained centers of genteel, cultivated life. Charleston, a community of 8,820 free whites and 10,000 black slaves in 1800,

> was a society rooted in a leisure unknown in Northern cities. . . . Charlestonians made gracious living their first business. The concerts of Mozart and Haydn given by the St. Cecilia society, the balls, the theatre, the race course, and in 1800 the only golf links in America provided endless diversion. In fine weather a promenade along the sea-wall, the 'Battery,' to exchange news with neighbors and visitors was a daily routine. Here were to be seen the latest European fashions in clothes, magnificent carriages, and fine blooded horses.[18]

---

[18] *Ibid.*, p. 25.

Between 1800 and 1860, however, the Atlantic port cities of the South did not grow as rapidly as northern and western cities. Savannah had only 11,000 residents in 1840; Richmond only 38,000 by 1860. Charleston, which numbered 40,000 in 1860 had dropped from being fifth among American cities to being twenty-second by this date.[19] In 1860 only New Orleans with 168,000 residents and Baltimore with 212,000 could claim the same kind of municipal status as New York, Philadelphia and Boston. In 1860, for example, New York already had one million inhabitants (including the independent city of Brooklyn) and Philadelphia numbered half a million residents.

The Southwest was the only region where cities showed vigorous growth. This region achieved importance as cotton cultivation spread westward and as western traders made the Mississippi into a major artery of trade. Here several cities grew up to provide port facilities, markets, and supplies and repair shops for rivermen. Memphis on the Mississippi grew with the river trade during the 1820s. Mobile, Alabama became an important Gulf port and grew from 9,000 in 1819 to 22,000 in 1850. The appearance of the steamboat on the Mississippi during the mid-1820s created a boom situation in many urban communities. New Orleans, for example, registered the most spectacular growth, from 17,000 in 1810 to 169,000 in 1860.

As a region, however, the South lagged behind the rest of the country in the pace and relative significance of urbanization. Southern cities were slow to develop the industries, commodity exchanges and financial institutions that characterized the major northern cities. Southern planters looked toward Europe for their principal market and did not promote their cities as railroad centers which could tap the wealth of the interior regions. The planter class, moreover, took great pride in the self-sufficiency of their plantations. Cities provided political and legal institutions and served as centers of relaxation and amusement but Southerners rarely regarded them as essential for the economic and social well-being of their society.

Another reason for the slow growth of cities in the South was the obsessive southern interest in tobacco and cotton cultivation. This specialization created the plantation system and the dependence on slave labor. It also created the demand for more and fresher land. Millions of southern dollars were poured into slaves and land instead of industry, transportation and city building. One side effect of the slave system was the elimination of a diversified urban middle class. Artisans and laborers emigrating from Europe avoided Southern cities where they would have to compete with slave labor.

---

[19] Charles Glaab and A. Theodore Brown, *A History of Urban America* (New York, 1967), p. 34.

The existence and wide acceptance of the slave system also marked "an ill-defined limit to the South's enthusiasm for urbanization."[20] As Richard Wade has shown, city life gave slaves substantial freedom; freedom to hire their own time, to meet and learn from free blacks, to shirk work or plan escape; freedom to develop illicit and illegal associations with white people. The circumstances of city life made it difficult if not impossible for whites to control and discipline blacks. Consequently, many slave masters saw danger in the city, perceiving it as a place where the bonds of slavery were loosened and where their wealth and status were threatened.[21]

The agrarian, slave-holding character of the South, then, inhibited the growth of large and influential urban centers. Without these the South became more and more dependent upon Northern commercial and industrial interests, a factor which contributed to the increasing hostility between North and South in the 1840s and 1850s. Hinton Helper, a Southern critic of the agrarian way of life, pleaded belatedly for the South to develop its cities in his book *The Impending Crisis of the South* (1857).

> Nothing is more evident than the fact, that our people have never entertained a proper opinion of the importance of home cities. Blindly, and greatly to our own injury, we have contributed hundreds of millions of dollars towards the erection of mammoth cities at the North, while our own magnificent bays and harbors have been most shamefully disregarded and neglected.[22]

Helper maintained that had the South abandoned slavery and built up her cities,

> how much richer, better, greater, would the South have been today! How much larger and intelligent would have been our population. . . . How much greater would be the number and length of our railroads, canals, turnpikes, and telegraphs. How much greater would be the extent and diversity of our manufacturers.[23]

Prophetically, Helper asked, "What then, must be the condition of those countries which do not possess the means or faculties of cen-

---

[20] *Ibid.,* p. 36.

[21] Richard C. Wade, *Slavery in the Cities: The South, 1820–1860* (New York, 1964).

[22] Quoted in Glaab, *The American City*, pp. 168–169.

[23] *Ibid.*

tralizing their material forces, their energies, and their talents? Are they not destined to occupy an inferior rank among the nations of the earth?"[24]

CITIES ON THE FRONTIER

In contrast to southern cities, especially those along the Atlantic seaboard, new towns on the western frontier grew vigorously during the first half of the nineteenth century. It is too often assumed that western cities were established only after farmers settled on the frontier when, in fact, the opposite was true. Cities emerged during the first stages of western expansion; they spearheaded the development of their hinterlands and shaped their economic futures. Pioneers frequently moved west to seek their fortunes in cities rather than settle on farms. Historians are finally abandoning the notion that cities played no part in nineteenth-century western expansion. City people opened up the American frontier along with trappers, miners, farmers and cowboys.

Without the appearance of steamboats on western rivers during the 1820s, the small settlements that began as military forts and fur trading centers would not have grown as rapidly as they did. The steamboats greatly increased the volume of trade; they created a demand for port facilities, warehouses, repair shops and skilled workmen; their crews and passengers required hotels and taverns for rest and relaxation as well as stocks of food and clothing. Immigrants who crossed the Alleghenies also had need of lodging and supplies of all kinds because many had converted their personal possessions to cash to make their trip less burdensome. Towns which before 1820 had served only trappers and boatmen found themselves pressed after this date to provide vital goods and services for a growing tide of western immigrants.

Towns situated at strategic points along the Ohio and Mississippi rivers benefited from the great upsurge in river traffic. Cincinnati increased its population between 1820 and 1850 from 9,000 to 115,000; Pittsburgh from 7,000 to 67,000; Louisville from 4,000 to 43,000; St. Louis from 4,000 to 74,000 and New Orleans from 27,000 to 120,000.[25] In the Ohio River Valley only Lexington, Kentucky, the home of Transylvania University, grew into an important urban community without benefit of the river trade.

Explosive population growth was fed by rich opportunities to be

---

[24] *Ibid.*
[25] Paul Kramer, "The River Cities 1800–1850," in Kramer and Holborn, p. 97.

found on the urban frontier. Real estate offered one way to get rich provided one had a little money and a head for fast dealing. One Louisville man watched the price of land rise from $700 a lot in 1812 to $300 a *foot* five years later.[26] In Cincinnati a public landing costing $2 in the 1790s was valued at $237,500 in 1841.[27] Labor as well as land commanded high prices because of the demand for new construction. "This town . . . is a fine place for mechanics," wrote a Cincinnati laborer to his brother in 1813:

> carpenters and masons can . . . make five to ten dollars a day; bricklaying is $3.50 a thousand . . . Mechanics here can make their fortune in four or five years.[28]

One observer in Lexington, Kentucky commented on "the decency and affluence of the trades-people and mechanics. . . . many of whom drive about in their own carriages."[29]

As frontier towns matured into cities in the 1830s they became more complex and diversified communities. The easy-going familiarity of the small town gave way to the impersonality of city life. The numerous occupations of the inhabitants eventually created social cleavages and a growing consciousness of class and status. Growth and maturity, on the other hand, meant the arrival of music and theater, libraries, museums, discussion groups and associations to advance the arts and sciences—all supported by a new class of merchants and professionals interested in promoting civic culture. Growth and maturity also meant increasing variety and opportunity to choose a particular church, newspaper, club or tavern.

Social distinctions soon found their expression in the physical appearance of frontier cities. By 1830 each city had its rich and poor sections with many gradations in between. The better residential districts were built farther and farther from the older commercial districts which tended to house the porters, bargemen, wagonmen and slaves. New economic forces also changed the city landscapes. By 1830 the semirural character of frontier towns disappeared as warehouses, factories and roads took the place of backyard gardens and forested open spaces. Ugly, shoddy buildings, houses built at random, and unpaved streets all bore testimony to an economic boom.

Only the imaginative mayor of St. Louis, William Carr Lane, grasped the importance of developing his city "according to some

---

[26] Richard Wade *The Urban Frontier* (Chicago, 1959), p. 164.
[27] Kramer, in Kramer and Holborn, p. 100.
[28] Richard Wade, *The Urban Frontier,* p. 117.
[29] *Ibid.,* p. 118.

general plan." He encouraged the town council to set aside money for "a market house, town house, public offices, and works to supply the town with water. . . ." He soon added to the list "Aquiducts (sic) or public fountains, public edifices and wharves, nay our pavements, which will last some twenty or thirty years."[30] Lane's ideas were slowly put into practice in St. Louis but not adopted by other frontier cities for many years.

Lane showed impressive foresight by stressing civic initiative at a time when cities were struggling to deal with the consequences of explosive growth. Suffering under the handicap of being denied adequate taxation and borrowing powers by state legislatures, western cities strained to clear swamps and provide adequate fresh water supplies for their communities. They moved slowly to initiate regular and efficient waste and garbage disposal. Their poorly staffed police and voluntary fire departments were inadequate for the burdensome task of protecting large populations in cities built of wood. Municipal authorities were aware of all these problems but lack of money and experience thwarted their successful solution.

During the middle decades of the nineteenth century the frontier cities of the West took on the appearance and function of older cities in the East. Their schools, newspapers, libraries and "opera houses" provided points of contact with education and culture in regions preoccupied with material development. Their merchant associations made decisions—such as subsidizing roads, canals and railroads—which affected the economic life of surrounding agricultural communities. Their wealthy citizens set standards of dress and behavior which created both envy and ridicule for those observing the urban scene. In sum, the frontier cities developed quite early into regional capitals exerting enormous influence over the economic, social and political life of their respective regions. This influence was sometimes resented by rural neighbors but often produced positive good. Cincinnati, for example, spearheaded the drive for tax-supported free schools in the state of Ohio. Transylvania University in Lexington, Kentucky, provided westerners with an alternative to traveling east for higher education and trained many of the first doctors, lawyers and clergymen to serve in the Mississippi region.

CITIES ON THE GREAT LAKES

A few decades after the cities along the Ohio and Mississippi emerged as urban centers, several towns along the Great Lakes began to ex-

---

[30] *Ibid.,* p. 279.

perience the same pattern of urban growth. The critical factor in this expansion was the completion of the Erie Canal in 1825 which made possible east-west trade on an unprecedented scale and encouraged immigrants to make their way toward the Great Lakes region.

The first community to feel the effects of the Erie Canal trade was Cleveland, Ohio, a tiny outpost begun as a trading settlement in 1796. In 1810 its population numbered only fifty-seven persons, but a visit by the first Great Lakes steamboat in 1818, a canal link with the Ohio River, and improvement of Cleveland's harbor in the 1820s launched its expansion.[31] By 1840 its population had increased to 6,000 and by 1850 it had 17,000 inhabitants. During the next decade industrial development and a railroad tie with the East enhanced its economic influence and helped sustain its growth.

Detroit, a port on Lake Erie like Cleveland, also benefited from the flow of goods on the Great Lakes and the Erie Canal. Settlers in Chicago and Milwaukee, two small towns on Lake Michigan, also found their communities changing under the impact of increased trade and immigration. These communities grew slowly in the 1830s until their strategic importance on the Great Lakes trade routes became apparent. Then boosters and speculators began to laud their virtues and real estate booms placed them on the map.

It was not until the 1840s and 1850s, however, that the Great Lakes towns evolved into full-fledged urban centers. During these years railroad building programs established trade ties with eastern ports. The exploitation of the vast natural resources of the region was begun. Industries such as Cyrus McCormick's reaper factory, built in Chicago in 1847, began to operate, servicing a growing midwestern farm population. Although the cities along the Great Lakes were to grow even more dramatically in the second half of the nineteenth century, their importance as commercial, financial and cultural centers was already manifest before the Civil War.

AMERICA BECOMES URBANIZED: 1860–1910

Although large and important cities appeared in the East before the Civil War, and city building proceded rapidly in the Mississippi Valley and the Great Lakes region before 1860, the most spectacular era of city building and urban development occurred during the second half of the nineteenth century. Between 1860 and 1910 the total number of Americans living in cities (communities over 2,500) increased

---

[31] Glaab and Brown, *History of Urban America*, p. 46.

from 6.2 million to 44.6 million. The number of cities with 100,000 or more people grew from nine in 1860 to fifty in 1910 and smaller cities in the range of 25–50,000 grew in number from fifty-eight to 369.[32] Whereas 19.8 percent of the American population lived in cities when the Civil War broke out, fifty years later 45.7 percent of the population were city dwellers.[33] This urbanizing trend marked the emergence of new political and economic forces, fostered new institutions and ideas and altered the entire social and cultural fabric of American life.

One of the regions to experience rapid urbanization during the post-Civil War years was the Midwest, where previously established cities grew into giant industrial centers and where new towns mushroomed on the open prairie. The most spectacular growth was recorded by Chicago, which grew from a city of 109,620 in 1860 to a metropolis of 2,185,283 in 1910. Chicago's growth was stimulated by her intense interest in railroads. Beginning in the early 1850s, Illinois senators and congressmen lobbied to obtain federal subsidies for building railroads; Chicago city fathers promoted railroad conventions, floated stocks and bonds and did everything in their power to bring railroads to the Lake City. By 1860 ten trunk lines connected Chicago with the East, South, and West; by 1880 Chicago stood at the center of a network of rails that stretched 15,000 miles into her surrounding region.

Chicago had more than railroads. Ideally located on the Great Lakes and connected since 1832 by a canal to the Mississippi, Chicago was a natural port and transshipping center. During the 1870s and 1880s her mills and factories began to process the agricultural produce and the minerals and resources of the Mississippi and Great Lakes region. Chicago also became a great slaughterhouse and meatpacking center and dominated the dressed-meat traffic to the East even before her merchants began utilizing the refrigerated railroad cars introduced in the late 1860s. All these activities attracted settlers, and wave after wave of immigrants fueled the city's economic development. Even a dramatic fire in 1871 which leveled two-thirds of the city did not thwart Chicago's growth. She met the challenge by rebuilding taller and more modern structures in brick and iron, and emerged at the turn of the century as the nation's second largest city.

Spectacular as Chicago's growth was, it was paralleled by many other Midwestern cities which grew up with the nation's expanding railroad network. The lake and river cities already mentioned—Cleve-

---

[32] *Ibid.*, p. 107.
[33] *Ibid.*

land, Milwaukee, Detroit, St. Louis—continued to grow rapidly. Smaller cities such as Kansas City, Missouri, Omaha, Wichita, Duluth, and Minneapolis grew three and four times their size during the 1880s. Although the South continued to lag behind the rest of the nation in its overall rate of urban growth, a few southern cities emerged as industrial and commercial centers after 1880. Birmingham, Alabama became a steel producing center with a population of 26,000 in 1890. El Paso, Texas multiplied itself thirteen times in the 1880s.

The building of the transcontinental railroad after 1865 opened up the Trans-Mississippi region and the Pacific North and Southwest for urban development. Cities such as Cheyenne, Wyoming and Reno, Nevada which began as small construction sites, managed to grow into small cities after the railroad crews moved on. Portland, Oregon, Tacoma, Washington and the urban complex Oakland-San Francisco experienced explosive growth when they became the termini for the great railroad lines connecting East and West. Several cities initially by-passed by the transcontinentals responded to the threat by building their own connecting lines or by offering large sums to the railroads to provide the necessary connection. Denver built a 106-mile line north to Cheyenne in 1870 which provided the vital link with the Union Pacific; Seattle fought a long battle with the Northern Pacific for a connecting line after that railroad chose Tacoma as its terminus; Los Angeles merchants offered the Southern Pacific a large cash subsidy and other inducements to build a line into their city, a link which was finally established in 1876.

It is evident from this description that railroads acted as the principal catalyst to urban development in the post-Civil War years. Railroads made it unnecessary for cities to be restricted to lake and river locations; they greatly accelerated the flow of men and material into hitherto inaccessible regions; they made possible a network of widely diffused urban sites and tied them to already established commercial and industrial centers. Railroad companies also generated urban growth by developing separate companies to promote and develop town sites along their right-of-ways. Glaab and Brown cite the case of the Illinois Central which chartered a company to speculate in town-site promotion. "The company's concern with town promotion contributed to considerable urbanization along the line of the Illinois Central. In 1850 there were only ten towns in the immediate vicinity of the railroad's route; ten years later there were forty-seven; in 1870, eighty-one."[34] All the other railroad companies promoted town building by purchasing virgin land, drawing up crude geometric town plans

---

[34] *Ibid.*, p. 113.

and then advertising their new cities in grossly exaggerated terms. In several instances, city lots were sold even before a single home or store was built or any tracks were laid.

Another factor that stimulated urban development after the Civil War was the accelerated pace of industrialization. Factory production meant centralization; industries required a large labor pool and transportation and warehouses that only cities could provide. Blake McKelvy argues in *The Urbanization of America: 1860–1915* that between 1865 and 1910 industry outstripped commerce as the chief source of urban growth and estimates that nine-tenths of industrial production occurred in urban factories. The link between industry and the city is clearly indicated by the rise of cities that received their initial impetus from industry and continued to be indentified by their principal manufactured product. Kansas City specialized in meat packing; Milwaukee in brewing; Rochester in photography; Pittsburgh and Birmingham in steel. In the early twentieth century Detroit became the automobile capital of America; Dayton the center of the cash register industry; Cleveland an oil refining center; and Schenectedy the home of General Electric Company. New York, while greatly diversified, was well known as the center of the garment industry.

In the alchemy that produced great cities, however, the essential ingredient was people. The United States had a large and growing population in the nineteenth century, a population fed by the great tide of migration coming from Europe. Between 1865 and 1915 about 25 million immigrants arrived in the United States, many of whom dreamed of establishing thriving farms in land-rich America. Many immigrants, however, found themselves caught in the vortex of the great eastern cities where they found jobs and remained. Many migrated west but settled in cities where they supplied industry with much-needed labor or managed to strike out on their own. "In 1890 the foreign-born population of Chicago almost equaled the *total* population of Chicago in 1880, a third of all Bostonians and a quarter of all Philadelphians were immigrants, and four out of every five residents of New York City were either foreign-born or the children of immigrants."[35] Almost every city in the United States after 1880 had its large number of immigrants; so many, in fact, that cities became identified in the native and rural mind with foreign manners, foreign ways, and alien religious ideas.

But foreign immigration, large as it was, was only one factor accounting for urban population growth after the Civil War. The other (aside from the natural increase of urban residents) was the migration

[35] John Garraty, *The American Nation, vol. II* (New York, 1966), p. 121.

of rural Americans to cities, a migration that has only recently received full recognition. The principal reason for this internal migration was depression in the farm economy brought on by the mechanization of agriculture which gained momentum after the Civil War. Farm technology made it possible to produce much more food, but it also reduced the need for farm labor and made it imperative for farmers to learn sophisticated methods of production. Many farmers found it hard to adapt to the demands of commercial farming. Many resented the commodity transactions in distant cities that fixed prices on their produce. Many felt frustrated by arbitrary railroad rates set by combinations and monopolies outside their control. Beginning as early as 1850, but becoming more pronounced after 1870, farmers felt increasingly dissatisfied as farm prices declined and as heavy spending for equipment and high railroad costs cut into their profits.

Cities, with their expanding economies and need for labor, provided natural outlets for a rural population which was economically hard pressed. The migration from farm to city began during the 1870s and swelled in the 1880s, depopulating rural townships across the nation. "Almost 40 percent of the 25,746 townships of the nation in 1880 reported a drop in population in 1890," writes Carl Degler.[36] "Almost 50 percent of Indiana's townships, for instance, showed a decline in population for the 1880s, though the state as a whole grew in numbers. Fifty-four percent of Illinois' and 58 percent of Ohio's townships lost people in a decade when the states as a whole were increasing in population."[37] The eastern states showed a similar pattern of rural depopulation with farms abandoned on an unprecedented scale. Glaab and Brown estimate that "about eleven million of the forty-two million city dwellers of 1910 had come from American farm homes after 1880; it also seems fairly certain that at least one third of the total urban population of 1910 were American natives of rural origin."[38]

With so many stimuli favoring urban growth it was inevitable that city building in itself would become big business. Here the boosters and real estate speculators held center stage, for they were the ones who stood to profit if their small town could attract industry and people or if their visionary plans for a new town could materialize. Sometimes planning for a new city was undertaken seriously as eastern capitalists poured money into a new city along a railroad route and planned for its orderly development. More characteristic of town

[36] Carl Degler, *Out of Our Past* (New York, 1959), p. 308.
[37] *Ibid.*
[38] Glaab and Brown, *History of Urban America*, p. 136.

building during these years was the promotion by unscrupulous speculators of towns which existed only on paper and had no internal logic for growth beyond their bold predictions of future greatness. "From January 1, 1887 to July 1, 1889, speculators laid out sixty new towns in southern California with estimated space enough for two million people, but at the end of the boom the sites had an aggregate population of less than 3,000."[39] The southern California land boom was only one example of real estate promotion that occurred throughout the less developed regions of the Midwest and Far West during the late nineteenth century. It could be argued that the growth of new towns was inevitable and that the real estate promoter was performing an essential service for communities beginning their development. But where these new towns had no natural geographic advantage or where they were not tied to the development of a larger city, they either remained rural outposts or simply disappeared from the map.

THE URBAN ENVIRONMENT

A person who grew to maturity in one of America's major cities during the last four decades of the nineteenth century witnessed profound changes in the urban environment, changes which altered the size and structure of the city, its physical appearance and the means by which city residents traveled and interacted. New techniques of building and the appearance of new urban structures was one dimension of this transformation as builders responded to the incessant demand for new housing and as corporations financed new structures to house their expanded operations.

The technique of using cast-iron instead of wood and masonry to build large sprawling buildings was already well developed by the 1850s. What was added in the following decades was a vertical dimension as architects began to explore the possibilities of building taller and taller buildings. This was necessitated by the skyrocketing cost of city property and facilitated by advancements in cast-iron and steel construction and the invention of the elevator after 1860. Chicago, which began to rebuild after the fire of 1871, led the way in new commercial architecture with William Le Baron Jenny's ten-story Mutual Savings Bank Building (1884), which employed a steel frame. New York built its first steel edifice five years later. By the 1890s skyscrapers

---

[39] *Ibid.*, p. 120.

were becoming a familiar sight in major cities, altering the city's landscape and changing the work patterns of millions of Americans.

> The new buildings were cities unto themselves. A tenant could eat, drink, have a haircut, obtain legal advice or consult a real estate broker without leaving the building. It was not unusual for the head office of a corporation to be housed in one sky-scraper, as in the instance of the Metropolitan Life. Life insurance companies, which were then growing rapidly, were the leaders in this practice of assembling their large clerical forces into one building. The handsome New York Life building (1890) in Kansas City . . . and the equally handsome Prudential Building (1894) in Buffalo . . . were typical. With these as a beginning America was later to make its most spectacular contribution to world architecture and to the urban scene. . . .[40]

The people who worked in these impressive buildings, and those who labored in urban factories and warehouses, however, continued to live in buildings that were cramped, dreary and unfit for human habitation. In New York, for example, four- and five-story tenements with poor ventilation and inadequate water and sanitation facilities provided the bulk of housing until the 1870s. After this date, dumb-bell tenements, so-called for indented air shafts on their sides, were built, but these dwellings were as airless and dreary as the buildings they replaced. In the dumbbells, toilet facilities were limited to one per floor, light and ventilation were poor, and shoddy workmanship meant constant problems and calls for repairs. The dumbbells, which were regarded as innovative and humane dwellings, were, in fact, substandard structures meant to return a high profit. Roughly a million and a half New Yorkers lived in them at the turn of the century. Tens of thousands more continued to live in older-styled tenements, in damp basements and in buildings without heat or toilet facilities.

In the absence of stringent and enforced building regulations, there were no sanctions against builders who erected shoddy, inadequate and unsafe structures. There was, consequently, no motive for business and technology to meet the challenge of building more commodious and healthful buildings. This was not the case, however, with urban transportation. Unlike buildings, horse cars and cable cars were not permanent structures. New methods of moving people and

---

[40] Christopher Tunnard and Henry Hope Reed, *American Skyline* (Boston, 1953), p. 125.

improved vehicles quickly gained recognition and financing. For this reason there was much more innovation and experimentation in the field of urban transportation.

The urban resident living after 1870 was able to travel much farther and in much less time than his counterpart in the Civil War and pre-Civil War years. The use of cars running on rails and pulled by horses was common in the 1850s; by the 1870s and 1880s steam railroads built on elevated platforms had appeared in major cities followed in short order by cable cars attached by pulleys to stationary steam engines. The harnessing of electricity for commercial use, however, provided a major innovation in urban transportation. Richmond, Virginia had the distinction of being the first city to install a fully electrified trolley system in 1887. The electric trolley was functioning in fifty-one cities by 1890. The building of large generating plants also made possible the use of electricity in railway travel. In 1895–1897 Boston built the first American subway which ran a mile and a half underground. New York completed the first link of its ambitious subway line in 1904.

To some extent technical advances in transportation solved the problem of overcrowding in already swollen urban centers. If not for the trolleys, the elevated trains and subways, cities would have been glutted to the point of strangulation. Instead, with the advent of new transport, cities expanded outward and suburbs began to evolve. In the 1880s and 1890s suburban growth followed the course of commuter railroad expansion and middle class families moved to areas immediately adjacent to city boundaries. In the 1920s the advent of mass travel by automobile accelerated the suburban trend and greatly extended the suburb's geographic limits.

Other technical innovations complemented the advances made in the field of transportation. Probably the most important of these was the telephone, invented in 1876, and developed commercially in the late 1880s. In 1891 there were 239,000 telephones in the entire United States, in 1899 there were 1,356,000, and in 1910 they numbered seven and a half million. Almost all these telephones were installed in cities, where they revolutionized commercial and financial transactions and enabled an increasingly dispersed population to maintain personal contacts. Another technical innovation was electric power transmission used to light homes and streets, run elevators and drive machines. Other technical advances included new techniques in tunnel and bridge construction which made possible subway travel and the growth of cities restricted by contiguous rivers and lakes.

By 1900 cities had become patchworks of industrial, commercial and residential sections. They were also patchworks of immigrant groups sharing little in common except their dreary tenements and crowded streets. No longer could an individual walk and know the entire city. No longer could he feel that he belonged to one community with a common outlook and values. The new metropolis was also a habitat of concrete and steel, made ugly over the years by complete disregard for the natural landscape. It was the artificiality of city life, its impersonality and lack of shared values, its poverty and vice, that awakened the humanitarian impulse in a number of urban reformers. Slowly urbanites became aware of how much their communities had been transfigured and transformed.

THE REFORM IMPULSE

American Protestantism was slow to respond to the challenge of the city.[41] Rural in outlook, with a theology interpenetrated by the ethos of individualism and laissez faire, it was difficult for it to adjust to an urban environment bearing so little resemblance to the traditional and homogeneous "village church on the green." How were Protestants to minister to immigrants ignorant of American values and American ways? How were they to communicate with the poor and the destitute and bring them into their congregations? Was the traditional method of preaching and the emphasis on sin, salvation and self-help appropriate to urban parishioners preoccupied with poverty, disease and simple survival? Some churchmen believed old-style evangelizing was the best way to reach the urban masses. Others avoided the urban challenge entirely by moving their churches from downtown locations to more stable and affluent areas. Among the manifold responses of American Protestantism to the rise of the city, however, one was clearly reformist and urban in spirit. It took its inspiration from the Social Gospel of Washington Gladden and Walter Rauschenbusch and found expression in the institutional church.

Gladden and Rauschenbusch were clergymen who became convinced that the mission of Christianity in the modern world was to address itself to social problems and their melioration. "The chief purpose of the Christian Church in the past has been the salvation of individuals," Rauschenbusch wrote in 1912. "But the most pressing task of the present is not individualistic. Our business is to make over an antiquated and immoral economic system; to get rid of laws, customs, maxims, and philosophies inherited from an evil and despotic

---

[41] For the religious response to the city see Robert Cross, ed., *The Church and the City 1865–1910* (New York, 1966).

past; to create just and brotherly relations between groups and classes of society."[42]

It followed from these assumptions that the mission of the church was to reach out to the community and find ways and means to improve the lives of people whatever their economic and social circumstances. Ministers inspired by the Social Gospel began to study and know their communities. They began to see that poverty and crime were less signs of individual moral failure than society's failure to correct inequalities. Protestant churches in working class neighborhoods began to sponsor clubs, recreation rooms, hostels and adult education courses. The idea behind these institutional churches was to do more than minister to people's souls. They attempted to communicate to the whole man and woman and deal with problems in their immediate environment.

Institutional churches gained acceptance among Protestant clergymen and their wealthy parishioners during the 1890s. A gift of money from the Vanderbilts helped build St. Bartholomew's Church in New York which became one of the most active in community affairs. Temple Church, erected in 1890 in Philadelphia, also pioneered in Social Gospel activities.

> The institutional church pushed its activities out into the city itself. Volunteer women went out into the streets and into the tenements to seek out the deserving poor; co-operative ventures among several churches were initiated in order to provide church services to those working people who had no nearby churches.[43]

By 1900 it was evident that the Social Gospel ministry of reform and concern had revitalized urban Protestantism.

The institutional church was only one facet of a broad religious response to the rise of the city. The Salvation Army, which crossed the Atlantic from England in the 1870s, was active in succoring the city's poor well before institutional churches were founded. The Young Men's and Young Women's Christian Associations were two semireligious organizations concerned with the well-being of Christian youth in urban centers. Catholics and Jews were also active in improving the lives of their coreligionists through clerical involvement in the community and through social welfare agencies. Catholic and Jewish clergymen found it easier than their Protestant counterparts to

---

[42] Quoted in Degler, *Out of Our Past,* p. 346.
[43] *Ibid.,* p. 343.

adjust to the problems of an urban ministry; their congregations were composed of immigrants and working-class people and their churches were urban in origin.

A response to urban problems similar in spirit to the Social Gospel was the settlement house movement which took root in American cities in the 1890s. Following the example set by British settlements opened in London in the 1880s, American settlements attempted to serve the poor by enlisting men and women who would live and work in immigrant, working-class communities. Jane Addams and Ellen Gates Staar, for example, opened Hull House in a Chicago slum in 1889; Robert A. Wood founded South End House in Boston in 1892; Lillian Wald opened the Henry Street Settlement on New York's Lower East Side in 1893. These settlement houses shared three main goals: 1) to create facilities for education, recreation and social welfare 2) to interpret American society to new immigrants, and 3) to create settings in which settlement workers could learn through experience about the lives of the urban poor.

Settlement houses were imaginative and innovative in developing programs to improve life in the slums. Hull House created a day nursery for children of working mothers; it launched a series of classes in music and art and offered theatricals; it eventually opened a gymnasium for community sports and recreation. Other settlement houses prepared community surveys which documented squalid slum conditions and agitated for improved schools, sanitation and recreation facilities. The settlement houses attracted college graduates, especially women, who were anxious to improve the quality of life in urban society. They were, in this sense, the precursors of Peace Corps, Action and civil rights activists today.

The pioneering efforts of settlement workers were supported by men and woman active in other areas of urban life. Jacob Riis in *How The Other Half Lives* (1890) applied his journalistic talents to vivid portrayals of slum life, especially accounts of how children were brutalized by poverty and ignorance in the slums. Scholarly and technical studies explored big-city problems such as W. E. B. Du Bois' *The Philadelphia Negro* (1899) and Robert Hunter's *Poverty* (1904) which fostered a new awareness of urban problems. Private foundations and universities also made important contributions to understanding the city by sponsoring research into various aspects of urban life. The University of Chicago Sociology Department worked with Jane Addams and her associates in preparing reports on Chicago's immigrant communities. The Russel Sage Foundation sponsored a study of life in Pittsburgh, published in six volumes as the *Pittsburgh Survey* (1909–1914). The *Survey's* methods of field work and analysis were soon adopted by church and philanthropic groups as well as municipal research bureaus which began to make their appearance in the early twentieth century.

In some instances reform activity was translated into reform legislation. Lawrence Veiller, a tireless critic of the evils of tenement life, campaigned to get improved housing in New York City and was instrumental in the passage of New York's Tenement Law in 1901. The law "was the first carefully drafted building code in the country and it was also to be the first carefully enforced one."[44] Reformers were also instrumental in the passage of better health codes, child labor laws and the establishment of municipal welfare agencies. But reform legislation was only a small beginning in the uphill fight to improve the quality of urban life. The slum, the sweatshop, crime and mental illness were too imbedded in the fabric of urban life to be eliminated by legislation alone.

The creation of urban parks and recreation facilities was another aspect of reform that gained adherents in the late nineteenth century. The outstanding figure in this movement was Frederick Law Olmsted who, with Calvert Vaux, designed and helped build New York's Central Park in the late 1850s. Olmsted believed that city dwellers were becoming increasingly cut off from the charms and tranquility of nature. Unchecked expansion of concrete and steel, he maintained, would eliminate the last vestiges of natural beauty and leave city people with no opportunity to rest and revitalize themselves in the bosom of nature.

As a consequence of Olmsted's achievement in New York, cities across the nation launched programs of park construction. Olmsted himself was instrumental in many of these. He worked on Buffalo's Delaware Park, Brooklyn's Prospect Park, Detroit's Belle Isle Park and helped landscape the grounds of the United States Capitol. In 1884 Minneapolis drew up a master plan for its city parks. A decade later Boston and Kansas City, Missouri hired outstanding landscape architects to further develop their park systems. City officials increasingly recognized the value of consulting architects and "city planners" before undertaking important municipal projects. The most important offshoot of the urban park movement, however, was the awareness it fostered that cities required planned growth and that planning should emphasize human needs.

One dimension of this new awareness was the creation of recreation facilities for urban youth. Play was not a major reform concern. But social workers, clergymen and educators gradually recognized the need to occupy the city's youth in healthful, engaging pursuits. As

---

[44] Glaab and Brown, *History of Urban America*, p. 177.

late as 1885 no city provided public play areas for children.[45] In that year, however, a group of Boston women dumped sand in empty lots, which launched a movement to provide recreation for the young. Gradually cities responded to an obvious need. In 1889 the New York Board of Education created thirty-one playgrounds attached to public schools.[46] Within a decade playgrounds with supervisory personnel were being created in many American cities. Playgrounds grew from a new awareness of children's needs in the city; they also reflected the belief, articulated by Olmsted, that cities could become ideal environments when they provided their residents with peace and beauty, rest and play.

GOVERNING THE CITY

As the pace of urbanization accelerated after the Civil War, the problems facing city governments grew in number and complexity. There were traditional problems exacerbated by explosive population growth: protecting citizens from fire, policing the city, paving and cleaning streets, providing clean water and efficient sewage. There were problems created by poverty and ignorance such as disease, crime and juvenile delinquency. Cities attempted to provide schools, regulate housing construction, set up boards of health, build parks and provide efficient transportation. Archaic municipal charters, and conflicts between city governments and state legislatures, posed formidable obstacles to efficient city administration.

Governing American cities after 1870 was also complicated by new social and economic factors. Fewer and fewer of the urban elite—men of wealth, education and aristocratic background—interested themselves in the problems of city life. They pursued careers in finance, construction and manufacturing and left city government to men of different backgrounds and interests. This abdication of civic responsibility occurred at the same time cities were absorbing millions of immigrants, unfamiliar with the language, economy and government of their adopted nation. Cities became islands of linguistic, ethnic and religious groups who shared nothing in common and had little knowledge of the city and its ways.

The post-Civil War era in American cities witnessed the rise of big city bosses and political machines, and corruption and venality at almost every level of city administration. Neither bosses nor cor-

[45] Degler, *Out of Our Past*, p. 355.
[46] *Ibid.*

ruption were new to American cities, but the power these bosses came to wield, the extraordinary sums they stole from the public till, and the openness and arrogance with which they pursued their goals was unprecedented in American life. Many of these politicians began their careers in the slums and immigrant neighborhoods as leaders in fire brigades or members of fraternal organizations. They won control of political clubs such as New York's Tammany and gradually extended their influence by finding people jobs and distributing money and advice to neighbors in need. Immigrants naturally identified with men who helped them directly. When the time came to vote they put these men—the bosses—into office.

In most major cities the party of the workingman and the immigrant was the Democratic party; the bosses, men of immigrant background who learned how to make the city work and work for them. As aldermen they let franchises for road building, street cleaning, transportation and utilities development from which they extracted substantial "kickbacks." They appointed police officials, tax commissioners and customs officers and received money and favors in return. William Marcy Tweed, the most famous of New York's bosses, ran a "ring" which defrauded the city of tens of millions of dollars within the space of two years. George Washington Plunkett, another Tammany Hall figure, boasted in 1905 that he had made a fortune from "honest graft"—buying and selling real estate on tips he gained from his political connections at city hall.

Corruption in city administrations ultimately brought forth a reform crusade whose objective was to restore honest and efficient administration and establish procedures for accountibility and control. Readers of Lincoln Steffens' *The Shame of the Cities* (1904) were shocked to read how city after city he visited was controlled by some boss, machine or ring and how "American" this corruption actually was.

> When I set out on my travels, an honest New Yorker told me honestly that I would find that the Irish, the Catholic Irish, were at the bottom of it all everywhere. The first city I went to was St. Louis, a German city. The next was Minneapolis, a Scandinavian city, with a leadership of New Englanders. Then came Pittsburgh, Scotch Presbyterian, and that was what my New York friend was. "Ah, but they are all foreign populations," I heard. The next city was Philadelphia, the purest American community of all, and the most hopeless. And after that came Chicago and New York, both mongrel-bred, but the one a triumph of reform, and the other the best example of good government that I had seen. The

"foreign element" excuse is one of the hypocritical lies that save us from the clear sight of ourselves.[47]

Exposed by muckraking journalists such as Steffens, and supported by moralists and businessmen anxious to clean up the city, the reform movement gained momentum in the two decades before World War I. Detroit, Toledo and Cleveland elected reform mayors who stressed honest accounting, control of utilities, the eight-hour day, and the construction of playgrounds, bathhouses and parks. Other city administrations introduced home rule charters, nonpartisan elections, regular independent audits, and the initiative and referendum that allowed voters to propose or kill legislation at the polls. Two popular alternatives to the old mayor-city council form of government was the commission plan and the city manager plan which empowered commissions and single individuals with talents in management to run cities honestly and efficiently. These administrative models were adopted in scores of cities after 1914. They took city administration out of the hands of politicians and placed it in the hands of businessmen.

Reform did not end the rule of bosses nor did it eliminate corruption and patronage; it did, however, infuse cities with new standards and ideals. Municipal civil service reform gradually eliminated the worst evils of machine patronage. A growing number of organizations concerned with honest and efficient government made their appearance after 1890 and placed their research and ideas in the hands of municipal administrators. Reformers, nevertheless, found their fight to clean up cities tough going. Frequently they were social types with whom working-class people and immigrants could not identify. Often they proposed remedies that had no meaning for the worker in the slum. It has been pointed out as well, that many of the reformers were more interested in what reform could do for business than what it could do for the man in the street. When business concerns were satisfied their reform ardor waned.

URBAN SOCIETY AND CULTURE

Although cities after 1860 were increasingly identified with crime, slums and a host of other urban problems, cities were also centers of

---

[47] Lincoln Steffens, *The Shame of the Cities*. Quoted in Richard Hofstadter, ed., *Great Issues in American History, From Reconstruction to the Present Day, 1864–1969* (New York, 1969), p. 246.

artistic and cultural life. Middle class urbanites were eager to learn from their European counterparts; eager too, to found institutions that would provide cultural enrichment and entertainment. In the graphic arts and science, in literature and learning, in music and theater urbanites strove to explore and appreciate a great variety of creative expression. The urban masses also experimented with new leisure time activities and evolved new forms of popular culture.[48]

In an attempt to make cities something more than commercial and manufacturing emporiums, wealthy urbanites gave generously to a wide variety of cultural activities. Washington's Corcoran gallery, Baltimore's Peabody Institute, Boston's Museum of Fine Arts and New York's Metropolitan Museum all emerged in the post-Civil War years as institutions of cultural importance. Symphony orchestras and regular operatic performances also made their appearance during these years. The middle class became ardent theater goers and supported a wide variety of dramatic entertainment. Whether it was burlesque or vaudeville, Shakespearean tragedy or drawing room comedy they all found a place in the diversified metropolis. New York's Broadway became synonomous with American theater after 1880. Every major city either supported some local theater or built elaborate homes for traveling companies.

Cities, too, were centers of scientific, academic and literary activity. Natural science museums, geographic societies and amateur societies of every type and description were founded to promote learning and scholarship. Urban universities enlarged their physical plants, built up great libraries and vied with one another to hire serious scholars and researchers. Cities also attracted artists and writers who thrived on the diversity and dynamism of urban life. Publishing houses, art galleries and literary journals provided new channels of expression. Cities also provided audiences of growing sophistication and cosmopolitan outlook.

The masses of city people, workers and immigrants, also found cultural enrichment in city life. The immigrant press and theater, popular musicals, vaudeville and the cinema offered entertainment that anyone could enjoy. Newspapers and mass circulation magazines provided cheap news and a steady diet of excitement and sensation. Public libraries and museums were another source of popular education and diversion. Public schools played an important role by offering opportunities for education and social advancement. City schools advanced the idea of compulsory attendance; they pioneered in vo-

---

[48] Blake McKelvy, *The Urbanization of America, 1860–1915* (New Brunswick, N.J., 1963), *passim*.

cational training, education for the disabled and initiated the first kindergartens and medical inspection of children. In the 1890s city high schools and colleges began the first night classes in the nation.

Leisure and recreation were also transformed by the urban milieu. Chicago opened the first park zoo in 1868, and zoos were gradually introduced in other major cities. Boston's sandlots opened an era of playground building at the same time park construction gained momentum. Although indoor gymnasiums and swimming pools grew in popularity towards the end of the century, urbanites also took to the outdoors to cycle, walk, play tennis, and go boating. They also enjoyed organized sports, especially baseball, which became an urban and a rural passion. Sports helped city dwellers of different backgrounds and outlook to meet and rub shoulders. In an increasingly impersonal city, sports provided one of the few community activities where people could share loyalties and enthusiasms.

TWENTIETH CENTURY TRENDS

When the *Denver Post,* in 1930, wrote "New York has been a cesspool into which immigrant trash has been dumped for so long that it can scarcely be considered American any more,"[49] it was expressing an antiurban bias as old as the nation itself. Jefferson had articulated his antiurban feelings on many occasions; William Jennings Bryan, speaking for the farmer in the 1890s, expressed himself similarly. But the statement from Denver in 1930 was more an echo of the past than a meaningful response to the present. The modern metropolis with its giant buildings, large populations and impersonal institutions had been part of the American scene for at least a half century. The transition from a rural to an urban society had already been made. By 1930 fifty-six percent of the American population lived in cities. Notwithstanding the *Denver Post,* New York *was* American as were the nation's other major cities.

What we discern as trends in American urbanization in the twentieth century actually had antecedents in the last decades of the nineteenth century. One of these was the growth of large metropolitan centers. This trend continued into the twentieth century with increases in the number of large metropolitan regions and increases in their respective populations. In the federal census of 1910, for example, twenty-five metropolitan districts were identified. New calcula-

---

[49] Quoted in William Leuchtenburg, *The Perils of Prosperity* (Chicago, 1958), pp. 226–227.

tions in subsequent census showed an increase in what was termed Standard Metropolitan Areas and an accompanying increase in population. The urban population of the United States grew from 24.1 million in 1900 to 84.3 million in 1950. By 1970, 140 million Americans were living in cities. Another trend with antecedents in the nineteenth century was the growth of suburbs. After 1920 the suburbs grew at a faster rate than the central cities.

The invention of the automobile and its wide scale adoption after 1910 had a profound effect on the course of American urbanization. Automobile registration jumped from around half a million in 1910 to almost ten million in 1920. By 1930 there were thirty-two million automobiles on the roads; by 1950 there were forty-eight and a half million. The number of trucks jumped from 700 in 1906 to eleven million in 1957. To accomodate this dramatic increase in motor vehicle use the United States government began providing money for highway development after 1916. By 1957 it had assisted in building and improving 780,989 miles of highways and roads.

The automobile accelerated the trend toward suburbanization which began with the commuter railroad back in the 1880s. New highways and access routes made it possible for real estate promoters to build residential sections ten and twenty miles from the centers where most urbanites worked. Home ownership, good rental values and the semirural character of the suburbs, attracted many middle class individuals who were anxious to leave the crowded and impoverished sections of the central cities. Suburban growth was one of the most important elements of twentieth century urbanization. Some suburbs grew four and five hundred percent during the 1920s. A similar growth rate was recorded after World War II when the suburban building boom revived. By 1970 there were more Americans living in suburbs (37.2 percent) than in central cities (31.4 percent). Together suburbanites and urbanites accounted for 68.6 percent of the total population.

The automobile and truck, however, were also responsible for accelerating the decentralization of industry begun in the late nineteenth century. Industrial communities built outside major cities became common in the early twentieth century, made possible by improved rail and motor vehicle transportation. As trucks came into common use, it became feasible for small industries to establish themselves on the outskirts of cities or make the move from the central cities to the suburbs. The trend toward industrial decentralization was accompanied by the decentralization of retailing as well. In 1922 the first out-of-town shopping center was built. The advantage of building retailing outlets away from congested downtown areas was quickly recognized and exploited.

The emergence of the automobile as the principal means of personal conveyance posed major problems for already established cities. Roads had to be widened and new traffic patterns created. The lack of parking space added to the already congested conditions on city streets. A reverse problem emerged in the newer suburbs and cities such as Los Angeles that developed after the advent of the automobile. These new urban and suburban entities had no centers and were so spread out that only great ribbons of highway and intense use of automobiles could hold them together. The price for this low density and decentralization was a dramatic increase in air pollution and traffic accidents that escalated in the years after World War II.

Another twentieth century urban trend was the increase in the number of black people who came to live in cities. The black population of the United States was overwhelmingly southern and rural until the World War I era. Then, as a response to crop failures and the demand for industrial labor in the North, Negroes began to migrate to northeast and northwestern cities in large numbers. After World War I the black population increased in cities at a faster rate than the native white population. "During the whole period from 1900 to 1950 the percentage of Negroes outside the South increased from ten percent to thirty-two percent and the percentage within cities rose from seventeen to forty-eight percent."[50]

New York, which increased its Negro population from 91,709 in 1910 to 327,706 in 1930, offers perhaps the best example of how a major city absorbed this new wave of migrants and how they fared. Initially the city's black population lived in relatively small sections and blocks interspersed with residential sections of white working class families. After 1915 black people were gradually forced to concentrate in Harlem, a large area to the north and east of Central Park. Racism created the Negro ghetto and racism made it almost impossible for black people to leave the ghetto even after their economic status improved. As a consequence of being jammed together rents skyrocketed, building conditions deteriorated and all the problems associated with poverty and adjustment to urban life emerged. "The most profound change that Harlem experienced in the 1920s," writes Gilbert Osofsky, "was its emergence as a slum."[51]

Largely within the space of a single decade Harlem was transformed from a potentially ideal community to a neighborhood

---

[50] Glaab and Brown, *History of Urban America*, p. 286.
[51] Gilbert Osofsky, *Harlem: The Making of a Ghetto* (New York, 1968), p. 135.

with manifold social and economic problems called "deplorable," "unspeakable," "incredible." "The State would not allow cows to live in some of these apartments used by colored people . . . in Harlem," the chairman of a city housing reform committee said in 1927. The Harlem slum of today was created in the 1920s.[52]

Slum life in Harlem of the 1920s was not very different from slum life today. Population density was higher than in other sections of the city. Poverty was pervasive and widespread. The incidence of crime, disease, and mental illness exceeded that of any other section of the city. Gambling, prostitution, drug addiction and bootlegging fastened itself on the community. The cohesiveness of the Negro family was severely strained by conditions in the slums. "Working mothers had little time to care for their children. Youngsters 'with keys tied around their necks on a ribbon' wandered around the streets until families came home at night."[53] It is little wonder that every possible nostrum from faith healing to black separatism gained followers in the slum. With little chance for physical and social mobility, Harlem's inhabitants nurtured their frustration and hatred.

The arrival of rural immigrants was not something new in the history of American cities. But because of racism and fear black people posed more of a threat to white urbanites than was posed by any other immigrant group. It is significant that the migration of black people to Manhattan Island coincided with the first out-migration of white people to other boroughs. "The population of that borough declined 18 percent in the 1920s as its Negro population increased 106 percent."[54] This population change was part of a larger movement of white people to outlying boroughs and suburbs that continued to accelerate in the mid-twentieth century. The pattern of Negro settlement was similar in other cities. In Philadelphia and Pittsburgh, Rochester and Detroit, Cleveland and Chicago, segregation established black sections and "black belts." The movement of white people to outlying sections intensified as the black population increased.

One entirely new development in twentieth century urbanization was federal involvement in solving urban problems. This began with the Great Depression and the New Deal when the President and Congress finally accepted the challenge of restoring confidence in the American economy.

---

[52] Ibid.
[53] Ibid., p. 147.
[54] Ibid., p. 129.

Although President Hoover initiated federal assistance to housing with the Federal Home Loan Bank in 1932, it was the administration of Franklin D. Roosevelt that used federal housing policy as a means of stabilizing and stimulating the economy. The Federal Housing Administration created in 1934, the Federal National Mortgage Association, and the Veterans Administration all helped with loans and insurance to enable people to purchase homes. The United States Housing Authority created in 1937 (later the Public Housing Administration) subsidized 114,000 units of public low-rent housing before the program was eliminated during World War II. The Housing Act of 1949, however, marked the decisive entrance of the federal government into the urban housing field with a one billion dollar program of "federal urban renewal assistance to localities in clearing and redeveloping slums." This program expanded in 1954 with additional money allocated for specific community projects and for housing construction for the elderly. By 1961 the federal government was involved in urban housing programs on many levels, searching for new ways to halt urban blight and to create, in the words of the 1949 law, "a decent home and a suitable living environment for every American family."

Federally assisted housing and urban renewal, however, were not without out their severe critics. Federal subsidies raised the specter of socialism and the welfare state to those still wedded to a laissez-faire tradition. Real estate interests disliked the power and economic leverage implicit in government intervention. Urban renewal came under attack for displacing poor people, for not providing enough low rent housing on renewal sites, for unnecessary destruction of sound structures and historic buildings and for not dealing with the human problems existing in impoverished urban areas. In sum, the federal government entered a field in which a great many technical, administrative and philosophical problems had to be resolved. Critics of urban assistance wanted federal subsidies curtailed, while city mayors and their constituents demanded more help and a firmer commitment to revitalize their communities.

This commitment crystalized during Lyndon Johnson's administration. In 1965 a highly controversial bill authorizing rent supplements for poor people became law. The same year a Department of Housing and Urban Development (HUD) was created to administer the increasing number of federal urban programs. A third law, passed in 1966, committed the federal government to solve the social as well as the physical problems in the slum communities (Model Cities Programs) by aid to education, antipoverty efforts, job training programs, aid to health facilities, and the creation of other people-oriented programs. In 1968 an omnibus housing bill containing seventeen titles was passed which included a plan to help poor people purchase homes, as well as provisions for mass transit aid, flood insurance, mortgage assistance for college housing and nonprofit hospitals and special mortgage insurance for low-income persons.

The landmark housing bills passed during the Johnson Administration emerged from the realization, long overdue, that cities required ongoing aid in their fight for survival and renewal. President Johnson, more than any other American president, articulated this new awareness and also affirmed the central significance of cities in modern American society.

> Many of you will live to see the day, perhaps 50 years from now, when there will be 400 million Americans; four-fifths of them in urban areas. In the remainder of this century urban population will double, city land will double, and we will have to build homes, highways and facilities equal to all those built since this country was first settled. So in the next 40 years we must rebuild the entire urban United States. . . .
>
> It is harder and harder to live the good life in American cities today. The catalogue of ills is long: There is decay of the centers and the despoiling of the suburbs. There is not enough housing for our people or transportation for our traffic. Open land is vanishing and old landmarks are violated. Worst of all, expansion is eroding the precious and time-honored values of community with neighbors and communion with nature. The loss of these values breeds loneliness and boredom and indifference. Our society will never be great until our cities are great. Today the frontier of imagination and innovation is inside those cities, and not beyond their borders. New experiments are already going on. It will be the task of your generation to make the American city a place where future generations will come, not only to live but to live the good life.[55]

It is a sad commentary that President Johnson's urban programs have not won sustained support and enthusiasm. During President Nixon's second administration many federally assisted urban programs began to be dismantled, replaced (in theory) by state directed programs funded through revenue sharing. Big city mayors in the mid-1970s found themselves pleading for at least the same level of government aid they had in the past, even though city problems multiplied

---

[55] Quoted in Congressional Quarterly Service, *Congress and the Nation, vol. II, 1965–1968* (Washington, D.C., 1969), p. 188.

and inflation advanced. Former President Nixon's assertions that "throwing money after problems won't make them go away" appears to be an oversimplification that finds support among people who are frustrated by the complexity and persistence of the urban crisis. Given President Ford's conservative economic views and congressional attempts to curb inflation, city leaders will find it increasingly difficult to elicit help from Washington.

THE CITY IN AMERICAN THOUGHT

From the beginning of American society cities featured prominently in our national development and cities provided an environment in which Americans evolved and tested their values and attitudes. To emphasize the frontier and pioneer life as exclusive determinants of the "American character," is neither accurate nor historically up-to-date. No doubt much of what we call American in values and ways of thinking bear the stamp of our frontier heritage. But our individualism, our pragmatism, our democratic ethos and our love of mobility and change also were shaped in city environments. In addition, the town promoter and merchant, the urban immigrant and journalist, the black laborer and urbanite must take their place beside the trapper and farmer as distinct American types. They also built America although their contribution has been clearly underplayed.

It is perhaps not surprising that there has been a deep current of antiurbanism in American thought that has shaped our attitudes and perceptions of cities. The tradition of antiurbanism began with Jefferson's oft quoted remarks on cities—"The yellow fever will discourage the growth of great cities in our nation, and I view great cities as pestilential to the morals, the health and the liberties of man."—and continued to be articulated in the writings of some of our most revered poets, essayists and novelists.[56] To be sure, this antiurbanism had its counterpart in the writings of men who lauded the city and viewed it as a stage for future wealth and progress, but antiurbanism continued to exert a powerful influence among urban intellectuals and among farmers who felt threatened by the rise of the metropolis. The antiurbanites held that cities were unnatural; that they corrupted individuals; that they were inhuman in scale and that they were totally impersonal. Variations on the antiurban theme may be found in the writings of Emerson, Thoreau, Whitman, William Jennings Bryan,

---

[56] Morton and Lucia White, *The Intellectual Versus the City* (Cambridge, Mass., 1962), *passim*.

Henry James, Henry Adams, Theodore Dreiser, and in the architectural conceptions of Frank Lloyd Wright.

We have not fully divested ourselves of these antiurban sentiments. To many the small town still seems more wholesome and more "American" than the city, the rural or suburban home more idyllic than the apartment "downtown." This adherence to pastoral ideals and myths, this conscious/unconscious antiurbanism affects the whole range of our responses to the city and its problems. There is far more hostility to urban welfare programs, for example, than to agricultural subsidies. There is far more support for highway development than for mass transit. There is waning support for public housing and no recompense for those who rent, while individuals receive substantial tax benefits from owning their own homes. There are but a few examples of how antiurbanism still affects our way of thinking and acting. Only when we fully acquaint ourselves with the facts of our urban history, will we work out more equitable arrangements and improve and revitalize our urban communities.

Suggestions for Further Reading

There are many books that discuss contemporary urban problems. Some of these are: James Wilson, ed., *The Metropolitan Enigma: Inquiries into the Nature and Dimensions of America's "Urban Crisis"* (1967); Edward Banfield, *The Unheavenly City: The Nature and the Future of Our Urban Crisis* (1968); Dick Netzer, *Economics and Urban Problems, Diagnoses and Prescriptions* (1970); Robert Liston, *Downtown: Our Challenging Urban Problems* (1965); Leonard Duhl, ed., *The Urban Condition* (1969); *Report of the National Advisory Commission on Civil Disorders* (The Kerner Commission, 1968); and *The State of the Cities, Report of the Commission on the Cities in the '70's* (1972). A useful, brief statistical source is U.S. Department of Commerce, *Pocket Data Book U.S.A. 1971.*

An excellent bibliographic source for American urban history is Dwight W. Hoover, *A Teacher's Guide to American Urban History* (1971). A book which provides an abundance of facts and interpretive information is Charles Glaab and A. Theodore Brown, *A History of Urban America* (1967). A complementary source is Charles Glaab, *The American City, A Documentary History* (1963). Other relevant books are Sam Bass Warner, Jr., *The Urban Wilderness: A History of the American City* (1972); Blake McKelvy, *The Urbanization of America, 1860–1915* (1963), . . . *The Emergence of Metropolitan America: 1915–1966* (1968); Zane Miller, *The Urbanization of Modern America: A Brief History* (1973); Constance McLaughlin Green, *American Cities in the Growth of the Nation* (1957), and *The Rise of Urban America* (1965).

Growth of the Nation (1957), and *The Rise of Urban America* (1965).

Useful collections of articles dealing with urban history include Paul Kramer and Frederick Holborn, eds., *The City in American Life, From Colonial Times to the Present* (1971); Alexander Callow, Jr., ed., *American Urban History* (1969); Allen Wakstein, ed., *The Urbanization of America, A Reader* (1970); James Richardson, *The American City, Historical Studies* (1972); and Raymond Mohl and Neil Betten, eds., *Urban America in Historical Perspective* (1970).

On city planning consult John Reps, *The Making of Urban America: A History of City Planning in the United States* (1965). On architecture see Christopher Tunnard and Henry Hope Reed, *American Skyline* (1953). Other specialized studies are Richard Wade, *The Urban Frontier* (1959); and Wade's *Slavery in the Cities: The South, 1820–1860* (1964); Oscar Handlin, *The Uprooted* (1951) and *Boston's Immigrants* (1959); Gilbert Osofsky, *Harlem: The Making of a Ghetto* (1968); Allen Schoener, *Portal to America: The Lower East Side, 1870–1925* (1967); and S. B. Sutton, ed., *Civilizing American Cities. A Selection of Frederick Law Olmsted's Writing on City Landscapes* (1971).

Our Littered Landscape

6

Nature and Ecology in American Thought

On April 22, 1970 Americans witnessed a curious phenomenon. People from all walks of life, of all ages and political persuasions, hailing from small towns and sprawling cities, met and heard speeches devoted to the problems of the deteriorating environment. They came armed with rakes and shovels, with brooms and litter bags and when the speeches were over they set to work cleaning streets, scavenging for bottles and tin cans, dredging streams of man-made debris. At day's end some felt that a new beginning had been made in focusing national attention on America's environmental problems.

For perhaps six or seven years prior to Earth Day 1970, Americans were becoming aware of a new problem, actually an old problem with a new name. It was variously referred to as the Ecology Issue, the Environment Issue or the Pollution Problem. Scientists were saying

that automobile exhausts and industrial smokestacks were making the air unfit to breathe. Some talked about radiation poisoning, pesticide poisoning and water pollution. Magazines and newspapers suddenly seemed to be filled with alarming stories about some aspect of environmental decay. New scientific terms came into popular use: biosphere, biodegradable, ecosystem, phosphates, ecology. One prominent biologist wrote an article predicting the death of the oceans—ecocatastrophe—not in the year 2000 but in 1976, right in the reader's own lifetime.[1]

[1] Paul Ehrlich, "Eco-catastrophe!" *Ramparts Magazine* 8 (Spetember 1969): 24–28.

American concern about the environment during these years was reinforced by widespread evidence of environmental decay. A catalogue of the findings of biologists and public health officials in 1972 included the following:[2]

—Industrial smokestacks, automobile exhausts, apartment house incinerators and construction equipment spew forth 200 million tons of contaminants every year. Black soot, carbon monoxide, sulfur oxides, hydrocarbons, nitrogen oxides and a variety of colorless but harmful gases circulate in our streets, our homes and our lungs.

—Synthetic pesticides have a broad range of harmful effects. DDT, in particular, does not break down and passes from one organism to another through all the links in the food chain. DDT may cause cancer.

—Noise and crowded urban living cause serious emotional and physiological stress.

—The nation's rivers and lakes are dying. Lake Erie has been biologically altered beyond repair. The lower Hudson is filthy; the Ohio, Mississippi and Missouri are heavily polluted; the Detroit River, the Cuyahoga River in Cleveland and the Houston Ship Canal are industrial sewers.

—Phosphates in household detergents are creating algal blooms which cause serious oxygen depletion in lakes, rivers and streams.

—Areas on the continental shelf are dying due to the dumping of raw sewage, sludge and other debris.

—Almost 100 million Americans drink water that is substandard and potentially harmful.

Confronted by this mounting tide of evidence, Americans were forced to acknowledge that an environmental crisis was at hand. People stopped taking for granted the inexhaustability of their resources. They became aware that industrial growth had unwanted and unexpected environmental consequences. They became aware that environmental harm was often irreversible, that it was nationwide and worldwide, and that it was created by subtle influences. Perhaps most disturbing was the new knowledge that pollution could not simply be blamed on big industries; people learned that they too polluted the environment when they threw away soda bottles and

---

[2] Compiled from statements in contemporary newspapers and magazines.

aluminum cans, and when they dumped their refuse in forests and lakes or washed their clothes with harmful detergents.

Popular awareness of environmental problems arose during the 1960s largely because scientists and journalists became alarmed about environmental deterioration and determined to do something about it. The science of ecology provided the foundation for the new criticism. In place of the rhetoric of nature love or the ethical and aesthetic arguments of conservationists, the ecologists put forward hardhitting data showing how modern industrial societies were altering and destroying life processes throughout the world. The ecologists proved, for example, that changes in the oxygen supply of lakes or changes in water temperature, changes in the composition of the atmosphere or the presence of pesticide residues in animals, altered life cycles that ultimately affected humans. The ecologists also pointed out that environmental decay had been accelerating rapidly since World War II.

These insights filtered down into the public consciousness in a variety of ways. Widespread discussion of the harmful effects of Strontium 90 in the press during the late 1950s generated popular concern about nuclear fallout. Rachel Carson's *Silent Spring* (1962) provided a chilling narrative of how DDT and other synthetic pesticides poisoned animals and entered the tissue of humans. Paul Ehrlich's 1968 best seller *The Population Bomb* attempted to prove that runaway population growth was dooming life on earth. In *Science and Survival* (1966) Barry Commoner discussed the origins and implications of ecological stress. A host of other books and articles appeared during the 1960s analyzing environmental problems. Conservation groups and activist organizations such as The Sierra Club, The Friends of the Earth, and the Environmental Defense Fund began legal and lobbying efforts to halt further environmental deterioration.

There was widespread agreement among scientists and ecologists regarding the dimensions of the problem. They all agreed that industrialists, farmers and consumers were pouring millions of tons of waste material into the water and air which those ecosystems could not properly absorb. They voiced special concern for the disastrous effects of runaway population growth, the effects of new technologies, the lack of adequate safeguards for the sea and the atmosphere, and the possibility of contamination in space.

When ecologists came to grips with assigning root causes for the environmental crisis, however, they disagreed. One group, whose best known spokesman today is Paul Ehrlich, believes environmental stress is the result of accelerating population growth. To quote Ehrlich: "Too many cars, too many factories, too much detergent, too much pesticide, multiplying contrails, inadequate sewage treatment plants, too little water, too much carbon dioxide—all can be traced easily to *too many people.*"[3] Ehrlich's thesis is that the earth cannot sustain population growth which doubles every thirty or forty years; that underdeveloped nations, in particular, face mass starvation because food production cannot keep pace with food demand; that population growth feeds industry's skyrocketing demand for natural resources and this demand leads to environmental plunder.

Ehrlich's solution to our environmental problems is simple: halt population growth. By slowing population growth, he argues, nations will need less food, less power and fewer natural resources to satisfy their citizen's wants. A leveling of population will raise standards of living, eradicate the immense difference between rich and poor nations and create a more peaceful international climate. Ehrlich recognizes, however, that limiting population size is difficult to achieve because people resist coercion and because social and medical solutions raise complex ethical and political questions. Nevertheless, leveling of population growth is the *sine qua non* of survival. "Somehow, we've got to change from a growth-oriented, exploitative system to one focused on stability and conservation."[4]

A variant of the population-causes-environmental decay argument is that affluence is the true source of evil. Some ecologists say it is not the populous underdeveloped nations of the world that cause pollution but the developed nations that use huge quantities of natural resources and that return billions of tons of waste to the environment each year. In support of this view, advocates of limiting affluence point out that the average American consumes three to ten times more natural resources in his or her lifetime than an individual in India or China and that increases in American population size, while small, have much greater environmental impact than increases in the underdeveloped nations. Those who favor a curb on affluence urge that people in industrialized societies reconsider their attachment to material wealth and stop worshipping at the shrine of economic growth.

A third interpretation of the world's environmental problems comes from Barry Commoner who differs sharply with those who believe population growth and affluence are the cause of the environmental crisis.

In *The Closing Circle: Nature, Man and Technology* (1971) Commoner shows that pollution in the American environment has far outstripped population growth since 1946; population grew forty-two percent since that date while pollutants increased between 200 and

---

[3] Paul Ehrlich, *The Population Bomb* (New York, 1970), pp. 66–67.
[4] *Ibid.,* pp. 169–170.

2000 percent depending upon the pollutant measured. He also points out that affluence measured in food intake, per capita housing, clothing and other essentials has not increased substantially since 1946. He therefore concludes that neither "affluence" nor population growth has increased enough to be responsible for the environmental crisis.

For Commoner the root of the environmental crisis is the shift from old to new technologies after World War II—technologies that have burdened the environment with new products and chemicals which are alien to nature and which cannot be broken down by normal life processes.

> New production technologies have displaced old ones. Soap powder has been displaced by synthetic detergents; natural fibres (cotton and wool) have been displaced by synthetic ones; steel and lumber have been displaced by aluminum, plastics, and concrete; railroad freight has been displaced by truck freight; returnable bottles have been displaced by nonreturnable ones. On the road, the low-powered automobile engines of the 1920s and 1930s have been displaced by high-powered ones. On the farm, while per capita production has remained about constant, the amount of harvested acreage has decreased; in effect, fertilizer has displaced land. Older methods of insect control have been displaced by synthetic insecticides, such as DDT, and for controlling weeds the cultivator has been displaced by the herbicide spray. Range-feeding of livestock has been displaced by feedlots.[5]

This displacement has occurred at a rapid rate without any knowledge or caring about how the environment might deal with new substances and chemicals. The result, according to Commoner, has been a disastrous stressing of the environment, a breakdown of the delicate balances formerly maintained in the soil, water and atmospheric ecosystems. "All this 'progress,' " he writes, "has greatly increased the impact on the environment."

> This pattern of economic growth is the major reason for the environmental crisis. A good deal of the mystery and confusion about the sudden emergence of the environmental crisis can be removed by pinpointing, pollutant by pollutant, how the postwar technological transformation of the United States economy has produced not only the much-heralded 126 percent rise in

[5] Barry Commoner, The Closing Circle (New York, 1971), p. 144.

GNP, but also, at a rate about ten times faster than the growth of GNP, the rising level of environmental pollution.[6]

It follows from Commoner's analysis that the only way to reverse environmental deterioration is to develop technologies and rates of economic growth compatible with the environment. (To the extent that this is not undertaken, he does say that population growth must drop significantly). He suggests that reconversion along ecologically sound principles would be a monumental task requiring a major commitment upon the part of industry, the farmer, the consumer and the government and that it would cost upwards of 40 billion dollars a year for 25 years.

> If we are to survive economically as well as biológically, industry, agriculture, and transportation will have to meet the inescapable demands of the ecosystem. This will require the development of major new technologies, including: systems to return sewage and garbage directly to the soil; the replacement of many synthetic materials by natural ones; the reversal of the present trend to retire land from cultivation and to elevate the yield per acre by heavy fertilization; replacement of synthetic pesticides, as rapidly as possible, by biological ones; the discouragement of power-consuming industries; the development of land transport that operates with maximal fuel efficiency at low combustion temperatures and with minimal land use; essentially complete containment and reclamation of wastes from combustion processes, smelting, and chemical operations (smokestacks must become rarities); essentially complete recycling of all reuseable metal, glass, and paper products; ecologically sound planning to govern land use including urban areas.[7]

Commoner believes that to avoid these reconversions is to invite major disaster within the next 50 or so years.

What evidence is there that people are beginning to listen to the Ehrlichs and Commoners? It there a discernable commitment to halt environmental overload?

Since the late 1960s more people than ever are aware of the environmental impact of industrial processes and of the products they use. Large segments of the public recognize the harmful effects of

---

[6] *Ibid.,* p. 146.
[7] *Ibid.,* pp. 283–284.

nondegradable containers, plastics, food additives, pesticides, dumping of raw sewage, oil spills, etc., on the environment. On a strictly personal level there is widespread evidence that people want safe food and want products that do not pollute. The organic food movement is one illustration of this, communities that collect aluminum cans and bottles for recycling, another. Municipalities have also taken the first steps to restore environmental quality. In 1970 several small towns and cities banned the use of phosphate detergents in an attempt to clean up their lakes and reservoirs.

Unfortunately, the public remains at the mercy of the industries that provide them with consumer goods, and these industries have shown a reluctance to develop ecologically sound methods and products. A gentle, but far from universal prodding has begun, however. Public recognition of the dangers of automobile emissions has led to federal legislation setting strict limits on emissions to go into effect no later than 1976. This was fought by the automobile industry, but when faced with new legislation, the industry responded by developing new engines which hold the promise of being pollution free. The federal government, to cite another example, has also begun to monitor the discharge of all industrial and sewage wastes in the nation's waterways. Industries must now catalogue the wastes they dump and request permission—so far being granted—to continue discharging these wastes. This does not solve the problem of water pollution, but it is a first step in the direction of restoring water quality.

Recognizing the mounting concern over the state of the environment, President Nixon asked Congress in 1969 to establish an Environmental Protection Agency and a Council on Environmental Quality. The E.P.A. is now responsible for a broad program of research and monitoring, an effort which, it is hoped, will produce environmental yardsticks which industry will be forced to follow. The Council on Environmental Quality is responsible for setting broad policy and for drafting a State of the Environment report each year. A third organization, the National Oceanic and Atmospheric Administration, within the Commerce Department, is mandated to conduct research programs dealing with the sea and the air. Pessimists believe these organizations will go no further than reprimanding the big polluters. Optimists believe that, at best, they will effect reforms only when they are consistent with the political strategy of the president and party in power.

It seems then that the environmental crisis is being perceived on the political level, as it were, through a glass darkly. Some legislation has been passed to correct environmental plunder, but the profound commitment asked for by Commoner and others has not yet crystalized. The individual can act but only in a limited way. Politicians may act but they are restrained by the conflicting interests of their constitu-encies. It may take an even greater sense of crisis, or broad acknowl-edgment that we are doomed to extinction, to force us to match our response to the nature and magnitude of the challenge.

THE ORIGINS OF POPULAR CONCERN

Popular concern with the state of the American environment is not unique to our own era; the intense preoccupation with the environ-ment that we are now experiencing was, in fact, characteristic of earlier periods when nature lovers, scientists and government officials awakened to the horrors being perpetrated against our resources and wilderness. One such period was the Progressive Era (1896–1915) when conservation became a national concern; another was the de-pression years (1930–1936) when advocates of strong government in-tervened to restore life to the dustbowls of the Southwest and zones of poverty in the Tennessee Valley. Well before these two periods, however, individuals were active in campaigning for national parks, forest protection and water conservation. Their attitudes toward the American environment, in turn, were influenced by the handful of nature lovers, explorers, writers and artists who first perceived the American environment as a treasure to be appreciated, protected and preserved.

NATURE AND THE AMERICAN

Long before the words conservation and ecology existed, Elizabethan Englishmen confronted the New World environment; they brought with them a broad spectrum of attitudes toward nature, shaped by their experiences in England, by their folklore and by their reading of the Bible. By the sixteenth century England had largely been cleared of dense forest and, except for the Scottish highlands, most of the British Isles was tame pasture and farmland. The English looked upon nature as a benign force, nature, that is, envisoned as a garden or pastoral countryside. Wilderness was viewed quite differently. For the Eliza-bethan, wilderness was a terrifying and lonely place, the abode of evil spirits and of the devil. Centuries of experience in taming the wilderness created a strong bias against nature in the wild. The Bible reinforced the notion that wilderness was a place of spiritual loss and longing.

Many early accounts of the New World describe the newly discovered lands as resembling a garden, comparable to the garden of paradise in Genesis. To Sir Walter Raleigh, the New World was an abundant garden, picturesque and beautiful. Michael Drayton, in 1605, wrote that Virginia was "Earth's only paradise where the soil yielded its fruits without toil and the land smelled sweet and fragrant."[8] Many poems, pamphlets and travel accounts of the Elizabethans evoked the garden as a controlling image. A New Eden had been discovered in the West, and the idea of an abundant garden captured the imagination of Englishmen and generations of settlers who crossed the Atlantic ocean.

The image of the garden, however, was marred by those who found physical and spiritual wilderness in the New World. To the Mayflower travelers the new world was a "hideous and desolate wilderness, full of wilde beasts and wilde men."[9] These weary travelers found no New Eden but rather cold, starvation and savage Indians. The strangeness of the New England environment, its untamed forests, unworked soil and barren coastlines threatened those who were accustomed to a more peaceful countryside. Michael Wigglesworth found no garden in America but a "howling wilderness / Where none inhabited / But hellish fiends and brutish man / That Devils worshipped...."[10]

The longing for a garden paradise and a fear of wilderness shaped early American attitudes toward nature. With little love for the wild and untamed, the first settlers set out to clear the land and cut the forests to make way for homes and farmland. The Bible said that man should "Increase & multiply, replenish the earth and subdue it" and this admonition the settlers took seriously. Nature was not something to be loved and appreciated. It was an adversary; only when it was subdued was it safe to be contemplated.

The Puritans, however, did occasionally contemplate nature, for in nature one could find evidence of God's perfection. He had designed the world, created all living things and therefore a measure of reverence and appreciation for the divinity of nature was necessary. But the Puritans also believed that God had placed nature and its abundant resources before man to use. There was less thought about replenishing the earth than subduing it, more exploitation than contemplation. In sum, "nature had both use and meaning. It was to be both exploited

---

[8] Leo Marx, *The Machine in the Garden* (New York, 1964), p. 38.
[9] Russel B. Nye, "The American View of Nature," in *This Almost Chosen People* (East Lansing, Michigan, 1966), p. 258.
[10] *Ibid.*

and contemplated; it was tool and symbol. These two attitudes have controlled the pattern of Americans' reactions to nature ever since."[11]

The emotional and intellectual attitudes toward nature brought from England to the New World were powerful formative influences; of equal significance, however, was the physical endowment of the North American continent and the settlers' reaction to its incredible size and abundance. The frontier worked like a giant magnet, drawing settlers farther and farther west. It encouraged hardihood, practicality, toughness of spirit. What was useful and necessary triumphed over what was beautiful. Trees were obstacles to be cut down and used; mountains were barriers to further expansion; animals and wild fowl were sources for food, fur and leather. The frontiersman was much too close to nature to derive any pleasure from its beauty. The French traveler De Tocqueville summed this up with great accuracy:

> In Europe people talk a great deal of the wilds of America, but the Americans themselves never think about them; they are insensible to the wonders of inanimate nature and they may be said not to perceive the mighty forests that surround them till they fall beneath the hatchet. Their eyes are fixed upon another sight. . . . the . . . march across these wilds, draining swamps, turning the course of rivers, peopling solitudes and subduing nature.[12]

One additional factor was operating during the period of settlement that influenced early American attitudes toward nature: the idea that property was privately owned and could be disposed of in any way an individual wished. Except for one or two early ordinances regulating deer hunting or reserving large trees for sailing masts, men were free to cut and clear their land even if this meant total despoilation. Ignorant of the facts of ecology and believing in the unending abundance before them, colonial settlers and frontiersmen tore away at nature with all the tools at their disposal. "Since wood ash was commercially more valuable than trees, Ohio settlers burned whole sections of forest for the ashes alone. Passenger pigeons, killed by the thousands, became hog food. California loggers . . . burned out smaller sequoias to get at the big ones, which they blasted into manageable pieces with gunpowder, wasting half the tree."[13] As the fron-

---

[11] *Ibid.,* p. 260.
[12] Roderick Nash, *Wilderness and the American Mind* (New Haven, 1967), p. 23.
[13] Nye, "The American View of Nature," p. 278.

tier was pushed farther and farther westward, the American forests gave way to the saw and axe. Students of the American forest estimate that in the nineteenth century four-fifths of all the prime timber in America was cut. Only a few hundred acres of redwoods remain today of the original two million.[14]

THE DISCOVERY OF NATURE

It was not until the middle decades of the eighteenth century, when the eastern United States had become a mosaic of cities, towns and hamlets, that small numbers of Americans began to look upon nature with appreciation. Urbanization had pushed out the wilderness, life was more stable, and nature lost its menacing quality. Educated people were learning new theories about nature which emphasized that nature was characterized by order and harmony.

The central figure in this transformation in attitudes was Sir Issac Newton who less than a century before had reduced certain laws of nature to mathematical formulae. Newton wrote that order and system reigned throughout the natural world; European philosophers embraced and popularized his mechanistic view of nature. No longer, they said, did a capricious God control the workings of the universe; no longer should storm and lightning be thought of as divinely inspired. Reason could penetrate the once dark veil of nature. God was a supreme being, the original creator, but nature worked according to its own regular laws.

The Newtonian conception of the universe found expression in Deism, a religious world view that was popular among many eighteenth-century American intellectuals. Deism emphasized the divinity of nature, and Deists believed that spiritual truths could be gleaned from the study and contemplation of nature. Like the early Puritans, the Deists saw God in nature, but He was not the harsh, demanding God of an earlier century. Because nature exhibited law, harmony and reason, the Deists argued that God must be a beneficent creator.

While Deism and Newtonian science opened up an intellectual channel for the study and appreciation of nature, a movement, loosely defined as Romanticism, opened up an emotional one. Romanticism was a literary movement that emerged in Europe during the late eighteenth and early nineteenth centuries. The Romantics rejected the emphasis on reason, progress and order championed by the eigh-

---

[14] *Ibid.*, p. 279.

teenth-century philosophers and, instead, infused their literary and artistic works with feeling, sentiment, passion and fantasy.

Romantic poets such as Wordsworth, Coleridge, Keats and Shelley sought out nature to escape the horrors of England's new industrial cities, and they found in nature the mystery, enchantment and depth of feeling they seemed to crave. Wordsworth told his generation to quit its books and to learn from nature. Those touched by his vision developed an entirely new attitude toward pastoral landscapes, wilderness and exotic places.

The impact of Romanticism, Deism and Newtonian science in America opened up new doors of perception onto the American environment. Men began to leave the cities to travel into the surrounding countryside where they could study, observe, meditate and record their impressions. During the eighteenth century, for example, a number of scientists and explorers toured the eastern United States to study its flora and fauna. John Bartram and his son William recorded their botanical observations, and the younger Bartram wrote his *Travels*, a serious scientific study and a glorification of American nature.

More interested in the magnificence and sublimity of nature were men of leisure and wealth who trekked northward to see Niagara Falls, or south to the Great Natural Bridge in Virginia which Thomas Jefferson described in rapturous terms in his *Notes on the State of Virginia* (1781). By the late eighteenth-century, descriptions of nature were included in the emerging national poetry, and literary magazines were filled with sentimental, romantic impressions of wild country. In the writings of James Fenimore Cooper and Washington Irving descriptions of nature and wild country were commonplace.

Just as nature became a subject for poets and writers, the scenery of the New World captured the interest of American painters. Landscape painting had few practitioners during the colonial period, but during the early nineteenth century a number of prominent artists turned toward American nature to immortalize its beauty. These artists rejected the idea that American scenery was inadequate because it contained no ruins of antiquity to enhance the viewer's mental associations (as in Europe) and instead began to paint the rivers and mountains of the Northeast which they considered sufficiently sublime and picturesque.

John Trumbull and John Vanderlyn painted romantic scenes of Niagara Falls; Thomas Cole encouraged a whole school of painters to record the beauties of the Hudson River Valley; Asher Durand, in addition to his paintings of America scenery, helped publish engravings and lithographs which captured the beauty of the American landscape.[15] On the frontier, Carl Bodmer and George Catlin recorded, for posterity, pioneer cabins and Indian rituals, while Alexander Wilson and John James Audubon painted the birds of America.

By the third decade of the nineteenth century, American nature found a permanent home in the nation's art, poetry and literature. It was, however, a romanticised and sentimentalized nature which made it more attractive to urban, sophisticated audiences. Americans retained an hostility to raw wilderness for many decades to come.

THE TRANSCENDENTALISTS: EMERSON AND THOREAU

Perhaps the two foremost exponents of American nature during the middle decades of the nineteenth century were Ralph Waldo Emerson and Henry David Thoreau. Both these men were essayists, lecturers and full-time critics of American culture; both were heavily influenced by the Romantic writers and poets of Europe; and both found in nature and wilderness something essential to the spiritual health and well-being of man and society. Transcendentalism, the intuitive, mystical philosophy which these men espoused, was a philosophical and emotional response to the rise of urban industry and the rampant materialism that characterized nineteenth-century America.

Emerson and Thoreau looked upon the advance of industry with suspicion and foreboding. Factory life demanded submission and conformity; the pursuit of the dollar dominated men's thinking and shaped their morality; wealth was destroying the enjoyment of simple pleasures and was poisoning human relationships. The transcendentalists believed that unless a balance was struck between individual and group needs, between material and spiritual values and between the city and nature, society would decay. Nature was indispensable because it strengthened the virtues of self-reliance and individualism.

Emerson and Thoreau were aware that industrial and technological progress was inevitable, but they decried the fact that it detached men from nature and made them "the tools of their tools." Nature offered a world of harmony and spiritual truths; nature was a link between man and God; if only men would go out into nature and allow themselves to observe its beauty they would find a correspondence between what they saw and the higher, moral laws of the universe. Man could transcend (go beyond) his reason to perceive spiritual truths. In nature men could also explore their mental and moral landscapes.

---

[15] Hans Huth, *Nature and the American* (Berkeley, 1957), Ch. 3, *passim*.

For Thoreau transcendentalism was not an academic exercise. He sought to live what he believed by retreating to his neighboring countryside (Concord, Massachusetts) for two years to live a life unencumbered by luxuries or even the necessity to work. In *Walden* (1854) he described how he set about finding the bare minimum of food and shelter; how he spent days on end walking and observing nature; how he felt revitalized by the wilderness. "Thoreau grounded his argument on the idea that wilderness was the source of vigor, inspiration, and strength."[16] He believed that "to the extent a culture, or an individual, lost contact with wilderness it became weak and dull."[17] His stay at Walden pond offered him an opportunity to test his capacities and mental resources; it was a perfect setting for an inward journey. At Walden Thoreau attempted to penetrate "the wildness . . . in our brains and bowels, the primitive vigor of Nature in us."[18]

Both Emerson and Thoreau viewed nature as a resource, a touchstone to human values. For this reason both denounced the exploitation of nature and articulated the earliest American philosophy of preservation. Thoreau was disgusted to find his neighbors cutting away pine seedlings to make way for vegetable crops. He feared that without forests and wild meadows men would have nowhere to go to feel deeply and experience spiritual renewal. The transcendentalists did not speak for nature in economic or ecological terms as later generations of conservationists were to do, because they saw nature largely in aesthetic terms. They were aware, however, that industrialists and land speculators were doing irreparable harm to the environment.

Emerson, Thoreau and their fellow nature enthusiasts were the first to perceive the value of wilderness to people. Their writings became an inspiration to others who witnessed even more fully the devastation of the American environment.

THE IMPACT OF INDUSTRIALIZATION AND WESTWARD EXPANSION

It should be emphasized that the growing awareness and appreciation of nature we have so far discussed was confined to the wealthy, intellectual, urban elite; the vast majority of Americans remained oblivious to the aesthetic qualities of nature and retained a purely utili-

---

[16] Nash, *Wilderness and the American Mind,* p. 88.
[17] *Ibid.*
[18] Quoted in Nash, *Wilderness and the American Mind,* p. 89.

tarian attitude toward the environment. While Thoreau was contemplating nature at Walden, American frontiersmen began settling and exploiting the lands west of the Mississippi. In the East, industrialists turned their attention to wresting oil, iron and coal from the land. During the post-Civil War era capitalist greed and the new technology combined to destroy a substantial part of America's natural wealth.

The exploitation of the forests and mineral resources of the trans-Mississippi West began during the Civil War when the national government decided to dispose of its huge remaining holdings of virgin land. After the South withdrew from the union, the Republicans repaid their western supporters by passing a series of laws designed to provide cheap land for prospective western settlers. The Homestead Act of 1862 granted 160 acres of land to any American citizen over 21 who was willing to cultivate his plot for five years; the Timber Culture Act of 1873 made a similar grant to a settler who would seed at least forty acres with trees. Under the Desert Land Act of 1877, 640 acres were offered to settlers who would irrigate them; the Timber and Stone Act of 1878 allowed anyone to claim 160 acres of forest land unfit for agriculture at $2.50 an acre.

Homestead laws were intended to throw open the West to democratic settlement, but they were frequently abused by land speculators and eastern monied interests. Pioneers defaulted on their debts and were forced to give up their holdings to wealthy creditors. Lumber companies frequently paid individuals to request settlement rights so that the deeds could be reassigned to their companies. Other tricks and subterfuges were used to concentrate land in the hands of the few. While many western settlers succeeded in holding on to their properties, hundreds of millions of acres passed into the possession of wealthy individuals and powerful corporations.

With large portions of the national domain thus disposed of, it was possible for private interests to exploit the land without restriction. Timber companies brutally thinned the Great Lakes forests before moving out into the northwest to do the same. Mining companies bought large tracts from disillusioned prospectors and then employed machines and railroads to gouge out mineral wealth. In the southwest, sheep ranchers grazed their sheep until the land was stripped bare, moving on and repeating the process wherever the prairie had grass. Even individual farmers who hoped for successful harvests ruined the land they tilled. Wasteful methods and lack of knowledge caused soil erosion and soil exhaustion and farmers were forced to move to new lands and begin cultivation again.

Further east a parallel process of exploitation took place. Enterprising businessmen recognized the burgeoning need for steel in the nation's growing economy and began mining the rich iron fields of Michigan, Wisconsin and Minnesota. Surface deposits were stripped from giant pits and deep mine shafts were dug to get at less accessible ores. Whole regions were scarred by steam shovels and railroads brought in to facilitate transport to eastern refineries. Similarly, as the demand for coal grew to feed blast furnaces, locomotives and factory steam engines, mining operations spread across Pennsylvania, Maryland, Kentucky, Ohio and Illinois. After oil was discovered to be a fuel and an illuminant in the early 1860s, large sections of Pennsylvania, West Virginia, Ohio, Tennessee and Kentucky became pockmarked by thousands of oil rigs and wells. Dirty, crowded cities grew up around these mining and drilling centers, contributing to the pollution of local streams and rivers. No ordinances protected these waterways and no thought was given to restoring fertility or beauty to areas wasted and drained of their mineral wealth.

The belief that government should interfere as little as possible in the social and economic life of the nation gave businessmen all the justification they needed in their quest for riches and power.[19] Laissez-faire meant that the government had no right to tell a man what to do with his property even if his practices wasted irreplaceable natural resources. With "let alone" the governing ethos, no laws were passed to protect forest and mineral wealth; not until 1891, when four-fifths of the standing timber was out of government control, did Congress empower the President to create the first forest reserves.

The sheer abundance of resources in America's mines and forests masked the fact that these resources were finite, that eventually the nation's growing population would consume them totally. Laissez-faire, ignorance, lack of foresight and the belief that nature should submit to man, all conspired to destroy important sectors of the American environment. In post-Civil War America, the engines of industry were fed, a large population was housed and clothed; but the price of this rapid increase in material wealth was deferred for future generations to pay.

THE IDEA OF CONSERVATION

In 1862, George Perkins Marsh, then United States Ambassador to the Kingdom of Italy, completed work on a book entitled *Man and Nature; or Physical Geography as Modified by Human Action.* Published

---

[19] Sidney Fine, *Laissez Faire and the General-Welfare State* (Ann Arbor, Michigan, 1956).

in America two years later, *Man and Nature* became the first scholarly work to discuss the American exploitation of nature in ecological and historical terms. Marsh attempted to explain in scientific terms how irresponsible land-use imperiled human civilization. His book influenced many individuals who, at a later date, figured prominently in the conservation movement.[20]

Marsh stated the thesis of *Man and Nature* simply: "Man is everywhere a disturbing agent. Wherever he plants his foot, the harmonies of nature are turned to discords." Laying particular emphasis on the destruction of forests, Marsh pointed out how removal of trees destroyed protective ground cover, hastened water evaporation, and altered the levels of sunlight conducive to successful forest life. By reckless thinning of the virgin forests, by hunting and destroying its animal life, the harmony of nature (we would say its ecology) was dramatically altered. The results of this destruction were already apparent in Marsh's day: soil erosion, drought, violent flooding and the disappearance of birds and animals.

Marsh came to his conclusions by blending historical insights with careful observation. As a mill operator in his native Vermont he had witnessed the cutting of the forests and the erosion and ugliness it produced. As a traveler in the eastern Mediterranean and Italy he saw parched rocky soil and desert land where he knew once mighty civilizations stood. Marsh reasoned that societies which destroyed their forests invited destruction of their agricultural lands by removing the roots and plants which retained necessary water. Maintaining a balance between wooded land and farmland was essential if societies were to exist and prosper.

Marsh was the first American to perceive the complex relationships among living things in the forest and the first to state emphatically that man was altering nature irrevocably. He was also one of the first men to suggest remedial action. Aware that in Europe forests were protected by governments which regulated timber operations, Marsh suggested that Americans should introduce similar practices. Although he considered government intervention desirable only where forests were particularly vulnerable, Marsh hoped that individual lumbermen would, as a matter of self interest, develop a conservation mentality. He suggested that "belts of woodland" be allowed to reproduce themselves spontaneously so that the valuable "network of fibrous roots" would remain in tact. He exhorted his readers to recognize that the most successful of the ancient societies had maintained

---

[20] David Lowenthal, *George Perkins Marsh: Versatile Vermonter* (New York, 1958).

elaborate irrigation networks to ensure the productivity of their soil. Marsh even recommended growing plants and trees along the coastal sand dunes to halt drift and erosion. He was not an exponent of wild nature; rather he recognized that wise land-use entailed thoughtful, scientific intervention so that men could continue to enjoy nature's bounty.

Marsh went beyond the transcendentalists in his condemnation of man's propensity to waste and over consume. "Man pursues his victims with reckless destructiveness" he wrote, . . . "he unsparingly persecutes, even to extirpation, thousands of organic forms which he cannot consume."[21] Marsh linked this negative quality with the American's "restless love of change which characterizes us, and makes us almost a nomad rather than a sedentary people." He recognized that abundance, an open frontier, and the absence of laws and restraints rooted in history encouraged the American's tendency to exploit nature.

Marsh believed it was essential that Americans recognize their "love of change" as a cultural defect before they repeat the mistakes of the Mediterranean civilizations. The latter's demise began when they destroyed their forests. "Let us restore this one element of material life to its normal proportions," he wrote, "and devise means for maintaining the permanence of its relations to the fields, the meadows and the pastures, to the rain and the dews of heaven, to the springs and rivulets with which it waters the earth."[22] Then, and only then, Marsh maintained could he foresee a well-ordered commonwealth in the New World; then he could call Americans a "people of progress."

Although *Man and Nature* was full of ecological insights and the conservation idea was stated explicitly, Marsh's admonitions went largely unheeded during his lifetime; not until the conservation movement gained momentum in the early 1900s was his book reread and pronounced prophetic. Between the publication of *Man and Nature* and the first Conservation Conference in 1908, however, a few steps were taken in the direction he had suggested. In 1873 Congress received a report from the American Association for the Advancement of Science asking for a thorough study of the forestry question; during the 1880s numerous bills were advanced in Congress calling for the creation of forest reserves and one was finally passed in 1891. This bill, generally called "The Forest Reserve Act" empowered the

---

[21] Quoted in Roderick Nash, ed., *The American Environment: Readings in the History of Conservation* (Reading, Mass., 1968), p. 15.

[22] *Ibid.*, p. 17.

president to set aside forest lands held by the government; in the succeeding ten years both presidents Harrison and Cleveland used this new power to reserve millions of acres of valuable timber land for government use and protection. A parallel development was the establishment of the first forestry schools in the United States. In 1898 Cornell University and the Biltmore Forest School at Biltmore, North Carolina began offering courses in scientific forest management; two years later the Yale Forest School was established at New Haven, Connecticut.

The federal government at this time also became active in the field of irrigation with the establishment of the United States Geological Survey in 1879. Headed by the ardent irrigationist John Wesley Powell, the Survey conducted studies of water power sites with the intention of reclaiming for cultivation millions of acres of arid territory in the Far West. An important precedent was also set in 1865 when the federal government gave Yosemite Valley to the State of California for use as a park. In 1872 Yellowstone National Park in Wyoming was created; in 1885 the State of New York established the Adirondack Forest Preserve; in 1890 Yosemite reverted to the federal government to become a national park and in 1891 the Adirondack Preserve became a state park open for recreational use.

These legislative creations were the product of diverse interests and motivations. The Yellowstone area was on the verge of being gobbled up by commercial interests when Congress decided its canyons, waterfalls and geysers were too valuable to be exploited by private investors. The Adirondack Preserve was largely the creation of commercial interests hopeful of maintaining an abundant water supply for New York's canals and rivers. In the case of Yosemite National Park, the entreaties of wilderness lovers such as John Muir and Robert Underwood Johnson helped win congressional approval. Whatever the motives behind the creation of the national parks and forest preserves, each act protecting nature from commercial exploitation was a victory for nature and for Marsh's ideas. In the final analysis, however, they were limited victories, for the nation's conscience regarding the disappearance of wilderness and the destruction of natural resources had yet to be fully aroused.

THE CONSERVATION MOVEMENT

Americans were not ready to support a true conservation movement until the 1890s for it was not until then that the disappearance of the frontier, growing alarm at depleted resources, hostility to industrial monopolies, and intensifying urbanization acted together to generate widespread anxiety.[23] This anxiety produced a beneficial effect because it goaded foresters, engineers, government officials and practical-minded landowners to espouse the cause of wise land use and conservation. During this period conservation was named and defined; it won the support of a popular president, and it became an important component of the reform movement known as Progressivism.

If anxiety is the correct word to use to characterize the closing decade of the nineteenth century, this anxiety was broadly experienced and emanated from a multitude of problems. Labor and farmer unrest, the rise of slums and municipal corruption, hostility to newly arrived immigrants, hatred of industrial monopolies—these and many more problems blossomed during the 1880s and 1890s. Among these problems, and in a sense related to all of them, was an awareness that America had recently ceased to be a frontier society. In 1890 the Bureau of the Census reported that the frontier, as a distinct line of settlement, had become so obscured that it would no longer be mentioned in subsequent census reports. For the first time Americans were forced to realize that their society had reached adulthood. Their borders were fixed, their resources limited; the area for new settlement had finally been obliterated.

The man who interpreted this event in its historical context was Frederick Jackson Turner, a University of Wisconsin historian, who delivered an address at the American Historical Association in 1893 entitled, "The Significance of the Frontier in American History." Turner argued that among all the ideas, institutions and events that shaped America and Americans most, the frontier was the paramount influence. The frontier spawned a spirit of equality and therefore democratic ideas and institutions. The frontier encouraged hardihood, individualism, inventiveness and permitted both physical and social mobility; frontier life made Americans pragmatists, materialists, believers in progress, optimists. Turner did not intend to say that the frontier was the *only* formative influence in American history, but initially this is how his ideas were understood. Those who read his books and essays saw the frontier in a new light. From a physical fact, it became a vital and beneficent influence. Without a frontier, without wilderness, Americans would become a different people.

Although Turner said nothing directly about preservation or conservation in his essay on the significance of the frontier, Americans who read his works could not help linking his ideas with these two concerns. Not only had the frontier all but disappeared by 1890, America's great abundance seemed to be disappearing with it. Forests

---

[23] *Ibid.*, pp. 37–38 and pp. 85–93.

continued to be cut as if the supply of timber was limitless; coal and iron were being mined at astronomical rates; an expanding population demanded more and more from the nation's store of natural wealth. Fear of depletion of national resources joined with a building hostility toward the exploiters of these resources.

The conservation movement that came to fruition at the turn of the century was thus inspired by many concerns. For some it was an effort to hold on to what was left of the frontier and the values and ideals it produced; for some it was an effort to save nature and provide adequate resources for the future; for a small group of engineers and planners it was a movement to introduce scientific ideas of management and to promote efficient resource use. For the great majority of people, however, conservation was thought of as a fight for democracy; a fight of the little man against the corporate giants. This ultimately was the source of its success, for without popular support, conservation would have remained an idea without impetus and without direction.

The brains and energy behind the conservation movement was Gifford Pinchot, chief of the federal Bureau of Forestry from 1898 to 1910. Pinchot was a New Yorker of independent means, a man of administrative skill and persuasive power. After studying scientific forest management in France and Germany, he returned to the United States determined to educate Americans in the wise use of their forests. Briefly he worked as a forester for George W. Vanderbilt on his North Carolina estate. During the Cleveland administration he surveyed western timberlands as secretary to the forest commission of the National Academy of Sciences; this brought him national recognition and an invitation to head the forestry division within the Department of the Interior. After 1905 the Bureau of Forestry was transferred to the Department of Agriculture, and Pinchot took the title of Chief Forester. Here he gathered around him men of similar persuasion and from this post lobbied for and pushed through his conservation program.

Pinchot relates in his autobiography, *Breaking New Ground,* that it was either he or his colleague Overton Price who decided to call their cause conservation, a name derived from British forest lands in India known as conservancies. Pinchot recognized the propaganda value of the word conservation, but it was a fellow conservationist, W. J. McGee, who gave conservation its precise definition. Conservation, McGee said, was the use of resources for the "greatest good of the greatest number for the longest time." "What *right* has any citizen," he wrote in 1910, ". . . to seize on sources of life for his own behoof that are the common heritage of all; what *right* has legislature or court to help in the seizure; and striking more deeply, what *right* has any generation to wholly consume, much less waste, those sources of life without which the children or the children's children must starve or freeze?"[24]

This language typified the crusading zeal of the conservation advocates, and Pinchot made sure that it was not mere rhetoric. Under his administration, 45 million acres of national forests were enlarged to 150 million acres. At his insistence, forest agents began to crack down on men who cut timber or grazed their flocks on federally owned property. In addition, westerners were forced to pay fees for grazing and irrigation involving the reserves. "Pinchotism" outraged many westerners, but the Chief Forester gained support from senators and governors in California, Nevada, Colorado, and the New Mexico territory.

Pinchot was a close personal friend of Theodore Roosevelt who rose suddenly to the presidency in 1901 when McKinley was felled by an assassin's bullet. Roosevelt was a nature-lover and conservationist long before he entered the White House. As a young man he had traveled widely in the West, drove cattle in the Dakota territory, and came away with a profound love of the plains and prairies. Roosevelt and Pinchot saw eye to eye on the need to protect the existing national forests; they agreed on extending federal protection over new forests, mineral deposits and water-power sites.

Roosevelt was not afraid to fight for conservation when wooing and placating ranchers and lumbermen failed. In 1910 when Congress denied the President the right to create forest reserves in six western states, Roosevelt told Pinchot to create or enlarge thirty-two existing forest reserves before he signed away his presidential power. By acting hastily, seventeen million acres of forest and mineral sites were brought under federal control. Western anticonservationists were outraged but also outwitted.[25]

From May 13–15, 1908, President Roosevelt hosted a Conference on Conservation at the White House, an impressive gathering of governors, congressmen, Supreme Court justices and men of influence who came to hear experts talk about wise resource management. The National Conference on Conservation was an important and historic meeting, the first of its kind since the inception of the nation. At the opening ceremonies Roosevelt spoke eloquently about the disastrous consequences of resource waste and exhorted all who cared about the nation's future to regard conservation as a sacred duty.

---

[24] Quoted in Nash, *The American Environment*, p. 45.
[25] Elmo R. Richardson, *The Politics of Conservation: Crusades and Controversies, 1897–1913* (Berkeley and Los Angeles, 1962).

Measured by what was said at the conference, conservationists could rejoice; subsequent congressional coolness to several of Roosevelt's conservation proposals, however, proved that publicity and good words were not sufficient to generate meaningful ongoing concern for the environment. When Roosevelt left office in 1908 conservation was a popular cause and conservationists could take pride in some important accomplishments. But government officials and the public at large needed to learn much more about conservation before they could grasp its critical importance for the future of the nation.

PRESERVATIONISTS VS. CONSERVATIONISTS

While conservationists won important victories during the Roosevelt era, a split in their ranks occurred that was never fully mended. Preservationists such as John Muir and Robert Underwood Johnson, both wilderness lovers and propagandists for a national park system, were disappointed that the concept of "wise use" had gained preeminence; what they had hoped for was legislation that would make selected forests, parks and scenes of primitive beauty permanently inviolable. Echoing the transcendentalists, Muir extolled the beauty and sacredness of wilderness: "Climb the mountains," he wrote. "Nature's peace will flow into you as the sunshine into the trees. The winds will blow their freshness into you, and the storms their energy, while cares will drop off like autumn leaves."[26] During 1890 the preservationists mounted a successful campaign to turn Yosemite Valley into a national park. In 1892, Muir and twenty-seven kindred spirits founded the Sierra Club in San Francisco, devoted to promoting wilderness values and winning popular support for their preservation goals.

Muir at first befriended Gifford Pinchot as a fellow preservationist but quickly became disillusioned. Pinchot had little use for simple nature appreciation; his view was that resources were meant for people's use and this meant commercial use if controlled by legal restraints. When the National Conservation Congress met, Pinchot saw to it that Muir and his fellow wilderness enthusiasts were not invited. Federal resource policy never wavered from the principle of utility and efficiency.

Preservationists and conservationists met head on after 1908 when the city of San Francisco asked the federal government to recede Hetch Hetchy Valley in Yosemite National Park so that it might be damned to create a much-needed city reservoir. For five years preser-

---

[26] Quoted in Nash, *Wilderness and the American Mind*, p. 128.

vationists fought to save the valley, but the opposition of senators and lobbyists wedded to the wise use idea was too strong to overcome. Hetch Hetchy was damned despite the valiant and well-orchestrated campaign of Muir, Johnson, and several sympathetic senators.

The fight to save the valley, however, gave substantial publicity to the wilderness ideal, offering preservationists strength for future legislative battles. In 1916 the National Park Service Act was passed, itself a vindication of Muir's ideas. By then preservation had a constituency and a momentum all its own, and thereafter developed quite separately from the conservation movement. In this sense, Hetch Hetchy was a beginning and not a defeat for those who valued nature undisturbed.

FROM T.R. TO THE T.V.A.

While preservation won modest recognition after Theodore Roosevelt left office, conservation grew in stature and gained support within federal and state bureaucracies. Harding and Coolidge were cool to the idea of extending federal protection to more and more resources because they believed steadfastly in the laissez-faire ideal. But Hoover, although equally conservative in this regard, strongly supported conservation measures, primarily because he believed that efficient resource management was good business, both for the nation and for private industry. Franklin D. Roosevelt, confronting an economic breakdown of catastrophic proportions, saw conservation as both intrinsically important and as part of a larger program of economic uplift. He enthusiastically endorsed the Civilian Conservation Corps and the Tennessee Valley Authority because they offered solutions to grave economic problems.

The period from the end of World War I to 1933 witnessed some significant conservation accomplishments.[27] The Forest Service increased its surveillance and established the first effective system of forest fire protection. The National Park System flourished. The Bureau of Fisheries and the Biological Survey began scientific investigation into wildlife conservation. Giant flood control programs were undertaken. The Bureau of Mines disseminated information that helped industries curb wasteful practices and the Department of Agriculture began the first systematic studies of soil erosion.

Substantial hostility to conservation principles and to too much

---

[27] Donald Swain, *Federal Conservation Policy, 1921–1933* (Berkeley and Los Angeles, 1963), *passim.*

federal intervention, however, persisted during this period. The Army Corps of Engineers, responsible for ensuring safe river navigation, disregarded sound conservation practices in conducting flood control. The Federal Power Commission, granted authority over federally owned hydroelectric sites in 1920, proved to be a handmaiden of the private utility companies. The devastation of fish and wildlife continued because federal agencies had limited power to protect these valuable resources. A combination of executive restraint, poor bureaucratic leadership and a continuing laissez-faire attitude toward the nation's resources, retarded the conservation program. Basic advances were made in the scientific realm, in technical studies and research, but exploitation of the environment continued.

Conservation gained fresh impetus when Franklin D. Roosevelt assumed the presidency in 1933. His two major conservation programs, the Civilian Conservation Corps and the Tennessee Valley Authority, placed the government directly in the forefront of the conservation movement. In contrast to Hoover who favored decentralized authority and voluntary cooperation, Roosevelt believed in strong federal leadership, something the nation desperately needed in a time of deep economic depression. His conservation program was part of the New Deal, a vast, federally guided effort to lift the nation out of poverty and misery.

The Civilian Conservation Corps, authorized by Congress in April, 1933, created an army of young men, many taken from relief rolls, who were assigned to various conservation tasks throughout the United States. Between 1933 and 1942 when the program ended, over 2,750,000 men living in 1,500 separate camps had engaged in conservation activities, the greatest concerted effort to improve the environment in United States history. The Corps planted one billion new trees; it fought fires, soil erosion, floods and agricultural pests; it helped improve drainage, build roads and recreational facilities, protect birds and animals, improve range conditions for livestock and reclaim arid land. While aiding the environment, the Corps gave people jobs and a new sense of purpose. By any yardstick, it was a brilliant success, the brainchild of an imaginative, pragmatic, conservation-minded president.

The Tennessee Valley Authority was another program Roosevelt energetically supported. The idea of building a series of dams and nitrate plants (for explosives) at Muscle Shoals on the Tennessee River originated in Woodrow Wilson's administration. At the end of World War I, work on the project was nearing completion and the government moved to lease the Muscle Shoals development to private electric power companies. When Henry Ford came forward as a prospective lessee, a Nebraska senator, George W. Norris, began a long and clever legislative fight to keep Muscle Shoals from becoming a Ford monopoly. Twice he won congressional colleagues to his side only to have his bills vetoed by Presidents Coolidge and Hoover. When Roosevelt entered office, however, he endorsed Norris's proposals. In April, 1933 the Tennessee Valley Authority was given Congressional approval and signed into law.

The Tennessee Valley Authority went far beyond the Muscle Shoals proposals in that it envisaged development of the *entire* Tennessee River Valley to rescue the region from poverty. The technique was to develop the whole valley with each part of the TVA project functioning within one system. Between 1933 and 1952 twenty new dams were constructed and five older dams were brought into use. These, in turn, helped rid the area of floods, make the river navigable for commercial vessels, and produce electricity for the entire region. The nitrate plants at Muscle Shoals began producing fertilizer; the Authority opened schools to teach farmers how to prevent erosion and how to develop good soil. The TVA culminated a half century of conservation thought. It employed the systems approach to resource use and sound scientific planning to promote wealth for human needs. As a comprehensive conservation program it has yet to be surpassed.

Serious objections were raised by opponents of the TVA. Some said it was socialistic, a threat to the free enterprise system. Manufacturers of electric power hated the fact that the government had a "yardstick" by which it could gauge how much it cost to produce units of electric power. Suits brought against the government during the 1930s failed to kill the TVA and it grew and prospered. Other regional projects were begun—the Grand Coulee Dam on the Columbia River in Washington, for example—but none approached the TVA in its total approach to regional conservation. The TVA and the CCC attest to the fact that conservation had finally become an issue of supreme national importance. It was no longer the cause of a few far-seeing citizens. In the popular mind it was identified with the preservation of a free and healthy society.

PAST AND PRESENT

In many ways the 1930s witnessed the high water mark of popular interest in conservation; the depression created a revulsion against laissez-faire capitalism and many people came to realize that America could not again be a land of abundance unless some form of economic planning or regulation was accepted. These insights, however, lost much of their force and significance when war broke out in 1941. Thereafter, national attention was focused on foreign rather than internal issues and interest in environmental problems waned. American resources were pressed into the service of war; the economy dramatically expanded and prosperity returned.

The society that emerged from World War II had neither the will nor the interest to revive the conservation crusade of the Progressive era and the depression decade. Industrial expansion and new technological achievements seemed to offer the possibility of a new frontier; atomic energy was hailed as the answer to man's search for power; new synthetics offered alternatives to using natural fibers; experiments with pesticides, fertilizers and new strains of seed held promise as means for providing food for growing populations.

It was not immediately apparent, however, that technological progress created grave new problems. Radiation and pesticide poisoning, pollution from automobiles, thermal and industrial pollution of lakes and rivers, noise, ugliness, all accompanied industrial expansion and the new prosperity. It was not until the 1950s that scientists began to realize the dimensions of environmental stress and not until the late 1960s that popular concern grew vocal.

Why Americans did not recognize these threats sooner, why they regarded conservation in an older, narrower sense, are difficult questions to answer. No doubt the traditional hostility to nature and wilderness was a factor. No doubt the belief that natural resources were in infinite supply shaped popular attitudes. The belief that science and technology were inherently good and that they held out all the promise that the frontier once held out also influenced American perceptions of environmental problems.

Perhaps more important than any of these factors was the illusion that the American stood in relation to nature as a master and conqueror. He had not yet learned that he too was part of nature, that he too was a biotic citizen of the earth. Taming an empty continent had created the fiction that nature was expendable, that it would forever bend and make accommodation. To a great extent it had done so in the past, but in the 1970s this was no longer possible. It was clearly time for reality to replace illusion and for the right lessons to be learned from the nation's past.

Suggestions for Further Reading

Newspapers and weekly news magazines report regularly on environmental problems and are a good place to begin to understand our contemporary ecological crisis. Also valuable are the annual reports of the U.S. Government, Council on Environmental Quality. Some recent books are: Barry Commoner, *The Closing Circle* (1971); Paul

Ehrlich, *The Population Bomb* (1970); Editors of Fortune, *The Environment* (1969); Gene Marine, *America the Raped* (1969); Garrett De Bell, ed., *The Environmental Handbook* (1970); and *Ecotactics: The Sierra Club Handbook for Environmental Activists* (1970). David W. Ehrenfeld's *Biological Conservation* (1970) is a highly readable study.

The history of American attitudes towards nature is discussed by Roderick Nash in *Wilderness and the American Mind* (1967), and, edited by Nash, *The American Environment: Readings in the History of Conservation* (1968). Also valuable are: Arthur K. Moore, *The Frontier Mind, a Cultural Analysis of Kentucky Frontiersmen* (1957); Russel B. Nye, "The American View of Nature" in *This Almost Chosen People* (1966); Hans Huth, *Nature and the American* (1957); and Arthur A. Ekirch, Jr., *Man and Nature in America* (1963). American perceptions of nature as expressed in literature are discussed in Leo Marx, *The Machine in the Garden: Technology and the Pastoral Ideal in America* (1964) and Henry Nash Smith, *Virgin Land: The American West as Symbol and Myth* (1950). On transcendentalism, see Perry Miller, ed., *The American Transcendentalists: Their Prose and Poetry* (1957) and Henry David Thoreau, *Walden* (many editions).

The waste of natural resources is discussed in Arthur Bining and Thomas Cochran, *The Rise of American Economic Life,* (4th ed., 1964). On the lumber industry see Richard G. Lillard, *The Great Forest* (1947).

The following books deal specifically with the conservation movement: U.S. Dept. of the Interior, *Highlights in the History of Forest and Related Natural Resource Conservation* (Bulletin 41, Revised, 1962); David Lowenthal, *George Perkins Marsh: Versatile Vermonter* (1958); Elmo Richardson, *The Politics of Conservation: Crusades and Controversies, 1897–1913* (1962); Donald Swain, *Federal Conservation Policy, 1921–1933* (1963); Henry Clepper, ed., *Origins of American Conservation* (1966); and J. Leonard Bates, "Fulfilling American Democracy: The Conservation Movement, 1907–1921," *Mississippi Valley Historical Review*, 44 (1957). Sidney Fine's *Laissez Faire and the General-Welfare State: A Study of Conflict in American Thought 1865–1901* (1967) is an analysis of the laissez-faire idea.

American Pastimes

7

Leisure, Recreation and Popular Culture in America

In America today leisure and its social implications are increasingly being discussed and analyzed. The reasons for this are not hard to find. A century ago the work week averaged sixty-six hours; in 1940 it dropped to forty-four hours and today it averages thirty-eight hours.[1] The decrease in time devoted to work is being accompanied by an increase in life expectancy which has risen from around forty-five years in 1900 to well over seventy years in 1974. It is now entirely

---

[1] Joseph S. Zeisel, "The Workweek in American Industry, 1850–1956," in Eric Larrabee and Rolf Meyersohn, eds., *Mass Leisure* (Glencoe, Illinois, 1958), pp. 145–153.

possible for men and women retiring at age sixty to contemplate a retirement which may last twenty to thirty or more years. When one adds to these factors the social effects of automation and increases in the standard of living it becomes clear that a leisure revolution is at hand.

Since the end of World War II Americans have been adjusting to large increases in leisure time. This new leisure is reflected in expenditures for recreation which have outpaced population growth for well over two decades. Between 1950 and 1969, for example, personal expenditures for recreation in the United States more than tripled, jumping from 11.1 billion dollars in 1950 to 36.3 billion in 1969. In 1950 13.9 million visits were made to national parks while 45.8 million visits were made in 1970. The number of Americans traveling abroad by plane increased from 1.3 million in 1960 to 4.4 million in 1969, a three-fold increase in only nine years. Not unexpectedly, spectator sports registered some of the most significant increases during these years. Americans paid 290 million dollars to gain admission to organized sports events in 1960; in 1970 they paid almost half a billion dollars to see their favorite teams play.[2]

As the time approaches when people will spend more time at leisure and recreation than at labor, some individuals have begun to ask how this situation will affect the way we live. At a recent symposium on leisure and human values the historian Arthur Schlesinger, Jr. asked, "What will man in advanced industrial society do with this new infusion of free time? Or rather, . . . what will this infusion of free time do to man?"[3] Schlesinger was asking an important and fundamental question, for never before in modern history had a society or civilization experienced the prospect of unlimited leisure for its ordinary citizens.

To put Schlesinger's question in perspective it is useful to know the way leisure was used and distributed in societies of the past. For centuries leisure was the sole domain of the wealthy and privileged classes. As a consequence aristocrats and the wealthy middle class educated themselves for a life of leisure. Not all their activities had artistic or intellectual merit, but the leisured aristocracy did cultivate poetry, painting, music and philosophy. They indulged in collecting valuable and beautiful items and for a long time were the only class to own and read books. Historically, a good deal of leisure was serious, purposeful activity, associated with higher learning and culture.

With the rise of industrial society and mass democracy, however, the definitions of leisure and leisure activities themselves changed. Leisure became more and more synonymous with time off from work, or time for rest and relaxation. It was less associated with creative work and inquiry and more with physical and emotional pleasure. Leisure in modern industrialized societies meant recreation, enjoying organized sports and commercial amusements, taking a break from work, or simply doing nothing. In this sense it lost its old meaning and became what it is today, free time.[4]

Modern American society has largely abandoned the old notion of

[2] U.S. Bureau of the Census, *Statistical Abstracts of the United States, 1971* (Washington, D.C., 1971), Recreation.

[3] Max Kaplan and Phillip Bosserman, eds., *Technology, Human Values and Leisure* (Nashville, N.Y., 1971), p. 75.

[4] For a discussion of leisure in history see Sebastian de Grazia, *Of Time, Work, and Leisure* (New York, 1964).

leisure as serious, creative activity. People are no longer trained in its meaning and use, wih the result that leisure presents new problems and challenges. In a sprightly and humorous book, *Super Spectator and the Electric Lilliputians* (1970), William O. Johnson describes how tens of millions of Americans—seventy million to be exact—watched the 1970 superbowl, a ritual engaged in by only slightly fewer Americans on other Sundays throughout the year. Implicit in Johnson's account is the question whether this is leisure well spent and whether Americans could and should be engaged in more active, intellectually rewarding pursuits.

It would be simplistic and unrealistic to suggest that a democratic society such as the United States should return, in the strict sense, to old notions of leisure and recreation. It is reasonable, however, to suggest that Americans can and should be educated to cultivate their leisure time in an intelligent and satisfying manner. Consider, for example, the active executive who retires to a "leisure village." Is he or she to spend ten or twenty years playing golf and cards? Does it make sense to encourage retirement at 60 or 55 when decades of free time stretch before potentially active and creative people. It will probably take some rethinking and personal reprogramming to get people to realize that what they do with their leisure is as important as what they do during their years of work.

LEISURE AND RECREATION IN COLONIAL AMERICA

It is not surprising that leisure, recreation and amusements meant something entirely different to our colonial forebears. They had to relax and seek what pleasures they could in a wilderness environment, devoid of any of the softening influences once found in England and Europe. In the early years no taverns dotted the landscape where warm friendship and food could be found. At Plymouth, Providence and Jamestown there were no theaters, traveling shows, musical societies or organized sports to take people's minds off the struggle for survival. Rich and poor, black and white toiled to build shelters and get crops into the ground. A pipe smoked after dinner, a dram of rum sipped near the fire might constitute the only moments of quiet leisure in a long day of wearying work. The Lord's day, to be sure, was set aside for prayer and contemplation but after church there were always home chores to perform. Boredom was probably unknown to the early Americans. When not working or praying, they hungered for sleep.

Had they had a good deal of spare time on their hands, however, it is unlikely that the early settlers would have been satisfied with idle amusements. In New England, where Puritanism was strong, and in the Middle Colonies, among Anglicans and Quakers, there was agreement that leisure was synonymous with idleness and that amusements were sinful and a waste of time. John Winthrop, the Governor of Massachusetts Bay, had early foresworn the temptations of idle recreation and he and his successors in office saw to it that the "City on a Hill" remained a colony of workers and worshippers. Strict bans were placed on Sabbath-day dancing, fiddling, card-playing, labor and travel. General laws forbade a host of innocent pastimes from bowling in the Commons to smoking in public places. Held up for particular scorn was Mixt or Promiscuous Dancing of Men and Women, even when performed at a celebration or wedding. The theater, too, was viewed as harmful to the morals of any good citizen. In Old England Puritan ministers had railed against the theater since the early 1600s. When the dour Cromwell overthrew the Stuarts in 1649 one of his first acts was to close all the theaters in London.

The Puritan distaste for indulgence in recreation had social and economic roots in the movement for religious reform begun in fourteenth-century England. Religious reformers and dissenters, usually from the lower strata of society, resented the wealth and pleasure-seeking which they perceived in the hierarchy of the Roman Catholic Church. This resentment found expression in English Lollardy, a fourteenth-century peasant movement aimed at cleansing and purifying the church. It found expression in continental Protestantism which gained support among the masses by condemning the wealth and ostentation of the Catholic Church. The Puritans also "were a party of reform, condemning the worldliness of the [Anglican] Church and damning as sinful many of the pleasures that the Church countenanced. They resented the amusements of the more wealthy, leisured classes, making a moral issue of their discontent."[5]

Class hostility was one of the factors that shaped Puritan theology and the Puritan's stern moral code. The heirs of Calvin stressed self-discipline, spiritual striving, and acceptance of Biblical authority. To seek pleasure for its own sake was a turning away from God; to spend time in idle amusement was a form of vanity and self-involvement. The Puritans, by no means, eschewed a good meal, meaningful conversation, or enjoyment of sex within marriage. They aspired, however, to moderation in all things and a constant awareness of God.

Puritan dislike of entertainment and amusements, however, could not stifle the human need for recreation and relaxation. In colonial America this need manifested itself in a variety of ways. Throughout

---

[5] Foster Rhea Dulles, *America Learns to Play* (New York, 1940), p. 9.

New England Sunday church meetings provided opportunities for people to meet their neighbors and exchange news and gossip. Mid-week lectures and sermons drew large audiences who came to break the monotony of constant work and rural isolation. Home amusements also provided New Englanders with moments of pleasant recreation. Hymn singing was popular. Books were often read aloud. Sewing, baking and home decorating had both the qualities of work and play. Puritan New England was not as barren of enjoyment and entertainment as was once assumed.

Although Puritanism influenced popular attitudes towards leisure and recreation for many generations, there were many non-Puritans in colonial America who did not share the Puritan's restricted point of view. In the Middle Colonies, the South and on the frontier, the Puritan influence was never strong. As more non-Puritans arrived in New England after 1660 more permissive attitudes emerged. By 1700 the colonists shared a number of common pastimes and amusements which were beginning to assume a distinctly American character.

As one might expect in a rural society many forms of amusement centered on outdoor games and activities. Fishing and hunting were popular in all the colonies, aided by the fact that even a poor shot could bag abundant game. Fishing required only a pole, a line and a hook, and the streams surrounding even the largest settlements were full of tasty species. Other outdoor recreation included skating, sleighing, picnicking, boating, and exploring on foot. With the wilderness virtually at the colonial settler's doorstep, it is easy to see how the outdoors beckoned to be tamed and explored.

Nature also provided the backdrop for the first colonial sports. Most of these were imported from Old England and gradually adapted to the American environment. Bear-baiting and cock-fighting were popular at all levels of society although they were periodically condemned and outlawed. Bowling was a favorite sport, thriving on the fact that in England it was prohibited to the "meaner sort of people." Stoolball, a form of croquet in which a ball was knocked from wicket to wicket was also popular, as was a crude form of football. Horse racing too was enjoyed, especially in the South and frontier areas. Whatever sports were performed were played informally and spontaneously. There were no teams, no uniforms and no paying spectators in colonial days.

Among indoor amusements dancing was perhaps the most popular form of recreation. Frowned on in New England, it found favor in the Middle Colonies and the South where the aristocracy had the leisure to practice and perfect their technique. Dancing masters were common in Virginia, Maryland and South Carolina in the early 1700s. Books on dancing made their appearance around the same time.

Philip Fithian who visited Robert Carter's plantation in 1773 left this description of his host's interest in dancing.

> After breakfast we all retired into the dancing room, and after the scholars had their lesson singly round, Mr. Christian very politely requested me to step a minuet; I excused myself however but signified my peculiar pleasure in the accuracy of their performance. There were several minuets danced with great ease and propriety, after which the whole company joined in country-dances. . . .[6]

Other, poorer households throughout the South loved dancing as much as the Carters. Contemporary descriptions of fiddling and dancing among poor whites and blacks indicate that dancing was one of the most popular forms of recreation in the tobacco and cotton states.

With the rise of cities in the eighteenth century patterns of leisure and recreation became institutionalized and took on a more sophisticated quality. In cities and towns the tavern became a gathering place where good conversation, drink and the availability of newspapers made up for anything the food might lack. Here one could find merchants gathering to discuss business and politics. A session of local government might be sitting in one of the tavern's large public rooms. Card playing, gambling, drinking and an occasional performance by a magician or strolling player was a normal part of tavern life. Taverns "served as a focal point for all comers and frequently were the places of meetings for civic bodies, committees, and councils of one kind and another. On muster days the militia converged on the nearest tavern, and on election days the tavern was the busiest spot in the community."[7] Taverns and coffee houses were also popular places for "auctions, real estate sales and transfers, and a variety of other business transactions."[8]

With their large populations and social cohesion, towns and cities helped broaden the possibilities for entertainment and recreation. By the early eighteenth-century, for example, music-making became a part of urban life. Choral groups formed in most colonial cities. Orchestral concerts made their appearance although the first paid orchestra, the St. Cecilia Society of Charlestown, was not founded until 1762. At Philadelphia "a talented young poet and musician, Francis Hopkinson, gathered about him a group of musicians who frequently

---

[6] Louis B. Wright, *Life in Colonial America* (New York, 1965), p. 193.
[7] Louis B. Wright, *The Cultural Life of the American Colonies, 1607–1763* (New York, 1962), p. 248.
[8] *Ibid.*

met to play a variety of instruments. . . . Peter Kalm, the Swedish botanist, in Philadelphia on Christmas Day, 1750, was impressed by the music heard in the Roman Catholic church there."[9] Music was only part of the variegated leisure activity of the new urban centers. Debating societies, literary clubs and philosophical associations came into existence. The Tuesday Club of Annapolis, Maryland, founded in 1745, emphasized "good conversation, raillery, good drink, and good fellowship," providing a model for other all-male clubs forming throughout the colonies. Subscription libraries also provided a new channel for leisure by promoting reading and research. By 1750 members of the urban elite were beginning to develop a taste for new entertainment and amusements.

The theater, however, had to overcome major obstacles before gaining acceptance in colonial America. As we have seen the Puritans condemned the theater and held all plays and actors in low repute. As late as 1750 the Massachusetts legislature reaffirmed its ban on "public stage-plays, interludes, and other theatrical entertainments, which not only occasion great and unnecessary expenses, and discourage industry and frugality, but likewise tend generally to increase immorality, impiety, and a contempt for religion."[10] In 1700 the Pennsylvania Assembly legislated against "stage-plays, masks, revels," and rude and riotous sports, although the English government refused to prohibit them.[11] The love for drama, however, could not be quieted by simple statute. Strolling players began to make their appearance in the various port cities shortly after 1700. Williamsburg had a rudimentary theater by 1718 and Charlestown officials "permitted the use of the Court House for the performance of plays in the 1730s before the opening of its first theater, in Dock Street, in 1736."[12] By the 1740s dramatic performances were still not commonplace but at least they were being tolerated in American cities outside of New England.

The urban upper classes were forced by the scarcity of dramatic performances to develop broad theatrical tastes. Lewis Hallam, whose company arrived at Williamsburg in 1752, performed Shakespeare's *Merchant of Venice,* Lillo's *The London Merchant,* Moore's *The Gamester,* Farquhar's *The Beaux' Strategem,* Cibber's *The Careless Husband,* Gay's *The Beggar's Opera* and many other Restoration plays.[13] The Hallam company's twenty-four play repertory, enormously large by today's standards, was typical for touring companies, which often per-

---

[9] *Ibid.,* p. 195.
[10] Dulles, *America Learns to Play,* p. 49.
[11] Wright, *The Cultural Life,* p. 179.
[12] *Ibid.,* p. 181.
[13] *Ibid.,* p. 182.

formed a new play every other night. Catholic taste in drama, however, sometimes masked a total lack of discrimination. Some urban sophisticates applauded the most trite comedies and plodding tragedies. Some ventured off to see the Punch and Judy shows, visiting manageries (elephants, camels, lions) and displays of mechanical inventions. That Puritan enemy of entertainments, Samuel Seward, noted in his diary that on May 12, 1714, "a large Dromedary seven foot high, and 12 foot long, taken from the Turks at the Siege of Vienna," was to be sold.[14] One wonders did Seward circulate quietly among the crowd and observe the bidding?

The last half-century of colonial life continued to witness a thawing of the rigid Puritan attitude toward amusements and recreation. By no means did the Puritan influence disappear, but it lost some of its appeal and meaning to the increasing number of non-Puritans and to Protestants of a less doctrinaire frame of mind. Leisure and amusements were still condemned. They were still restricted within fairly narrow limits. Yet the desire for recreation was asserting itself on many fronts and when Americans threw off the colonial yoke, they also abandoned some of their traditional notions concerning the sinfulness of pleasure, recreation and entertainment.

ENTERTAINMENT FOR THE DEMOCRACY

The first half of the nineteenth century witnessed important changes in many areas of American political and social life. The phrases of equality and opportunity, which filled the rhetoric of the early national years, began to be taken more and more seriously. Educators felt the demand for free public schools. Politicians were told to make the ballot box more accessible. Capitalist entrepreneurs were forced to recognize the principles of competition and economic opportunity. Everywhere the new and sometimes crude democracy of America seemed to be asserting itself. It was only a matter of time before leisure and recreation would respond to the democratic impulse.

These years were also years of dynamic economic growth. New cities were rising on the frontier. Canals were being dug; steamboats made their appearance. By the 1840s the infant railroad was already revolutionizing American transport. New factories, now run by steam, also heralded a new age. These forces altered social conditions and with them traditional patterns of leisure and amusement.

Visitors to America commented on the way the twin forces of

---

[14] Dulles, *America Learns to Play*, p. 39.

democracy and industrialization influenced American recreation. Sir Charles Lyell thought Americans were too busy to enjoy their free time and observed that "we seemed to have been in a country where all, whether rich or poor, were laboring from morning till night, without ever indulging in a holiday."[15] Frances Trollope wrote on several occasions about the lack of American amusements and agreed with her contemporary, Mrs. Basil Hall, that Americans "are so constantly at work with real business, that they have no time to think of little minor things that constitute refinement." One European visitor after another painted a picture of an America devoid of pleasure or amusement. With considerable exaggeration an English cynic described New York:

> But how quiet the streets are! Are there no itinerant bands; no wind or stringed instruments? No, not one. By day are there no Punches, Fantocinne, Dancing Dogs, Jugglers, Conjurers, Orchestrinas, or even Barrel-organs? No, not one. Yes, I remember one, one barrel-organ and a dancing monkey, sportive by nature, but fast fading into a dull, lumpish monkey of the Utilitarian school. Beyond that, nothing lively; no, not so much as a white mouse in a twirling cage.[16]

Doubtless there was some truth in these observations. Americans were chasing the dollar during years of fast-paced development. They were more interested in markets, buildings, corporations and railroads than in museums, theaters, opera or public parks. Yet to suggest that during the early nineteenth century recreation and the love of amusement disappeared in the scramble for riches is to overemphasize one tendency in American society. Refined and sophisticated leisure may have been rare, but love of entertainment was very much in evidence in republican America.

In the developing urban centers the theater continued to provide one channel for entertainment, mirroring many of the changes occurring throughout the society at large. Once an institution for the urban elite, the theater now became an institution for all to attend and enjoy. In major cities theaters were erected which could accomodate several thousand people. Admission prices, ranging from twelve cents to two dollars made an evening's entertainment within every person's reach. Theaters began offering a great variety of programs which focused more and more on subjects which appealed to the great mass

---

[15] *Ibid.*, p. 87.
[16] *Ibid.*, p. 88.

of citizens. A crude star system emerged which focused people's attention as much on personality and flamboyance as on solid performance.

The average citizen continued to enjoy Shakespeare and some of the colonial favorites but wanted a dash of excitement and spectacle to round off an evening's entertainment. Equestrian dramas featuring troops of live horses enlivened many a play with a dull plot. Elaborate sets and machines to raise and lower actors, simulate changes of locale and climate and allow the hero or heroine suddenly to appear or disappear were all used to good effect. Several theaters offered entertainment between acts of a scheduled play or topped off a serious drama with short skits, dancing or singing. An uneducated and frequently illiterate audience hungered for anything novel, exciting and edifying. "The program at the Franklin Theatre on one occasion included Chemistry, French plays, Magic, Mesmeric Clairvoyance, beautiful and admired Astronomical Diagrams, and Diaphanous Tableaux—a selection clearly dsigned to meet all tastes, including the educational."[17]

As the American theater matured it ceased simply to reflect the tastes of the multitude. Playwrights and directors began to instruct and educate the audiences as well as entertain. Many Americans who never cared about the evils of slavery, for example, were moved to tears by a performance of *Uncle Tom's Cabin* in the 1850s. Eager but illiterate townsmen on the frontier had a chance to see Shakespeare performed, even if the performance was by some second-rate touring company. The theater became a vehicle for moral reform as in the case of *The Drunkard,* a temperance play which had a long and successful run at the Boston Museum theater in the 1840s. The theater also helped elevate common tastes by exposing people to new forms of entertainment. Americans began to appreciate the ballet after Fanny Elssler made her triumphant tour in the 1840s.

The urban masses that flocked to the new theaters brought their bad manners and zeal for enjoyment with them. Mrs. Trollope who observed one such audience in the 1830s described them as a motley group, who spat incessantly, removed their coats and smelled of onions and whiskey.

> The bearing and attitudes of the men are perfectly indescribable; the heels thrown higher than the head, the entire rear of the person presented to the audience, the whole length supported on the benches, are among the varieties that these ex-

---

[17] *Ibid.,* p. 119.

quisite posture-masters exhibit. The noises, too, were perpetual, and of the most unpleasant kind; the applause is expressed by cries and thumping with the feet, instead of clapping; and when a patriotic fit seized them, and 'Yankee Doodle' was called for, every man seemed to think his reputation as a citizen depended on the noise he made.[18]

On at least one occasion such raucous behavior resulted in full-scale riot. In 1849 a New York mob stormed the theater of a famous British actor, intent on proving that their favorite, an American rival, was a better performer. Troops were called to restore order and in the ensuing battle twenty-two persons were killed.

The theater gained and suffered from its new-found popularity. The crude variety shows and coarse entertainments gained favor among the urban masses but alienated the cultivated and well-to-do class who formerly supported dramatic endeavor. The theater expanded its offering of entertainment but forced serious drama into a more secluded niche. By encouraging the star system producers made fast money but downgraded the concept of excellence in ensemble work. The theater, however, was only responding to the prevailing forces of social change. To become a vehicle for popular entertainment it had to experiment and respond to the tastes of its new audience. It temporarily lost the support of the urban elite but it found warm approval in the emerging democracy.

Although much more popular and diverse than during colonial times, the theater could not answer all the entertainment needs of the growing urban populace. As a result new forms of entertainment began to appear, as businessmen, during the middle decades of the nineteenth century, recognized the money-making opportunities in urban amusement. No individual more shrewdly capitalized on the hunger for entertainment than Phineas T. Barnum. He provided city-dwellers with a dazzling variety of curiosities, amusements, spectacles and entertainment only rivaled in later years by the circus which bore his name.

Barnum's principal entertainment center was the American Museum, situated in New York City in the 1840s. There one could see jugglers, acrobats, rope-dancers and magicians. A gaping audience watched elephants and trained animals, a 600-pound giant and a midget known as General Tom Thumb. Exhibits included mechanical dioramas depicting scenes from North America, a wax works and an ingenious working model of Niagara Falls. Into his museum, Barnum

---

[18] Marshall B. Davidson, *Life in America*, vol. II (Boston, 1951), p. 20.

crammed any act or device that would excite wonder and amusement. His intent was to make money while catering to popular tastes. "No one did more to promote the leveling influence of popular recreation."[19]

Barnum also pioneered as a promoter and impresario. He organized a tour for Jenny Lind, a Swedish soprano who captured American hearts in the 1850s. Skillfully advertising the "Swedish Nightingale" in newspapers and broadsides, Barnum created a groundswell of popular acclaim which followed the singer wherever she performed. Thousands attended her first recital at Castle Garden in New York on September 11, 1850, some paying as much as $200 to see and hear the unknown singer. Encouraged by this success Barnum took Jenny Lind on a whirlwind tour that earned the singer large sums and Barnum over half a million dollars. Barnum's genius for promotion moved easily from the sublime to the ridiculous. On one occasion he offered New Yorkers a free buffalo hunt in New Jersey, first making sure he leased all the Hudson ferries for that particular day. Thousands flocked to Hoboken for the wild-west event and Barnum made his own killing by collecting thousands of dollars in ferry receipts.

In the 1840s and 1850s entertainment centers modeled after the American Museum sprouted in city after city. Traveling exhibits also made their appearance during these years. These traveling shows were first modest affairs which gradually took on the characteristics of the modern circus. They included acrobatics, performing animals, fancy horseback riding and the usual curiosities and freak shows. "By the 1830s some thirty rolling shows were regularly touring the country. Buckley and Wick had eight wagons, forty horses, thirty-five performers, and a tent holding eight hundred people. Soon the Zoölogical Institute advertised forty-seven carriages and wagons, one hundred and twenty matched gray horses, fourteen musicians, and sixty performers."[20] Once Barnum decided to transform the American Museum into a full-scale circus, however, the full potential of the traveling show emerged. In the 1850s he created the Grand Colossal Museum and Menagerie featuring spectacular acts and elephants from Ceylon. Decades later he allied with other circus promoters, most notably James A. Bailey, whose skill as a circus man outshone even Phineas T. The great days of the circus followed these mergers and in the 1880s and 1890s Barnum and Bailey's Greatest Show on Earth became a household word. By this time scores of other circuses traveled around

---

[19] Dulles, *America Learns to Play*, p. 123.
[20] *Ibid.*, p. 133.

the country bringing to out-of-the-way towns and villages the dazzling parades, animal spectacles and displays of courage in the center ring.

Commercial amusements like the theater and the circus provided an outlet for urban dwellers with few alternatives for recreation. Cities built for commerce had few parks or playing fields. The anonymity of city life made it all but impossible for people to participate in neighborly play. For this reason games and sports in urban communities also developed along commercial lines. People watched more and participated less and the age of spectator sports slowly dawned.

If the days of baseball and football still lay in the future, there were, nevertheless, exciting sports to watch in pre-Civil War America. One of the most popular was horse racing, which drew crowds ranging from twenty to fifty thousand spectators as early as the 1820s. Horseracing had always been popular in a nation where horses provided power and transportation. Early horse races, however, were amateurish affairs with improvised tracks and part-time jockeys. The horse races run after the 1820s, however, were fully professional events, promoted by men with good business sense. Tracks were well-maintained. Celebrated horses and jockeys competed for large purses. Races were advertised in advance and free transportation to the track was occasionally provided. The only unsavory aspect of horse-racing was the large numbers of gamblers who circulated in every racing crowd.

Horse-racing had that quality of competition and excitement which pleased Jacksonian America. Cities had their favorite horses which competed with one another. Intersectional rivalry expressed itself in regional favorites and North-South competition. Horse-racing was also a democratic sport where rich and poor mingled with easy familiarity. The track had an air of ritual and provided a setting for conspicuous display. In the South racing events were great social outings where the aristocracy could watch their horses as well as each other.

Prize fighting was also popular in nineteenth-century cities. Much more brutal than the sport as we know it today, prize-fighting had few rules or safeguards to prevent injury and even death. For this reason boxing was frequently outlawed. Fights were held outside city jurisdictions to prevent legal intervention. Secrecy and subterfuge were often employed. "When Yankee Sullivan and Tom Hyer fought their championship bout in 1849, they had to hold it in the woods on Maryland's Western Shore, having been driven away from the chosen site. . . . "[21] Notwithstanding legal obstacles and moral disapproval,

---

[21] *Ibid.*, p. 145.

boxing maintained an ardent, if somewhat coarse, following. It was not unusual for ten or fifteen thousand people to gather for a boxing "exhibition," so titled to keep the sheriff away.

Two other sports enjoyed popular support in pre-Civil War America. One was foot racing, which drew large crowds to cheer on their favorites "peds." Foot races were popular because they were easy to see and enjoy. City streets provided the first race courses until formal tracks were built so that promoters could collect admission fees. While offering little in the way of spectacle, foot-racing had an intimacy and immediacy that other sports lacked. Each racer had his special colors and local following. Each relied solely on his own strength and swiftness. Foot races of five and ten miles were common during these years. Prizes ranged from one hundred to one thousand dollars for a particularly strenuous race.

The other popular sport was boat racing, made possible by the many fine rivers and harbors lying along the nation's cities. Sailing vessels, representing clubs and boating associations, competed regularly. Regattas became a common feature of Sunday entertainment. In 1824 a boat-race in New York harbor for a one thousand dollar purse attracted some 5,000 people. Boat-racing was popular in a day when waterfronts were still accessible and relatively uncluttered and unpolluted. City dwellers enjoyed the opportunity to escape cramped dwellings and shops and to enjoy fresh air and graceful competition.

THE RURAL SCENE

The commercial influences transforming urban recreation in nineteenth century America were at work elsewhere in the United States. The age of steam introduced paddle-wheelers to the interior rivers bringing with them traveling minstrel shows, variety acts and gambling which soon became a part of river life. In the Far West, in frontier towns, the tavern owner and proprietor of the hurdy-gurdy house provided miners and cowboys with drink, women and gambling. Only in farming regions, where men and women continued to invent their own forms of recreation, was the commercial influence held in check. Without theaters, amusement centers and spectator sports, country people were forced to rely on imagination and ingenuity to devise ways to fill their leisure hours.

We get some idea of the variety of rural pastimes from paintings which record the life of the yeoman at play. There is Eastman Johnson's painting *Corn Husking* (1860), depicting men and women working and chatting as they prepare corn for storage and sale. There is John Stokes' painting *Wedding in the Big Smoky Mountains* (1872), a riotous scene of country-folk celebrating with all the gusto at their command. There is John Ehninger's *Turkey Shoot* (1879), a canvas which expresses the delight and seriousness with which communities took marksmen events. There are George Caleb Bingham's scenes of life on the Mississippi—men enjoying the quiet of the river, men playing cards on a keelboat (*Raftsmen Playing Cards*, 1851), men passing time in contemplation and play.

The artists who painted rural America recorded scene after scene of people enjoying moments of leisure. We have paintings of children fishing, families picnicking, whole communities celebrating the Fourth of July. We have paintings of duck shoots, beef shoots, buffalo hunts and women picking flowers and boys playing ball. We also have pictorial records of the religious camp meetings which were popular in rural areas and on the frontier. A. Rider's *Camp Meeting*, for example, shows us a circuit preacher with arms outstretched imploring his audience to repent and be saved. Women wail and shout. One faints into a man's arms. Scores of listeners react to the speaker's emotional appeal. These camp meetings were a regular feature of rural life throughout the nineteenth century. Isolation in the wilderness accentuated people's desire for human contact and spiritual sharing.

Rural leisure provided satisfactions increasingly denied city inhabitants. Farmers could still fish and hunt relatively near their homes. They knew their neighbors well enough to join in spontaneous play. Recreation was often tied to some community event such as a barbecue, election or house-raising, which gave people a sense of belonging and participation. Although farmers worked hard and long, sometimes fourteen hours a day, they still found time to rest, socialize and enjoy their free time. With leisure at a premium, attending a fair, shooting at a mark, or simply reclining under a tree took on special meaning and provided many moments of pleasant recreation.

THE PLEASURES OF THE PRINTED AND SPOKEN WORD

As literacy became widespread in nineteenth-century America, more people than ever before turned to books, newspapers and magazines to fill their leisure hours. Reading as a leisure activity had always been popular in the United States, but the limited numbers of books and bookstores in colonial times made it impossible for a truly mass reading audience to develop. All this changed dramatically in the 1820s and 1830s as new techniques of printing books were introduced. New paper-making processes, new book-binding machines, and more efficient methods of printing turned publishing into a major industry,

capable of producing millions of inexpensive books and magazines.
Bookselling also became much more widespread. By 1860 "there were ·
575 magazines published in the United States, 372 daily newspapers,
2,971 weekly newspapers, and ten million dollars' worth of books
each year."[22]

The revolution in publishing made it possible for businessmen to
reach a large audience and charge very little for their product. Bound
books sold for as little as fifty cents. Newspapers carried literary supplements—actually book installments—which could be purchased for
as little as ten cents. The potential of reaching a vast audience encouraged a new class of writers who wrote exclusively for a popular
audience. Before long thousands of novels, short stories, and essays
came gushing from the printing presses.

One popular form of fiction enjoyed after 1830 was the domestic
novel, a literary form which focused attention on personal and family
life. Written primarily by women, these works taught females how to
cope with the burdens of marriage, child rearing and living within
"woman's sphere." They generally had standard plots such as "The
Domestic Tragedy Plot [dealing] with erring husbands, broken homes,
tragic illnesses, and adversity."[23] They had stock characters—"the
other woman; the loose woman; the handsome seducer; the sick
husband; the crude husband; the weak husband; . . . the old sweet-
heart, the dying child."[24] Domestic novels were full of sentimental-
ism and moral teaching. Authors worked and reworked the themes
of suffering and renunciation, struggling against great odds, the
triumph of reason and virtue over passion, and trusting in God's
wisdom.

Many prolific, albeit prosaic authors, made fortunes from writing
domestic novels. First edition runs of twenty to fifty thousand copies
were common. Mrs. Emma Southworth's first novel, *Retribution,* sold
200,000 copies and she wrote sixty-one others before she died. In
the 1870s and 1880s Laura Jean Libbey cranked out novels of girls
fighting off seducers and marrying only for "true" love whose sales
exceeded sixteen million copies during her lifetime. None of these
novels were literary masterpieces, yet in their time they were im-
mensely popular. Perhaps their popularity derived from the fact that
they allowed people to read about love and sex and yet remain within
the framework of conventional morality.

Although domestic novels had millions of readers in mid-nine-

---

[22] Russel Nye, *The Unembarrassed Muse: The Popular Arts in America*
(New York, 1970), p. 24.
[23] *Ibid.,* p. 27.
[24] *Ibid.*

teenth-century America, there were other works which also appealed to a wide audience. Timothy Arthur's *Ten Nights in a Barroom; and What I Saw There* (1854) was a didactic, moral tale which emphasized the horrors of drink and the benefits of abstinence. Harriet Beecher Stowe's *Uncle Tom's Cabin* (1852) was an instant best seller that did much to make antislavery sentiment popular. Religious novels, action novels, western stories, historical romances, travel narratives, exposes and patriotic tales also enjoyed success during the post-Civil War era. *Ben Hur: A Tale of the Christ,* which appeared in 1880, was enormously successful and still remains popular today.

Reading as a leisure activity was greatly stimulated by the mass production of books. It was also popularized by the appearance of hundreds of cheap and easy-to-read magazines which appeared in the post-Civil War decades. The 700 periodicals published in 1865 increased to 3,300 in 1885.[25] Inexpensive printing techniques reduced prices thereby increasing circulation. One New York magazine, the *New York Weekly* boasted a circulation of 350,000 in 1874. In the 1870s The House of Harper had two magazines with circulations over 100,000. Leading the list in the next decade was the *Ladies' Home Journal* with a circulation well in excess of 250,000. Such different magazines as the *Police Gazette* and the *American Agriculturalist* also had sales in the area of 150,000 copies.

The successes of new magazines during the post-Civil War decades proved that publishers correctly judged the public's desire for entertainment and information in an inexpensive format. Magazines of every description appeared on the market, targeted for different tastes and educational levels. *The Nation* appeared in 1865 followed by *Harper's Bazaar* in 1867. *Scribner's Monthly, Popular Science Monthly* and *Puck* also appeared during these years. After 1880 *The Ladies' Home Journal, McCall's Magazine, McClure's Magazine, The National Geographic Magazine* and the *Saturday Evening Post* began their steady climb to popularity. Magazines were exciting and timely and cheap enough for everyone to read. They were illustrated with engravings, color plates and cartoons which made them attractive and pleasant to browse through. The new periodicals served as the nineteenth century equivalent of our radio, television and motion pictures. Along with novels, they turned reading into a universal pastime.

Despite the successes of books and magazines, public speaking retained its influence and popularity in nineteenth-century America. Listening to people speak, preach, lecture and debate was a traditional

---

[25] Frank L. Mott, *A History of American Magazines, 1865–1885,* vol. III (Cambridge, Mass., 1938), p. 5.

form of amusement. It lost none of its appeal as the nation grew and expanded.

The nineteenth century was a great age of public speaking, largely because there was no radio or television to provide entertainment and amusement. At camp meetings, Sunday services, campaign pic‐ nics, and political debates, men and women spoke forcefully and elo‐ quently on the issues of the day. Skilled orators prided themselves on their ability to convince hostile audiences of the validity of some par‐ ticular cause. Wendell Phillips, Theodore Weld, the Grimké Sisters, Frederick Douglass and William Lloyd Garrison spoke for the aboli‐ tionist movement. John C. Calhoun was the orator most identified with slavery and the southern cause. Ralph Waldo Emerson, Henry David Thoreau, Horace Greeley and Daniel Webster also spoke out on the great issues of their times.

After 1820, when the movement for educating the common man gained momentum, public lectures provided a unique channel for education and entertainment. One man who understood their po‐ tential was Josiah Holbrook, a Yale graduate who established learning centers for workers interested in expanding their cultural horizons. Holbrook's lyceum, begun at Millbury, Connecticut in 1826, attracted large audiences who came to hear lectures on everything from magne‐ tism to Shakespeare. The Millbury Lyceum was so successful that other lyceums were quickly founded. "So swiftly did the lyceums spread that eight years later, there were three thousand town lyceums, scores of county lyceums, and eight state lyceums, culminating for a time in a national lyceum in New York City. Massachusetts alone had 137 in 1839 with an average annual attendance of 33,000. Lyceums existed in practically every state in the Union, in frontier towns and Southern cities. . . ."[26]

The public lecture was the heart of the lyceum movement. For a small fee, citizens could attend lectures, suited to popular taste, which introduced them to the latest developments in science, mathematics, geography or medicine. They could hear skilled orators speak on the great issues of the day: abolitionism, pacifism, feminism, transcen‐ dentalism, socialism, prison reform or the temperance crusade. Ralph Waldo Emerson's lecture, "The American Scholar," was heard in hun‐ dreds of lyceums. Horace Greeley's utopian ideas were spread by repeated appearances on the lyceum circuit. Lyceums reaffirmed the idea that everyone in a democracy was entitled to be educated and

---

[26] Harvey Wish, *Society and Thought in Early America*, vol. I (New York, 1950), p. 445.

informed. They were the precursors of many of our twentieth-century adult education programs.

Although the lyceums did not survive the Civil War, destroyed in part by concessions to entertainment and by the challenge of cheap magazines and newspapers, public lectures continued to play an important role in popular education. They were incorporated most effectively into the chautauquas that flourished in America after 1880.

The Chautauqua Movement was a system of popular adult education that took its name from a summer school program begun at Lake Chautauqua, New York in 1874. Begun to upgrade the education of Sunday school teachers, the chautauqua gradually developed into a full-scale program to enrich the cultural lives of ordinary citizens. The New York Chautauqua, for example, combined conferences, classes, lectures, physical recreation, musical and dramatic performances in a potpourri of education, entertainment and amusement. Participants studied foreign languages, classical and modern literature, speech, theology, theater and library science. They were entertained with operas, poetry readings, square dances and orchestral performances. Well-known persons spoke on a great variety of social, political, economic and religious topics. In 1909, at the height of its popularity, the New York Chautauqua offered 188 courses attended by 2,300 people. Thousands of nonstudents also attended chautauqua lectures and public events.

The chautauqua idea proved so successful that it was quickly introduced in communities throughout the United States. The Chautauqua Institution, as it was called after 1902, coordinated the activities of local chautauquas and provided them with ideas for courses and public speakers. A program of home reading was introduced, and a magazine, the *Chautauquan*, was published to stimulate education and discussion in the home. Local chautauquas expanded their activities to include dramatic and musical performances, and the creation of literary societies and all kinds of clubs. By 1920 there were few Americans who had not attended or heard of a chautaugua program.

The advent of radio and motion pictures in the 1920s, however, had an eroding effect on the popularity of the chautauquas. The radio brought the spoken word into the home and entertained millions at the flick of a switch. A revolutionary entertainment medium, motion pictures, captured a good part of the old-time chautauqua audience. Chautauquas themselves were corrupted by traveling showmen who traded on their name to bring circus entertainment and evangelical tent shows to small towns and villages. For these reasons the chautauquas gradually died out, having fulfilled for four decades an important education-recreational function. The concept of adult education, extension courses, in-service courses, home-reading programs and dissemination of culture which they pioneered, was taken over in the twentieth century by other institutions, most notably colleges and universities.

BASEBALL, BICYCLES AND BURLESQUE

An America that was enjoying dime novels, magazines, lyceums and chautauquas was an America eager to experiment with new forms of leisure and recreation. This eagerness seemed to increase as the nation became more urbanized and industrialized. "Who will teach us incessant workers," asked Horace Greeley, "how to achieve leisure and enjoy it?" How, indeed, asked other Americans, was a large population, bound to machines and crowded in tenements, to find meaningful recreation amidst the steel and concrete of the expanding city? Answers to these questions were provided in the late nineteenth century by businessmen who grasped the profit potential in leisure and play. They were provided, too, by an urban population ready to try any new idea or invention that would give them fun and relaxation. For these reasons the American recreational scene became more complex and diversified as the nineteenth century drew to a close. This was an era of baseball, bicycles and burlesque.

In the "Gilded Age," as in past eras, class and status shaped recreational choice. The wealthy had their distinctive pastimes and amusements, which became more extravagant and ostentatious with each passing year. Opera became the entertainment of the rich, and opera houses, temples of conspicuous display. The urban aristocracy founded museums, orchestral societies, and country clubs, they traveled to resorts and spas, took the grand tour in Europe, and frequented the finest restaurants and hotels. The balls and banquets of the urban rich, however, told more about the tastes and style of this class than any other activity. "The new plutocracy gave dinners at which cigarettes were wrapped in hundred dollar bills."[27] For the Bradley Martin ball in 1879 "the ball-room of the Waldorf-Astoria Hotel was converted into a replica of Versailles and sumptuously decorated with rare tapestries and beautiful flowers."[28] One social event, a horseback dinner, featured displays of horsemanship right within the dining room itself! These events were reported in great detail on the "society pages" of newspapers and magazines.

---

[27] Dulles, *America Learns to Play*, p. 233.
[28] *Ibid.*

While the upper tenth remained in their isolated world, the urban masses continued to decide the direction of popular amusement and recreation. For some time, as we have seen, Americans were in the process of adapting to the circumstances of city life. The lack of parks, the long hours spent in factory and office, the difficulty of leaving the city, forced people to turn to commercial amusements to pass away their idle hours. This tendency became more pronounced as the city grew and its poor population increased. Saloons, gambling halls, and dance halls proliferated. The dime museum, prize fights and variety shows took center stage. The theaters threw off the last vestiges of cultural pretension in an attempt to entertain the masses. As a consequence their popularity soared.

The three most popular forms of theatrical entertainment in the 1880s and 1890s were melodrama, burlesque and vaudeville. Each had its special appeal. Melodrama played on audience emotions, evoking sympathy and terror for victims and villains. Melodrama plots were hackneyed and repetitive but, the crowds still roared their approval as the hero arrived for a last minute rescue. Vaudeville presented a lighter theatrical side, delighting audiences with songs, comedy, dancing and acrobatics. Burlesque, mixing female exhibitionism with minstrel-comedy routines, also emerged in the 1890s as a popular entertainment medium. The gay music, the simple humor, the "50—Pairs of Rounded Limbs, Ruby Lips, Tantalizing Torsos,"[29] excited and titillated male audiences wherever burlesque could be found.

While vaudeville and burlesque packed them in on Broadway and Main Street across the nation, a new entertainment phenomenon emerged on the city's outskirts. This was the amusement park. Initially built along beaches and rivers surrounding large cities, amusement parks provided recreation for summer visitors and vacationing urbanites. The invention of the electric trolley and the subway in the late 1880s, however, suddenly placed these playlands within easy traveling distance from central cities. Shrewd businessmen bought up plots of desirable land and began erecting fun houses, mechanical rides, race courses and marinas. They bought carousels, the giant revolving wheel invented by G. W. G. Ferris, and created colossal replicas of distant and exotic places. By the 1890s there were amusement parks in every major American city, accessible to the masses, inexpensive and endlessly exciting.

The quintessential amusement park was New York's Coney Island, which stretched along a five-mile beach on Brooklyn's south shore. There, in the late 1890s and early 1900s, millions flocked to ride the

---

[29] *Ibid.*, p. 217.

giant ferris wheels, experience the excitement of an aquatic toboggan ride, or gape in awe at Luna Park, lighted at night by one million electric bulbs. The Barnum of Coney was George Tilyou, whose Steeplechase Park became an amusement Mecca when it opened in 1897. "The premier attraction at the park, then as now, was the Steeplechase Horses: an undulant, curving metal track over which wooden . . . horses ran on wheels, coursing down by gravity and soaring up by momentum, in tolerable imitation of a real horse race."[30] Steeplechase Park also boasted the Wedding Ring, a giant circle of wood suspended by wires, which rocked people back and forth; the Barrel of Love, a revolving drum, which rolled people down one incline and up another; and the Earthquake Staircase, which moved in two directions at once, upsetting the climber to the merriment of all. Luna Park, Steeplechase's competitor, also attracted large crowds to ride the Giant See-Saw and its cyclorama, A Trip to the Moon.

> By 1905 a child who went to Coney Island could, thanks to Luna and Dreamland [another amusement park] . . . arrive at a fairly approximate idea of the universe around him and, in the bargain, be magnificently entertained. He could visit an Indian durbar, the streets of Cairo, an Eskimo village, an island in the Philippines . . . a garden in Japan, the Alps of Switzerland, or the canals of Venice . . . he could go under the sea in a submarine or whirl giddily aloft in an airplane . . . he could see a petrified whale . . . ride a camel or feed an elephant.[31]

This was Coney Island at its best; a playland for the masses, only a subway ride from home.

As amusement parks opened up recreational opportunities on the periphery of cities, recreation *within* cities underwent important changes as well. City governments recognized the need for more parks and playgrounds and began setting aside land for nature appreciation and play. Lakes, playing fields, horse trails and bowling greens became part of the urban scene; families could take Sunday strolls, picnic or visit a zoo or botanic garden without leaving the city proper. Churches, settlement houses, and philanthropic organizations also contributed to the health and welfare of city people by building gymnasiums, Y.M.C.A. and Y.W.C.A. recreation centers and theaters for musical and dramatic presentations. The sabbath tradition in the

---

[30] Peter Lyons, "The Master Showman of Coney Island," *American Heritage* 9 (June 1958): 14–20, 92–95.
[31] *Ibid.*, p.93.

city was gradually eroded and Sundays were given over to recreation and play.

With a zest for fun and recreation unparalleled in previous decades, Americans of all ages adopted the bicycle as their pleasure vehicle *par excellence*.[32] The bicycle was known in America since the Civil War, but its giant front wheel and precarious balance made safe riding possible for only the most skilled and adept. In the 1890s, however, the development of the safety bicycle, which had equal sized wheels and pneumatic tires, turned bicycle riding into a popular pastime. Americans thrilled at an opportunity to move swiftly around parks and city streets. Farmers could bike to nearby cities; boys and girls could ride out into the country; doctors and policemen could effortlessly make their rounds. For approximately six or seven years after 1890 America was swept by a bicycle craze. In 1895, 300 bicycle manufacturers were turning out bicycles, but their production was still not sufficient to satisfy popular demand.

For a brief while the bicycle was unrivaled as a popular form of recreation and amusement. City parks were filled with bicycle enthusiasts and municipalities were petitioned to build bicycle right-of-ways. Armories, roller-skating rinks and dance halls were converted into riding academies and riding clubs were formed across the nation.[33] Women loved the new invention because it gave them the same mobility as men. In the 1890s it was common to see men and women cycling into the country for a picnic or nature ride.

The bicycle released the energies of a people who had always valued freedom and mobility. The circumscribed life of the small town gave way to town and city interaction which would be further strengthened with the advent of the automobile. Night travel became possible with the invention of improved carbide lamps which made even the darkest country lanes reasonably visible. What Americans seemed to like most about their two-wheeled vehicles, however, was the almost infinite uses to which they could be put. They were used for delivering mail, riding to work, shopping and racing; they were used for physical exercise, sightseeing, long-distance travel and for military puposes. Finally, the classless character of bicycle riding won it a permanent place in American recreation. Rich and poor, farmer, and city worker, each found it useful for pleasure and work.

It remained only for spectator sports to become a national passion to complete the revolution in recreation begun in the 1880s. Baseball

---

[32] Robert A. Smith, *A Social History of the Bicycle* (New York, 1972).
[33] Fred Kelly, "The Great Bicycle Craze," *American Heritage* 3 (December 1956): 69–73.

was in the forefront of this phenomenon. Known to Americans since colonial days, baseball emerged in the 1890s as *the* American sport with its star teams, home run heroes, impressive stadia and special jargon. Two associations, the National League and the American League gradually brought order to the jumble of amateur, semi-professional and professional teams. Internal competitions leading to "pennant races" and interleague "world series" became standardized by the early 1900s. Baseball "emerged as a highly organized activity involving heavy expenditures, detailed rules of operation, player contracts, and an intricate system of club agreements."[34] Notwithstanding its commercial character, Americans flocked to see home teams defeat rival clubs and local favorites bat the ball out of the park.

Baseball caught on because it was suitable entertainment for big-city crowds. The new stadia had tickets priced for every social class; games played on weekends permitted even the most overworked urbanite to see his team in action. The game's emphasis on talent and discipline appealed to Americans who enjoyed seeing immigrants and farm boys catapulted to baseball fame. Equally important was the opportunity for city people to share a common interest in the successes and failures of their local teams. The ups and downs of the Pittsburgh Pirates, the Philadelphia Athletics or the New York Giants provided a subject for discussion, and an opportunity for wagering among the most diverse social types.

College football also reached a mass audience in the 1890s as more and more colleges sent their elevens onto the field. Football had to lose some of its roughness and brutality before it was accepted as a genuine sport. Refashioned in the 1880s as a game emphasizing precision and strategy, it won an enthusiastic following at eastern colleges and later at southern and midwestern schools. Football offered a spectacle of team play and individual daring. Its bigness and ritualized aggression appealed to youthful audiences who followed their teams with frenzied enthusiasm. The first Princeton-Yale game played in 1878 was watched by some 4,000 students; a decade later the same contest had forty thousand spectators. In the twentieth century college football reached new heights of popularity; ninety-one thousand fans attended the 1939 Rose Bowl at Pasadena, California to see Southern California defeat Duke University. Football became such a major enterprise that colleges poured millions into building stadia and searched the country for the finest high-school players. Some educators decried the emphasis on sports to the exclusion of academic

---

[34] Harvey Wish, *Society and Thought in Modern America* (New York, 1962), pp. 277–278.

work, but administrators knew a winning team meant prestige, alumni support and large stadium receipts.

Baseball and football were but two of the spectator sports that grew in popularity as the twentieth century dawned. Prize fighting became more respectable and drew larger and larger crowds. Horse racing continued to be a popular favorite even though betting was illegal and had to be done through "bookies" and other shady types. Spectatorship, however, did not triumph in every area of recreational life. Dr. James Naismith's invention of basketball in 1891 was an immediate success and volley ball, invented soon after, quickly gained a following. Gymnasiums, Ys, settlement house facilities, and public playgrounds continued to multiply, meeting some of the needs of play-hungry youth. Baseball's popularity was attested to by the hundreds of diamonds found on vacant lots in cities, towns and villages. Americans may have been watching more sports in the 1890s, but they were also playing wherever and whenever they could.

LEISURE IN AN AGE OF MOTION

"Why on earth do you need to study what's changing this country?" said a lifelong resident and shrewd observer of the Middle West. "I can tell you what's happening in just four letters: A-U-T-O!"[35] It was the 1920s when this individual gave his analysis of social trends and had he said M-O-V-I-E-S, as well, he would have accurately described the two most important influences on leisure and recreation in the twentieth century. Today we have only to add R-A-D-I-O and T-V to round out this capsule social commentary. These four inventions transformed the pace and quality of leisure and recreation in our time.

Had there not been a drastic decline in the average work week, however, the impact of these inventions in the post-World War I era would not have been as significant as they were. In 1896 the average work week was fifty-nine hours, not much different from Civil War days. Progressive legislation and union activity helped reduce the average to fifty-five hours by 1914. During the 1920s however, the twin innovation of the assembly line and scientific management increased productivity to the point that employers could voluntarily introduce the shorter working day. "In 1923 United States Steel abandoned the twelve-hour day and put its Gary plant on an eight-hour shift; in 1926 Henry Ford instituted the five-day week,

---

[35] Robert and Helen Lynd, *Middletown, A Study in Contemporary American Culture* (New York, 1929), p. 251.

while International Harvester announced the electrifying innovation of a two-week annual vacation with pay for its employees."[36] Within a few years after these pace-setting changes, a large number of industries and small businesses switched to the eight-hour day. By 1940 Americans were working an average of forty-four hours a week and taking for granted that they would receive at least one week off, with pay, for rest and relaxation.

The technological innovations and improvements that helped shorten the average work week also created a new abundance in American life that marked the 1920s as a decade of prosperity. The average income of Americans increased by over forty percent between 1900 and 1929. Real income—what income could actually buy at the store—also went up. This meant that families with modest incomes could buy the latest gadgets and inventions, items that ostensibly would save labor and provide new leisure for homemakers. Vacuum cleaners and washing machines, electric sewing machines, toasters and refrigerators, store-baked goods and canned foods all became part of American home life during the 1920s. Americans also bought tennis rackets, golf equipment, small craft, camping accessories and outdoor games, leisure items they would not have considered purchasing twenty years earlier.

In the years following World War I a good part of leisure spending in the United States went into the purchase of automobiles. Still a novelty and a plaything of the rich before 1914, automobiles became increasingly commonplace as mass production brought down their price. Henry Ford transformed the industry with his assembly line production at Highland Park; the two million cars of 1914 became nine million by 1921 and in 1929 alone American factories produced 4,800,000 cars. As the price of a new automobile leveled off at seven to eight hundred dollars, Americans of even modest means found the new innovation relatively easy to purchase. By the 1930s two-thirds of American families owned automobiles. By 1950 there were 40,333,591 registered cars on American roads, one car for every three Americans.

The automobile's potential as a recreation vehicle was immediately apparent as Americans of all social classes took to the roads. Unlike the bicycle, the automobile could transport people long distances, opening a new frontier for pleasure travel and tourism. The motor car took city people out "into the country," and swelled the numbers who visited national and state parks. It brought the country

---

[36] William E. Leuchtenburg, *The Perils of Prosperity, 1914–1932* (Chicago, 1958), p. 179.

club, beach resort and sports arena within easy reach of the big city and broke down the barriers of rural and small town isolation. The automobile created motor-lodges, drive-in movies and made possible distant weekend travel. As the ultimate leisure vehicles, people enjoyed sitting in them, showing them off, or simply taking them on random trips for the excitement of the ride.

The automobile disrupted old leisure patterns and created new ones. Leisure time spent with one's family was transformed into an evening out at a roadside tavern, a drive-in movie, or a visit to a neighboring community. "In the nineties we were all much more together," said one midwestern woman. "People brought chairs and cushions out of the house and sat on the lawn evenings . . . We'd sit out so all evening. The younger couples perhaps would wander off for half an hour to get a soda but come back to join in the informal singing or listen while somebody strummed a mandolin or guitar."[37] In addition to competing with home entertainment, the automobile changed the way people spent their Sundays, especially in small towns where church-going was still traditional. A minister in the Midwest denouced "automobilitis- the thing those people have who go off motoring on Sunday instead of going to church. If you want to use your car on Sunday, [he declared] take it out Sunday morning and bring some shut-ins to church and Sunday School; then in the afternoon, if you choose, go out and worship God in the beauty of nature."[38] In other ways, too, the automobile altered patterns of leisure and recreation. Cross-country travel became common in the 1920s. No distance seemed too far for a ski trip, hunting trip or fishing weekend as roads were constructed into hitherto inaccessible places. In the long run the automobile also created recreational opportunities outside urban centers that competed with theaters, opera houses and cultural institutions. On holidays and throughout the summer, city dwellers routinely deserted downtown areas for the pleasures of the beach, the weekend cottage and outdoor recreation.

At the same time that Americans were becoming accustomed to moving faster and farther in their new automobiles, they were also getting used to more motion in their entertainment. This was due to the invention of motion pictures which Americans first saw in the nickelodeons of the 1890s. The first Kinetoscopes, Bioscopes, and Vitascopes were certainly more exciting than the moving dioramas and magic lantern shows of the preceding decades, but until the techniques of mass viewing were perfected they remained artistically and

---

[37] Robert and Helen Lynd, *Middletown,* p. 257.
[38] *Ibid.,* p. 259.

commercially limited. In the early 1900s, however, enterprising businessmen bought the first one-reel movies and projected them on screens in store fronts and makeshift theaters. When the raised stage and piano were added in succeeding years, all the components of the modern motion picture theater were already in place.

The excitment generated when audiences first saw actors and actresses move about a screen in a darkened room was tremendous but would quickly have waned were it not for directors who explored the magnificent potential of the new photographic medium. Short one-reelers in which a woman danced, a man walked a tight-rope, or a horse jumped over a fence, were replaced by longer films with plot, action and characterization. Edwin S. Porter, for example, in *The Life of an American Fireman* (1902–03) and *The Great Train Robbery* (1903) "put together what was probably the first motion picture in the modern sense—that is an entire film governed by a single narrative conception, created by combining all the techniques of directing, editing, cutting and filming known to that time."[39] David's Griffith's, masterpiece *The Birth of a Nation* (1915), "used the devices of lighting and camera manipulation to suggest emotions, set moods, and convey abstract ideas—thus enabling the movie language to be more subtle and expressive."[40] As Porter and Griffith showed what could be achieved through the new medium, other directors began turning out commercially successful films. The feature film made up of five or more reels made its appearance in 1912. Novels and famous plays were adapted for the screen. Before long, Hollywood, where the film industry had concentrated after 1909, began using stars to attract people to the box office. Harold Lloyd, Charlie Chaplin, Douglas Fairbanks, Gloria Swanson, Tom Mix and Mary Pickford, to name but a few, were known to almost every American in the 1920s.

The movies, as the new entertainment medium was universally known, proved to be a commercial success right from the start. In 1909, New York City had 340 theaters "with a quarter-million daily attendance and a half-million on Sundays."[41] In 1916, 21,000 new theaters were erected across the country and before long movie palaces like New York's Strand (thick rugs, chandeliers, paintings and an orchestra) and the Roxy (6,214 seats and 125 ushers) made their appearance. In 1939 it was estimated that 65 percent of the national population went to the movies at least once a week.[42] Just before the

---

[39] Nye, *Muse,* p. 365.

[40] Robert Gessner, "The Moving Image," *American Heritage* 11 (April 1960): 35.

[41] Nye, *Muse,* p. 364.

[42] *Ibid.,* p. 384.

advent of television in 1947 movie attendance reached an all-time high of 85 to 90 million a week.

Movies were popular because they were made to conform to popular tastes. The films of Chaplin, Max Sennett, Harold Lloyd and Buster Keaton, for example, were models of comedy and characterization which were understood on the most basic level. The westerns, love stories, historical spectacles, musicals, crime thrillers, horror stories and war pictures that poured out of Hollywood were styled to reach the widest possible audience; producers rarely worried whether the product they were selling was high or popular art. It was the unreality of the motion picture, its larger than life quality, that drew audiences to see such epics as De Mille's *The Ten Commandments* (1923), *The King of Kings* (1927) or Rudolph Valentino in the *Sheik* and *Four Horsemen,* and Greta Garbo in *Flesh and the Devil.* Hollywood understood that what sold were films that transported people out their everyday world.

The advent of sound in motion pictures, the "talkies" of the late 1920s, only made the cinema more popular and exciting. Already unrivaled as an entertainment medium, its popularity grew as music, sound effects and the human voice were joined to action. Al Jolson's *The Jazz Singer* (1927) ushered in the era of sound motion pictures. A torrent of musicals, classical adaptations, "singing westerns," and historical epics using the new sound techniques soon followed. Another cinematic technique, the animated cartoon, made its appearance in 1928 when Walt Disney distributed *Steamboat Willie,* starring none other than Mickey Mouse. Sound and animation gave Hollywood two more techniques to alter, distort, or change reality, creating a world of make-believe that audiences seemed to want. "Go to a motion picture . . . and let yourself go," read one *Saturday Evening Post* advertisement of the 1920s. "Before you know it you are *living* the story—laughing, loving, hating, struggling, winning! All the adventure, all the romance, all the excitement you lack in your daily life are in —Pictures. They take you completely out of yourself into a wonderful new world. . . ." It was this quality of motion pictures that made them so popular in America and throughout the world.

To be entertained at the local Bijou or Pix, or at a movie palace in a big city was considered a treat by any right-thinking American in the 1920s. Imagine, however, the excitement generated when another electronic marvel, radio, brought music and drama right into the home. This occurred in the mid-1920s as small experimental radio stations were converted into powerful commercial enterprises through mergers and consolidation. In 1926 the Radio Corporation of America formed the National Broadcasting Company and in 1927 the Columbia Broadcasting System was created. Paid advertising began during these years. The eight stations of 1920 became three hundred stations and two chains by 1929.[43]

The medium of public broadcasting was unknown territory in its early years and it took much creative thought and experimenting to find out what the listening audience enjoyed. In the 1920s the proven successes were "special events" broadcasts such as the Dempsey-Carpentier fight (1921), the Rose Bowl games (first national hookup, 1927), and the regular broadcasts of baseball begun in 1923. Broadcasts of popular dance bands ("brought to you live from the Hotel. . . .") and singing were also popular. But it was not until radio stations started to explore what they could do in their own studios that the era of home radio entertainment really arrived. Serialized melodramas made their appearance with the "soap operas" of the 1930s; millions tuned in daily to listen to "Our Gal Sunday," "Mary Noble, Backstage Wife," and "Road of Life." The panoply of sound effects and music that embellished these dramatic presentations were soon adapted to thriller series such as "The Lone Ranger," "The Shadow," and "Treasury Men in Action." The most popular radio programs of the 1930s, however, were the nightly comedy shows starring such well known figures as Bob Hope, Jack Benny, Fred Allen, Jimmy Durante, Fanny Brice and Milton Berle. It is estimated that three quarters of American radios were tuned to "Amos 'n Andy" when the comedy team of Freeman Gosden and Charles Correll came on the air.

Virtually anything that could be communicated through the medium of sound was sent across the radio waves. Detective stories (The Thin Man, Sam Spade), adventure stories (The Green Hornet, Sergeant Preston of the Yukon), quiz programs (Truth or Consequences, The Quiz Kids), and disc-jockey shows (The Make-Believe Ballroom) all commanded huge listening audiences. Opera, symphony concerts, news programs and presidential "fireside chats" were regularly broadcast as the medium explored new horizons. Like the movies, however, the popularity of radio rested firmly on the fact that programming was tailored to the "average" American listener. Producers rarely experimented with "high-brow" or educational programs because advertisers wanted to reach the widest possible audience. "American radio," said J. Harold Ryan, president of the National Association of Broadcasters in 1925,

> . . . is the product of American business. If the legend still persists that a radio station is some kind of art center, a technical

---

[43] *Ibid.,* p. 391

museum, or a little piece of Hollywood transplanted strangely to your home town, then the first official act of the second quarter century should be to list it along with the local dairies, banks, bakeries, and filling stations.[44]

Clearly, the business of radio was business.

When television arrived to mesmerize American viewers in the late 1940s, the passive character of American leisure was given additional reinforcement. Here was radio and movies combined, aural and visual stimulation all at the touch of a switch. Viewers could now *see* their radio heroes and heroines. They could have their fare of westerns, melodramas, variety shows, and detective stories, without leaving their living rooms and without paying an admission fee. Television was so popular that the number of TV sets owned by Americans soon exceeded the number of bathtubs, refrigerators and telephones in the nation: 200,000 TV sets in 1947; five million in 1950; thirty-six and a half million in 1954; forty-eight and a half million in 1958; eighty-one million in 1970. Inevitably, radio listening and movie going declined for a time, but new programming and higher-priced movies enabled these traditional media to survive and prosper.

Television actualized everything that radio left to the imagination. Its strength (and also its weakness) stemmed from its ability to take the viewer right into the action. Motion pictures were quickly adapted for television so that no detail of reality would be left out of a given program. Interviews were conducted not only in studios but right in people's homes, as Edward R. Murrow did regularly on his program *Person to Person*. When Milton Berle was hit with a custard pie, Lucille Ball did a double-take, or Captain Video rocketed into space, all the action was literal and explicit. Sex was almost never shown on television but violence regularly was.

From an aesthetic point of view, the problems of television were the problems of radio all over again. Television took over radio's format of programming, interrupted by frequent commercial advertising; it took over all the standard soap operas, detective serials, situation comedies, quiz programs and added little besides a heavy dose of grade B Hollywood movies. Because the costs of producing a program were much higher than radio, television producers and directors were willing to take few risks, and opted for the programs that earned them the highest ratings. "Television must . . . always see its audience not only as an audience but as a market," writes Russel Nye. "What it presents is not only entertainment but adver-

---

[44] Quoted in Nye, *Muse,* p. 394.

tising. . . . Studies have shown that a program that requires too much thought, elicits too much excitement, or stirs up too much controversy is likely to make the viewer neglect the sponsor's message; the element of mediocrity thus has a certain importance in programming."[45]

Television mediocrity led to criticism that it was a "wasteland" in the 1960s. Sophisticated viewers looking for something edifying or uplifting agreed with this assessment. Daytime viewing was dominated by old movies, audience-participation shows, and soap operas. Evening "prime time" was filled with look-alike westerns, detective thrillers, situation comedies, and musical variety shows. Occasionally the networks produced a serious drama or ran a special on some subject of national interest but these were the exception rather than the rule. In the late 1960s and early 1970s the only bright stars on the television horizon were programs aired on National Educational Television, and the in-depth reporting by muck raking journalists.

Television inevitably had its impact on the leisure habits of Americans of all ages. Millions of hours were spent before the "tube" each day, with individuals averaging six, seven and eight hours a day. The passive character of television viewing created fears that Americans would become a nation of soft-bodied, soft-headed individuals, capable of doing little else besides switching channels and adjusting volume controls. Exaggerated as these claims were, they did point up the fact that spectatorship in the comfort of the home led to all kinds of passivity and indolence that could hardly be considered healthful or a creative use of leisure time. Television was clearly reinforcing the habit of looking, and discouraging the habit of doing.

THE FIVE-DAY WEEKEND

While television had a major impact on patterns of leisure and recreation after World War II, the new communications medium by no means stifled enthusiasm for other forms of play. Average viewing time rose to record highs in the 1970s (10.5 hours per week in 1972) but predictions that TV would turn America into a nation of spectators proved exaggerated and untrue. Reading as a leisure activity was reinforced by the appearance of inexpensive paperbacks in the 1950s, and sales of periodicals, notwithstanding the demise of *Look* and *Life*, remained strong. In fact, as Americans worked fewer hours, received more pay and took longer vacations, a veritable recreation explosion took place. Sociologists began writing about the "leisure problem"

---

[45] *Ibid.*, p. 408.

and businessmen began asking how they could cash in on recreation and the leisure market.

The extent of this recreation explosion was reflected in spending for recreation which jumped from $33 billion in 1967 to $50 billion in 1972. In the latter years Americans poured $18 billion into recreation-sports equipment, $10.2 billion into radios, TV sets, records and instruments, $9 billion into books, magazines and newspapers, $4.7 billion into admissions to sports, movies and cultural events and $1.3 billion into clubs and fraternal organizations. Garden purchases accounted for $1.6 billion of leisure spending, race-track receipts $1.1 billion and other "personal consumption" activities totaled $4.1 billion. In 1972 Americans also spent about $48 billion on domestic and foreign travel and another $7.5 billion on vacation land and second homes. "The money Americans are now spending on spare-time activities," proclaimed *U.S. New & World Report* in April, 1972 "exceeds national-defense costs. It is more than the outlay for construction of new homes. It surpasses the total of corporate profits. It is far larger than the aggregate income of U. S. farmers. It tops the over-all value of this country's exports."[45]

Spending, of course, was only one indicator of the extent to which leisure and recreation were becoming part of the American way of life. Time devoted to leisure and level of popular participation was another. One government study, for example, reported that in 1966 Americans averaged 5.1 hours of leisure time per day, with 1.5 hours devoted to TV, 1.5 to visiting, 0.6 to reading, 0.1 to sports and 1.4 to "other leisure" activities.[47] Another study reported that in 1970 Americans averaged 23 participation days in social activities (i.e., picnicking, walking, concerts, bird watching, sports attendance), 20 participation days in active sports, 15 in water activities and 3 in camping.[48] A survey for 1972 indicated that almost half the population participated in picnicking and swimming, one third participated in playing outdoor sports, viewing sports and walking for pleasure, and roughly a quarter of the population fished, boated, cycled and camped. Zeroing in on just one of these activities, *Fortune*, magazine reported that during 1973 Americans bought 15.2 million bicycles and that bicycle ownership (65 million) was rapidly catching up with that of cars (93 million).[49] *Fortune* also reported that the bicycle boom of the 1970s

---

[46] "Leisure Boom: Biggest Ever and Still Growing," *U.S. News & World Report* 72 (Aprl 17, 1972): 42–45.
[47] Executive Office of the President: Office of Management and Budget, *Social Indicators,* 1973 (Washington, D.C., 1973), p. 215.
[48] *Ibid.,* p. 216.
[49] *Fortune* (March 1974): 112–121.

opened the way for public financing of bikeways, a formula used by 15 states in 1974. Within a few years cycling had lost its status as an adolescent hobby and had joined the ranks of adult activities such as tennis, boating and golf.

That Americans in the 1970s were spending more for leisure and participating in a greater variety of recreational activities than ever before was apparent. As for the future, it seemed that increasing amounts of free time, heavy spending for recreation and more diversity in leisure activities would characterize American society for the foreseeable future. The prospect of a society in which people spent more time at leisure than at labor, however, challenged people and government institutions to find ways to make leisure satisfying and creative. It was one of the paradoxes of American life that a nation built on the ethos of hard work now had to find meaning in leisure, recreation and play.

CONCLUSION

The conclusion that one inevitably comes to after surveying the diverse currents of American leisure and recreation is that Americans gave up the Puritan notion of detesting leisure and idleness quite early in their history and chose instead to enjoy themselves in as many ways as they could. Those pastimes which could be enjoyed by the great masses of citizens, those most democratic in style and spirit, were those embraced most spontaneously and wholeheartedly. To a significant extent this explains why baseball is our national sport, why Americans still do not like opera, and why the automobile and television became the instruments and symbols of democratic leisure. We have a rich heritage of play and recreation, shaped by our belief that no class has the privilege to be amused, enlightened and entertained.

Suggestions for Further Reading

The following books offer insights into leisure and recreation in contemporary American society; Eric Larrabee and Rolf Meyersohn, eds., *Mass Leisure* (1958); Sebastian de Grazia, *Of Time, Work, and Leisure* (1964); Charles K. Brightbill, *The Challenge of Leisure* (1960); Pauline Madow, ed., *Recreation in America* (1965); Max Kaplan and Phillip Bosserman, eds., *Technology, Human Values and Leisure* (1971); and Riva Poor, ed., *4 Days, 40 Hours, Reporting a Revolution in Work and Leisure* (1970).

Still the best source for studying leisure and recreation in American history is Foster Rhea Dulles, *America Learns to Play* (1940). Other valuable works include: Ralph Andrist, *American Century: 100 Years of Changing Life Styles in America* (1972); Louis B. Wright, *Life in Colonial America* (1965) and *The Cultural Life of the American Colonies, 1607–1763* (1957); Foster Rhea Dulles, *Americans Abroad: Two Centuries of European Travel* (1964); Russel Nye, *The Unembarrassed Muse: The Popular Arts in America* (1970); Marshall B. Davidson, *Life in America*, Vols. I and II (Boston, 1951); Harvey Wish, *Society and Thought in Early America* (1950), and *Society and Thought in Modern America (1962);* Robert and Helen Lynd, *Middletown* (1929), and *Middletown in Transition* (1937); and Frederick Lewis Allen, *Only Yesterday* (1931).

Frank Luther Mott surveys American magazines and newspapers in *A History of American Magazines* (5 vols., reprinted 1966–1968). Robert A. Smith writes engagingly about the bicycle in *A Social History of the Bicycle* (1972). The magazine *American Heritage* has a number of articles on social history relating to leisure and recreation. See the Index.

Index